#speakyourtruth

THE
OBEDIENT
DAUGHTER

A MEMOIR

THE OBEDIENT DAUGHTER

A MEMOIR

AMBER NICOLE HAYES

Copyright © 2024 by Amber Nicole Hayes
All rights reserved.

No part of this publication may be reproduced, stored or transmitted in any form or by any means, electronic, mechanical, photocopying, recording, scanning, or otherwise without written permission from the publisher. It is illegal to copy this book, post it to a website, or distribute it by any other means without permission.

ISBN 978-1-0689950-0-2

CONTENT WARNING

This book contains references to childhood sexual abuse, sexual assault, domestic violence, generational trauma including borderline personality disorder, and suicide.

DISCLAIMER

The following is based on true events and reflects the author's present recollections of experiences over time. To protect the privacy of certain individuals their names and identifying details have been changed. Any resemblance to actual persons, living or dead, or actual events is purely coincidental.

For Monroe & Quinn,
you are my greatest gift

PROLOGUE

"Amber?" she asked.

A tall blonde woman in her late forties looked at me as I sat alone in the waiting room. She had an accent that I couldn't quite identify. I stood up, holding my Yeti of coffee in my hand. I rarely left the house without it. I had exactly one hour and forty-five minutes before I needed to pick up my youngest daughter from preschool. My oldest daughter started first grade a week earlier. This was the first time in years that I had a consistent schedule of time to myself.

"Hi, I'm Dr. M. It's nice to meet you," she said.

I smiled and nodded. We walked side by side together as we approached her office. She wore a long cardigan and dress pants and held a cup of coffee. She seemed approachable and reminded me of an elementary school teacher. I sat down on a grey linen couch. Two matching armchairs were on the opposite end of the room. There was a coffee table and small accents, including table lamps and teal artwork, that made her office feel homey. I could tell everything was from Ikea, but I liked that she appreciated a beautiful space.

She was the third therapist I'd seen in a year. The first therapist was for depression. The second helped me unveil a secret I'd kept for twenty-five years. Now, I was seeing a third therapist in the hopes of releasing some of the pain attached to that secret. This therapist specialized in post-traumatic stress disorder and worked with war veterans. I wondered if she could handle my story and my trauma. I didn't serve a term in Afghanistan, but I wondered if that might have been easier to endure than the last thirty-seven years.

Dr. M. explained her process of therapy. She used eye movement desensitization and reprocessing (EMDR) in addition to various other forms of therapy.

"Will it help erase my memories?" I asked.

"No. It won't erase your memories, but it will can help with releasing the emotions that are attached to them," she said.

I agreed to her process. It seemed better than nothing. At this point, I would do anything to take away the pain and the reoccurring thoughts that had been simmering in my brain for the last three years. I took a sip of my coffee. It brought me comfort and kept my hands occupied.

"Before we get to work on EMDR, I'd like to understand your trauma a bit more," she said.

She opened a fresh notebook to the first page.

"Ideally, we'll spend a few sessions understanding your childhood and any moments that have contributed to your PTSD."

I knew this was coming. It was the standard first session of therapy where you regurgitated your story while they sat and took notes. No tools or thought-provoking questions. Just silence. At the end of the hour, they bill you $220. She was the seventh therapist I'd sat with in my lifetime. I knew the routine. I took my boots off and sat back on the couch.

"Where do you want me to start?" I asked.

"Let's start at the beginning. Tell me about your childhood and any key memories you believe shaped you and your trauma. I want to know about your family dynamics, each member and what makes them tick."

I curled my legs behind me and tried to get more comfortable. I knew we would be here for a while.

BROTHERS

My mom always said that my brother Chad and I were the best of friends all through our childhood. I suppose we were. I'm the third child and the only daughter. I have two older brothers: Jason, who is nine years older, and Chad, who is fifteen months older. As children, Chad and I played together and told each other everything. He was the person I trusted most in our family. He seemed to make my mom the happiest, which I thought was a superpower. When an argument broke out between my parents, he was there to comfort me.

We had separate interests, though. He was into hockey and dirt bikes. I loved figure skating and Barbie dolls. He was inherently clumsy, frequently breaking bones and getting concussions.

At the age of six, Chad was diagnosed with a benign tumour in his jaw and was hospitalized to have it removed. I spent the night at home with Jason. I remember the night vividly. Jason opened a can of stew and warmed it on the stove. We sat down at the table and ate dinner in silence. I took small bites, pushing my meal around with my spoon.

"Ew, what is this?" I asked, prodding something in my soup.

It was the size of a golf ball, and it looked like a mouse.

"It's nothing. Just eat it," Jason said.

"I'm not eating this. It's hairy!" I said.

Jason grabbed my bowl and used his spoon to pick up the wet chunk of fur in my stew.

"Jesus! That's disgusting!"

"I don't have to eat it, do I?" I asked.

"No. I'll make you some Kraft Dinner," he said.

Jason set the chunk of fur aside on a piece of paper towel. He started a pot of water to boil and within fifteen minutes he placed a warm bowl of creamy, orange macaroni in front of me.

"Aren't you going to have some?" I asked.

"No, I'm not hungry anymore," he said, as he dumped the rest of it into a Tupperware container.

I didn't think much of it and delved happily into my favourite meal. We didn't really say much that night and it wasn't long before Jason put me to bed, said goodnight, and turned out the light. The house was eerie and quiet. It was never just the two of us.

The chunk of fur was shown to our parents and eventually sent to the company for testing. It ended up being a chunk of cowhide, and we were reimbursed for the can. They sent us a bunch of coupons for free stew but needless to say, they were never redeemed, and stew was never on the menu again.

•

The next day, we visited Chad at the hospital. He was swollen and it looked as though he was keeping a baseball in his cheek. We delivered cards from his classmates and a few things that Mom asked us to bring from home. His slippers, his robe, his teddy, his pillow. This developed into a systematic routine as we got older and Chad continued to get injured. Just over a year later, he crashed into the boards at the outdoor skating rink at school. He hit his head. A stranger drove him home and explained the incident to my parents.

"He's got a concussion!" Mom yelled.

They brought him into the house, still in his hockey gear. They undressed him at the door, removing his skates, jersey, and equipment.

"Amber, go get his slippers," Mom bellowed as she sat him down on the couch.

"How many fingers am I holding up?" she asked him.

This seemed like a stupid question to me.

"Fingers? Uh, six?" he said.

He was way off. There were only four. He couldn't see properly.

"He needs to go to the hospital. Amber, get me his jacket and his boots. Ben, get the keys," Mom instructed.

That was how every Chad crisis went. We stayed calm and dropped whatever we were doing at the time, waiting for instructions from Mom. She was outstanding in a crisis. If you were seriously injured or needed to be taken care of, she was the perfect person to help.

Chad held a certain intangible power in the house. He was Mom's favourite, even though she would never admit it. This became very apparent as I got older. Growing up, Chad represented different personas to me. He was my friend and my protector. He represented safety. He was the first person I would seek out if my parents were fighting or if someone was picking on me at school.

Unlike Chad, Jason and I were never that close growing up. We fought a lot. We sat across from each other at the dinner table where a permanent milk carton or cereal box needed to be placed between us. It prevented us from exchanging unwanted glances and getting under each other's skin. He loved blaring Guns N' Roses or Nirvana and screeching at the top of his lungs while he strummed his air guitar. It overwhelmed me. Jason and Chad got along just fine. They shared similar interests like hockey, football, golf, and music. But Jason and I shared nothing.

FORTS AND FLASHLIGHTS

We lived in a bungalow on the west side of Saskatoon. It had four bedrooms upstairs, one bedroom downstairs, and one additional room in the basement that we used as a playroom. We had a stack of three old mattresses that we used for kids to sleep on when they visited with their parents. Dad would sit on the stack of mattresses and make us bend over his knee for a spanking if we gave our mom a hard time while he was at work. There was a chalkboard on the wall that I used for my pretend classroom. Occasionally, I would get friends, cousins, and sometimes Chad to sit with me and let me teach them, but that was rare. They didn't love school as much as I did.

We had a family room with two couches, a chair, and a TV that was adjacent to a freestanding wood fireplace. On the other side of the room there was a pool table and two full-size arcade games: Pac Man and Space Invaders. I wasn't much of a pool player. I was only five and could barely see over the top of the pool table. Chad and I would spend hours making it into our fort. We would cover it with blankets, crawl underneath and turn on flashlights. We had Fisher Price Playskool flashlights that changed colour from red to green and back to white again. One day, we crawled underneath and turned our flashlights on to light up the fort.

"The baby needs to sleep. And we need food," I said.

I changed my baby doll's diaper and wrapped her up in a blanket before putting her in her playpen.

"Okay, I'll go get us a deer," Chad said.

He grabbed his toy pistol and left the fort on a hunt for game. Moments later, he returned empty handed, and it was time for bed.

"The baby is hungry," I said, reaching for my doll and a bottle.

"No, she's not. It's bedtime," Chad said.

I put the doll back down and pulled a blanket over myself, pretending to sleep.

"Wait!" Chad said.

"What?" I asked.

"Stand up for a second," he said.

My head hit the top of the pool table as I attempted to stand. I crouched and started to rub the spot on my head.

"Come out here," Chad said, ushering me to leave our fort.

We stood at the back of the room, behind the pool table.

"Pull down your pants," he said.

"What for?" I asked.

"I want to see something," he said.

I stood up and did what he said.

"Your panties, too."

I dropped my pink Care Bear panties to my ankles and stood there in the lightless basement. I had left my flashlight in the fort with my baby.

He took his flashlight and switched it to white. Then he buried the light directly on my vulva.

"Turn around," he instructed.

I did one quick spin, trying not to fall over.

"Slower," he said.

I listened and completed another full turn, shuffling my feet slowly while his flashlight shone on my private parts. I didn't understand why Chad needed an up close and personal view of my privates.

It wasn't like he hadn't seen them before. Chad and I bathed together every week for as long as I could remember.

"Chad! Amber! Supper!" Mom yelled from the top of the stairs.

I quickly pulled up my panties and pants. Chad turned off his flashlight and bolted toward the stairs.

"Wait for me!" I yelled.

I reached back into the fort to turn off my flashlight. Chad had already made it to the top of the stairs. I walked carefully but briskly toward the light that cascaded down from the kitchen.

"What were you guys doing down there?" Mom inquired.

"Playing house." Chad responded before I could say anything.

I remembered that I left my baby doll downstairs and stood up from the table to go get her.

"Where do you think you're going?" Mom asked.

"Just getting my baby," I said.

"Oh no you're not. You get back here and eat your supper. You can play later."

I sat back down and rushed through my supper. My baby doll was the only thing I could think about. She was alone in the dark. If she cried, I wouldn't be there.

"STOP YOUR CRYING AND SAY CHEESE!"

Mom and I sat together in the doctor's office. It was a busy waiting room with patients flooding to one of three doors: the doctors' offices, a dentistry practice, and an X-ray department. I scuttled onto the floor and over to the wooden abacus and bead maze. I pushed a red wooden ball through the maze as if it were a roller coaster.

"Those toys are for babies," Mom said.

I got up and sifted through a pile of magazines on the coffee table until I found an issue of *Highlights*. Mom was already flipping the pages of a *Chatelaine*. I suppose Mom was right, I was not a baby; I was five. I hopped back up onto the chair and dangled my feet below while flipping through the magazine pages, pretending to read.

"Amber?" a young nurse called my name.

"Come on, that's you," Mom said.

We put our magazines on the coffee table and walked through the doors that led to the doctors' offices. Numerous doors were closed, all numbered, and all with patient charts in pockets on the doors. Mom and I were ushered into a room. The nurse assured us that the doctor would be in shortly, and closed the door behind her. I was there for my yearly checkup.

"Okay, get your clothes off and then hop on up there," Mom said.

I took off my winter boots and jacket and gave them to her. Next, I removed my corduroy jeans and a plaid shirt. I hopped up on the table, the paper crinkling below me. It was cold. We sat there in silence. Mom came to everyone's doctor appointments, even Dad's. She was the one to make the appointment, and she made sure to accompany you into the room. She needed to know what was being said. There was a knock at the door and an older man entered the room. He had grey hair, and his hands shook as he opened my medical chart. He reminded me of a grandpa.

He removed his stethoscope from around his neck and listened to my chest and back.

"Take a deep breath in. And again. One more time," he said.

I took repeated deep breaths in and out as instructed.

"Okay, now open your mouth and say ahhh."

"Ahhgghhh."

"Okay, let's have you lie down on your back," he said.

I stretched out over the table, the paper shifting and ripping slightly. He put his hands on my stomach and started to press and then without saying anything he lifted my panties and placed his hand just above my pubic bone. I froze. I looked over at my mom and she was staring back at me with a blank expression. The doctor left the room and I got dressed. We exited the waiting room, which was now even busier than when we arrived.

We sat together in the car.

"Mom, I didn't like when his hand touched me in my panties," I said.

"Well, that's what doctors do," she said.

She clicked and shook her lighter repeatedly as she tried to light her cigarette until finally a puff of smoke filled the car.

"But he's an old man. Don't they have any girl doctors?" I asked.

"He's a good doctor, Amber. You will go to him for your check-ups. End of discussion."

I sat there, defeated. She didn't care how I felt.

We drove home and got ready for my cousins to arrive. They were flying in from Vancouver. My uncle, aunt, and their three boys ages two, three, and six. We didn't get to see them a lot but when we did, my dad was happy. They arrived, and we spent all afternoon playing together outside. My youngest cousin was sweet and wouldn't leave my side. I felt like a big sister, and he was mine to take care of like a real baby, even though he was two.

We ate supper outside on the patio: hot dogs, macaroni salad, and potato chips. As we cleared our paper plates and placed them in the garbage, Mom declared it was bath time. I sat there disgruntled. It was a Friday and Sundays were bath days. Mom bathed Chad and me every Sunday since we were babies.

"It's not Sunday!" I complained.

"No, but you're full of dirt. Let's go!"

The four of us followed my mom to the bathroom. We undressed and climbed into the tub. My mom, my aunt, and my youngest cousin watched while the rest of us bathed. My youngest cousin sat at the edge of the tub and wanted to come in. It was already crowded but Mom insisted it would be fun. She undressed him, removed his diaper, and put him beside me. He stood behind me, holding onto my hair.

"Let me get the camera," Mom yelled.

I heard her as she ran down the green carpeted hallway into the kitchen. She came running back and took multiple pictures. My baby cousin started to pull my hair hard. I couldn't move, and I wanted to get out. Tears streamed down my face.

"I don't think Amber is having fun," my aunt said.

"Oh, she's fine! Amber, stop your crying and say cheese!" Mom said.

They took my cousin out and I insisted I was done, too. It was enough to bathe with Chad every week, but too much to have three more boys with me.

MARLENE

I sat on the edge of my bed staring at the picture inside the frame. It was a photograph of a woman. She had a slim build and donned a floral, tea-length dress, and gloves. Her dark brown hair was tucked up into her sun hat. She smiled softly. She had an air of femininity and class that I had never seen before in my six years of age. She seemed playful and kind. I wondered what it would be like to have her as a mom. There was a tenderness in her eyes, so inviting and warm.

It was the picture that came in the frame. I took it out and placed it in the back of my photo album for safe keeping. She would be my dream mom. It became apparent to me that my relationship with my mother would always be complicated. Mom was complex and unpredictable. I would learn at a very young age to tiptoe around her always fearful of setting her off.

My mom was raised in an Anglican family with six brothers and six sisters. Her mom sought to enrage her own mother by having thirteen children. A baker's dozen. Their relationship was destructive and explosive. "I should have listened to my mother and stopped at five," my grandmother once told my mom. My mom was number six in the lineup, so undoubtedly, she took this personally.

Mom worked for my grandma for many years, taking care of her foster children. She made a small wage but nothing significant. Mom always said how much Grandma loved children; that was why she had so many and needed to have more through fostering. But I wasn't convinced that Grandma loved children.

She lived in an older house on the west side of Saskatoon. She filled the house with foster kids. Some were in wheelchairs with severe disabilities, some were on the spectrum. She also had young babies, sibling groups, and teenagers. At any given time, she could have twenty kids living with her. She relied on her own daughters to help her care for the foster kids.

We spent a great deal of time at my grandma's house. One afternoon when I was four, my mother said I needed to go upstairs and take a nap. I resisted.

"Four-year-old kids don't have naps anymore!"

I was convinced I wasn't tired, but she persisted. She took my hand, and we walked up the rickety stairs to the nursery. The door was ajar because it would stick if closed all the way. My mother made a bed for me by placing a blanket and a small decorative pillow on top of a wooden toy box.

"There. Now lay down and go to sleep," she whispered.

It was exceptionally uncomfortable. I tossed and turned. I was trying to sleep when I heard a shuffle in the room. I looked over to see three cribs with babies sleeping in them. One of them was stirring. I froze so I wouldn't wake them. I drifted in and out of sleep and eventually awoke as noises came from the cribs. I looked at the babies. They were all awake and rolling around. They grabbed the bars of the cribs and squished their chubby faces in between them, letting out cooing sounds. A small girl with fiery red hair and rosy cheeks grabbed a yellow rope that was dangling from the top of her crib. It was used to tie a sheet of plywood to the tops of the cribs. They were in cages. I got up and walked over to them. My hand reached out to touch theirs. So soft and small. I felt guilty leaving them, but

I wasn't big enough to set them free. I went downstairs and told my mom that they were awake.

•

It wasn't long after that when one of Grandma's foster kids invited me down to his bedroom in the cellar. I had never been down there before and hadn't spent much time with him. He was sixteen. The stairs to the cellar were outside the house so he had his own separate entrance. The ceiling was low, and it smelled of damp mould. Exposed pipes and cracked cement formed a pathway to a small area that was shaped with makeshift walls. The area was decorated entirely with Star Wars items.

"You can sit on my bed," he said.

I sat down. His bed was covered with a navy Star Wars comforter and white sheets that had R2-D2 and C-3PO on them. He showed me various models that he built, meticulously detailing their names and which character they belonged to. As we sat together on his bed, the door at the top of the stairs opened.

"Amber, you down there?"

It was Chad. I wasn't sure how Chad knew to find me there or how long he had been looking for me.

"I have to go," I said and quickly ran up the stairs.

Chad and I ran to meet Mom who was waiting in the car. She drove an older, silver station wagon with a dark red interior. I crawled into the backseat and Chad sat in the front.

"Where was she?" Mom asked as Chad buckled his seat belt.

"Down in the cellar," he replied.

"Amber, I don't want you down there again, do you understand me?"

She lit a cigarette. It was the first thing she did every time she got in the car.

"Yes," I said.

I let out a cough as the backseat flooded with cigarette smoke. She rolled down her window an inch and pulled onto the road to go home for supper.

•

Mom was raised in an exceptionally traditional family. The girls were expected to cook and clean, while the boys were allowed to go to work and play sports. There were enough chores around the house to do and younger children to look after that the opportunity to get a job wasn't an option for many of the girls. If ever in my childhood there was a time that I felt life wasn't fair, Mom always reminded me how much harder her childhood was. Hers was a childhood full of abuse, demeaning comments, and favouritism of the boys. I learned quickly that I should just be thankful for what I had because it could always be a lot worse.

BEN

Mild-mannered and meek, with a slim five-foot-nine frame. A full head of dark, curly hair and a moustache that surrounded his sweeping smile. His dark eyes twinkled and narrowed every time he laughed. He was soft-spoken and always agreeable. This was my dad, Ben. He was my constant growing up. He was the one whom I could predict, the one whom I never wanted to disappoint. He was subtle and easygoing.

He was born in Tsawwassen, British Columbia. He had one older brother and one older sister. They were raised in a conservative Christian family. His parents divorced when he was twelve and this left a lasting impact that shaped the way he lived his life. He moved to Saskatoon and met my mother when they both worked at the restaurant in Zellers. He was five years her junior, and she had a son, my brother Jason. Not long after they started dating, they became engaged and six months after they married. My dad adopted Jason. From that point on, he would be known as Dad and Jason would always be his.

My dad's truest passion was old cars. Always a Chevrolet man and never a Ford. I would happily tag along with him to car shows or watch hot rod TV, just to spend extra time with him. He was the ultimate handyman, with an endless supply of tools and the knowledge to repair anything. He shared all his tips and tricks for fixing things around the house. I idolized him. We became close when I was young. It was the little things. The single rose he would throw on the ice after a competition, or the Sarah Lee teddy bear he'd bring home from a food convention. He always let me know that he cared and that I mattered to him.

Our relationship grew as I got older. We exchanged our emotions and hopes. I helped him with spreadsheets and flyers for his sales representatives. We spent time joking and laughing, something we never did as a family. He was always carefree and not at all like my mom. I found comfort in knowing I was more like him than her. He watched me cheerlead and would rewatch my competitions long after I was done competing. He was my biggest fan. He always pushed me to keep going and celebrated every win with me. He was the opposite of my mother. He was the glimpse of love that I received in my life and the reason why I am who I am today.

SPARE ROOM SECRETS

Mom was exceptional at sewing. I started skating when I was two. Each year there was a year-end carnival performance that required a handsewn costume to coincide with the theme. One year, the theme was country and western with red fringe and cowgirl hats, the next year it was under-the-sea mermaids, and the year following that it was trolls with fluorescent fun fur wigs. She worked diligently into the late hours in the downstairs spare bedroom where her sewing machine was set up. She would call me down sporadically to fit me for various items and occasionally I was curious and ventured down to visit her.

"Hi, Mom," I said as I stepped into the room.

I put my head on her shoulder as I did each morning and took a deep breath. She smelled of cigarettes and cinnamon Dentyne gum.

"Come stand over here," she directed.

She wrapped the troll fun fur around my head for measurement and then sprayed it with hairspray to keep the fur from falling out. I looked at the wall. There was a large picture of a man walking on a beach. He was dressed in white and cream linen and had dark hair down to his shoulders.

"Is that Daddy?" I asked.

"No, it's not," she said.

"Oh. It looks like Daddy. Wouldn't that be cool if it was?"
"Yeah. Okay, there, you're done for now."

•

We rarely went into the spare room, but one evening Chad asked if we could have a sleepover downstairs. Mom agreed and we changed into our pyjamas and brushed our teeth. I reached for a couple of stuffed animals and my baby doll but was told to choose one. I had never slept downstairs before but since I was now seven, I guess I was old enough. We crawled into the double bed, pulling up the floral comforter that had a ruffled trim. The sheets were coarse, and a mid-weight blue blanket itched my chin. Mom and Dad gave us a kiss and turned off the lights.

"Now you two go to sleep," Mom said, as she walked out of the room and up the stairs.

Immediately, I wanted to go back to my room. It was cold, dark, and it smelled of basement.

"Hey," whispered Chad. "Do you want to know something?"

"What?" I answered, hoping it would take my mind off my new surroundings since he didn't seem as anxious as I was.

"Do you want to know what sex is?"

"Okay," I said.

Chad always seemed to know so much about adult stuff.

"Take off all your clothes," he instructed as he started undressing himself.

I took off my shirt and pulled down my pants and panties. I left them around my ankles and hoped he wouldn't notice. It was freezing in the basement spare room. With the blankets still over us, he crawled on top of me, his fully naked body on top of mine. He moved back and forth repeatedly, creating friction between our bodies. My airway felt as if it was collapsing with the weight of his body on mine. I let out a small cough. I wasn't yet forty pounds. I wanted to go back upstairs.

I looked over at the wall and saw the picture of the man on the beach again. It brought me a sense of calm, and I imagined what it would be like to be with my dad on the beach in that very moment. A couple of minutes seemed like hours, but Chad soon fell off to the side.

"That's what the grown-ups do," he said with confidence.

"How do you know that?" I asked.

"Cause, I just do," he said.

I shimmied up my pyjama bottoms and panties and grabbed my shirt from the floor. I rolled onto my side, away from Chad, and looked up one more time at the man in the picture. I held my Cabbage Patch baby tight, closed my eyes, and eventually fell asleep.

CHANGES

I laid down on the cement floor in our basement. I felt a dampness and the grit of cement that escaped from the cracks in the foundation. The washing machine was rumbling during its spin cycle. The smell of bleach filled the basement from the load of whites that were stretched out on the umbrella clothesline.

Chad came over and buckled me into a pair of old leather goalie pads. They came up to my waist, but I made them work. I never used a hockey stick as it distracted me from blocking the shots that Chad and Jason took at me with rubber pucks and occasionally the hard orange balls. Music was blaring and I felt confident. Chad and I always found things to do together. If it wasn't hockey, then it was letting him practice wrestling moves on me. He usually put me in a DDT, a sleeper hold, or a figure-four leg lock. We challenged each other on the trampoline, and I wore my black spandex shorts because it made me look like Jean-Claude Van Damme from *Bloodsport*, a movie we'd recently rented from Blockbuster.

After a solid forty-five minutes of hockey, my face was flushed, my hair was damp, and a new odour came from my underarms. I was eight and this had never happened before. I was nervous to mention it to my mom. I spent the rest of the day trying to work up the courage to ask her about deodorant, but I couldn't do it. I thought about sneaking into her room to borrow her Arrid Extra Dry, but the smell was strong, and she would know I used it. Instead, I grabbed a small address book that she'd given me a while back. I tore out the pages that had senseless drawings on them and started to write in the leftover pages of the book. *Dear Mom, I thought this book would be a good idea for us to be able to talk. I've started to notice that I smell. What do you think about me using deodorant? - Amber*

I placed the thin book under her pillow and hoped she'd find it before she went to bed. The next day the book showed up on top of my pillow. I eagerly opened it to find her response. *Amber, if you feel you need deodorant, I will pick some up at the store for you. - Mom*

Success! I avoided the inevitable and embarrassing conversation. Three days later there was a baby powder-scented Teen Spirit deodorant on my dresser. A couple of months later, I wrote in the book again. *Mom, I noticed that my boobies are starting to hurt. Why is this?* She wrote back that it was all part of growing up and that on the weekend, we would shop for a bra.

•

"C'mon let's go!" she said as she ushered me out the door.

"Where are we going?" I asked.

"Bra shopping!" she said, as if it was completely obvious.

We sat in silence as we drove downtown to Sears.

"How'd you like to get me a piece of gum?" she asked.

If you sat in the front seat, you had to hold Mom's purse. It was a large, black leather tote that was heavy and full of mom things. She had two wallets: a large red one for holding receipts, coupons, and money, and a chequebook for recording all her expenditures. She also had a coin purse, sunglasses, a handful of toiletries such as Vaseline and hand lotion, and a wad of tissues. She was always certain that the tissues weren't used.

I handed her a piece of gum. As we pulled into the parking lot, she lit another cigarette. We made our way to the front doors and paused outside so she could take another long drag. Then she stomped the cigarette butt out with her foot and we went into the store.

"Can I help you find anything today?" a saleslady asked.

"We're looking for bras," Mom said.

I cringed in embarrassment.

"What size are you needing?"

The saleslady was larger in size and wore a conservative floral button-up blouse. She looked my mom up and down, trying to guess what size she would be.

"Oh, not for me, for her," she said.

The saleslady looked down at me and I immediately flushed.

"Oh, I see!" she said.

She adjusted her glasses and then asked me to follow her to the changing rooms to get measured. She allowed me to keep my T-shirt on and placed the measuring tape around my chest. She took my measurements and then escorted us to a small section of boxed bras in my size.

Mom and I browsed through the options and purchased three different bras. We got back into the car and drove home. As we pulled into the front of the house, Mom looked over at me.

"We don't need to tell your dad about this, alright?"

I nodded and snuck my bag of bras into the house. I placed them in a drawer with my panties.

·

I used the notebook one last time shortly thereafter. I wrote a note to her about Chad and how he made me feel when he bugged me. I was nervous to place it under her pillow but hopeful it would be the start of a loving bond. I waited for three days in hopes of finding it on my pillow, but she never wrote back. It was the last time the notebook would ever be used. I learned then that Chad was not up for discussion.

ERRAND GIRL

The extent of time I spent with my mother was limited. We enjoyed our shopping trips, and I helped with running errands. For as long as I can remember, I was Mom's runner to pay the bills. She'd pull up outside the office building downtown, and I'd run in with that month's cheques for the water, electricity, and phone bills.

"Don't forget to get me a receipt!" she yelled as soon as I got out of the car.

I proceeded to the first floor where the tellers were located and waited impatiently in line. Mom was circling the block, and I hated to make her wait. As my turn came, I stepped up to the counter on my tiptoes and presented the cheque and the bill together.

"Well, hello there. Aren't you such a good little helper?" she said.

Little! I was nine.

"Would you like a receipt?" she asked.

"Yes," I said with confidence.

I took my receipt and ran outside to find Mom sitting in a parking spot, windows down and a cigarette burning in her fingers over the edge of the door.

"What took you so long? I had to circle the block five times before I found this spot."

"There was a lineup."

I hopped into my seat, put my seatbelt on, and we were off to pay the next bill before getting a few things from the store. We pulled into the Co-op, and she handed me a list of six items: bread, buns, milk, sour cream, yellow onions, and cigarettes.

"Here's my debit card and here's a letter for the smokes. You know what kind they are, right? Lights?"

The first time Mom sent me into the store I forgot to say lights and was sent out with the wrong carton. She had to go back in and plead with the cashier for an exchange.

"Yes, Mom. Number seven king-size lights."

"Okay, good girl. Quick like a bunny."

I ran into the store and grabbed a small basket. Then I made my way through the bakery and to the refrigerated section. I put all my items onto the circular conveyor and placed a separator behind my items, like Mom taught me.

"Are you shopping alone today, miss?" the cashier asked.

Her name tag said *Susan*.

"Um, no. My mom's in the car. Oh, and I need a carton of number seven king-size lights, please."

She raised one eyebrow before telling me I'd need to go to customer service for that purchase. I carried my two bags of groceries to the customer service counter. I again requested the carton of cigarettes. I showed them my note and told them my mom was waiting in the car. They processed the payment on her debit card, and I made my way out to the parking lot.

I placed my grocery bags in the backseat.

Before closing the door, Mom said, "Pass me the cigarettes."

She opened the carton and put two packs inside her purse, then put her purse back on my seat.

When we arrived home, I grabbed the bags from the back of the car and put away the groceries. I took the rest of the cigarette packages out and put them in the freezer, lined up together inside the door.

"Amber!" she called from the bathroom.

She was sitting on the toilet, reading one of her *Chicken Soup for the Soul* books.

"How'd you like to get me a cup of tea and some smokes?" she asked.

"Okay," I said.

"You'll have to heat it up in the microwave," she added as I turned the corner.

I went to the kitchen and placed a cup of earl grey tea in the microwave for two minutes. Usually there was tea in the pot but on occasion I would need to make a new pot which required two tea bags and a full kettle of boiled water. While I waited for the microwave, I reached into her purse and grabbed a new pack of smokes. Mom was very particular about how she liked to receive them. Take the plastic off on the outside, open it up and pull out the two foils inside, then toss the foil in the garbage before handing the pack over.

I grabbed her tea and put one and a half centimetres depth of milk into it, just the way she liked it. It was full to the top. I tiptoed back to the bathroom and handed it to her cautiously, to not spill any tea on the carpet.

"Thank you," she said, handing me an empty package of cigarettes to put in the garbage.

I went back to the kitchen and got all the ingredients out to make perogies and sausage for supper.

•

As I got older, the distance between Mom and me became more prevalent. It was apparent to everyone who knew us that things were difficult between us. However, if you didn't know us, you'd have no idea. We never spoke about the important things, and it was a general understanding that I was to be proper and polite. A perfect lady. A respectable wife in training.

AUNTIE BETH

Auntie Beth was one of my mom's younger sisters; she was also my godmother. She had two young kids: a boy and a girl. I loved her like a second mom. Auntie Beth was always fiercely protective of her kids, and if we were in her care, then she was protective of us as well. Chad and I would often have sleepovers at her house, and during the day we'd head over to the playground. It wasn't unusual for older kids to give us trouble. One of us would run back home and tell Auntie Beth that there were bigger kids being mean at the playground. She would run over in her housecoat, cigarette in hand, hair a mess.

"Which ones are they?" she'd ask, and we would confidently point them out to her.

"Hey! Listen here you little shits. If any of you even speak a word to one of my kids again, I'll come back out here so fast and beat your ass until you're black and blue. Ya hear me?"

The kids would stare at her sheepishly, stunned. They'd nod their heads while the three of us stood a little taller, knowing she always had our back. This was Auntie Beth. My ferocious protector.

Our relationship flourished as I got older. She never missed a birthday, and she became someone I could confide in about my relationship with my mom. Auntie Beth knew how unstable my mom was, but she had a way of keeping her calm with her laissez-faire attitude. Her style of mothering was laid back. She was carefree, and her kids laughed a lot. On the rare occasions they did argue with each other, Auntie Beth never took it personally and never let it fester. She was a version of motherhood I admired growing up, so different from what I knew. I kept that knowledge inside, that not all mothers were like my own.

STRIPPED SIBLINGS

Tension in our family spiked when Dad was transferred two and a half hours south to Regina for his job. Mom was angry and upset that she had to move. We were leaving our home and all her family members. I was entering fifth grade and Chad sixth grade. Jason had already finished high school but needed to take a few classes to upgrade his marks so he could go into physiotherapy.

We moved down to Regina and stayed in a hotel for a couple of weeks before moving into our new home. The hotel was one room with two queen beds and a cot for the five of us and our dog, Sheena. It was cramped. Chad and I were always in the same bed whenever we travelled or went camping.

When we moved into our new home, Chad and Jason got huge bedrooms downstairs. Jason had his own full bathroom ensuite, and Chad had full-size gymnastics parallel bars, a punching bag, and a built-in desk. My room was modest in comparison, but Mom decorated it with pink-and-purple floral wallpaper. We spent a good month renovating and repainting the entire house. I was a quick study to learn how to paint and reattach baseboards. I followed behind Dad and used a nail punch on every baseboard nail before we filled, sanded, and painted. For weeks, we worked late into the evening, listening to

Meatloaf at full volume, making this house our home. A black and grey room for Jason and black, grey, and red room for Chad. Mom recently discovered sponge painting, so it was a consistent theme throughout our house.

•

"C'mon you two, get in the bath," Mom said.

We had just finished applying a first coat of beige paint in the living room. It was a Sunday night and Chad and I still bathed together once a week. We were nine and eleven. Mom ran the bath while Dad and Jason continued working in the living room. I could hear Sheena barking and Jason growling at her. He taunted her with his hand shaped like a claw. I wanted to rescue her, but I knew my mom would object. Chad and I stripped down, leaving our clothes on the bathroom floor. I stood with my arms folded over my chest. I had been wearing a bra now for almost a year. We began to fight about who had to sit in the back, closest to the taps.

"Get in!" Chad argued as he stood there naked.

"I always have to sit in the back," I said.

I hated sitting closest to the taps. The glass shower doors were always closed on that side, and it felt claustrophobic and hot. The humidity made it hard to breathe, and I couldn't see through the frosted glass. Chad got mad every time I tried to open my side of the doors and allow some cooler air in.

"Amber, get in the tub!" Mom said, as she came back to the bathroom to wash our hair.

I said nothing and reluctantly got into the tub. I crossed my arms over my chest and sat down, feeling the scalding water on my bottom. I immediately pulled my knees up to my chest and wrapped my arms around myself as Chad got in after me. Mom washed my hair. My breasts were now pronounced, and they shook as she vigorously scrubbed my scalp. Chad watched with interest.

Then she shampooed his hair. When Mom was done, she exited the bathroom and instructed us to finish bathing and wash ourselves. I stayed with my knees up to my chest as I pulled soapy water onto my arms. Chad had always been comfortable with his body. He liked to show me his newly developed pubic hair and his ability to pull the skin from the shaft over the head of his penis. He only did this when it was just the two of us.

"Okay you two, time to get out," Mom said when she returned to the bathroom.

Chad stepped out of the tub, and she wrapped him with a towel.

"Stay on the mat!" Mom yelled.

She hated water being tracked through the house.

"Okay, Amber, your turn," she said.

Chad made some room for me on the mat, and I got out of the tub. I turned my back to her, and she wrapped me in my towel. I held it tight to me, wiped my feet on the mat and hurried off to my room to put on my pyjamas.

If I didn't have a bath with Chad, I showered with my mom. She would wash my hair and then take the bar of soap to my body, washing my back and under my arms. Her hand dipped between my buttocks and then between my legs, washing my vulva. She followed up by washing her body the same way. I never bathed alone.

FINITE FREEDOM

The skating rink became my escape. I started skating when I was two years old. My mother always said it came naturally to me. She said I was graceful. What I loved most was the sense of calm and ability to be alone. The sound and feeling of a sharp blade cutting through the fresh ice. The cold, crisp air hitting my face. The feeling of flying as I glided on my skates at full speed. I was free. I loved getting to the rink and being the first one on the ice. Those few moments were everything to me, the silence and stillness. Skating was therapeutic.

When we moved to Regina, I joined the CanFigure program and worked with a Russian coach who had taught Olympians from Russia. He was extremely strict and expected everyone to be diligent with their training. He had a thick accent and was difficult to understand most of the time. His wife was much younger, and was soft-spoken. She knew how to speak English quite well and helped with translation. I practised twice a week with a small group of girls and my coaches' son.

I learned very quickly that socializing with the other kids wasn't allowed. I made the mistake of pausing during practice to join a conversation with a couple of the girls in my group.

"Hurry up!" Mom said.

I had just gotten off the ice and was heading to the changing rooms to take off my skates. I could tell from the ice that something was wrong with her. She had an upset look on her face, but I had no idea what I had done wrong. She didn't say anything until we got into the car.

"Listen here, missy. I'm not paying for you to stand out there and socialize," she said. "Do you have any idea how much skating costs?"

I sat in the backseat, feet dangling off the edge. I lowered my head and feelings of despair came over me. Mom always called me missy when she wasn't happy with me. I hated it. She reminded me of the cost of ice time and skating lessons. The price for a private lesson had just gone up to $2.80 for a fifteen-minute lesson and those only happened once a week.

"I'm sorry, Mom. I won't do it again."

"You better not!"

I immediately switched the conversation to something I knew would make her blood boil. It was a surefire tactic to get her aggression focused on someone other than me.

"Did Jennifer's mom say anything to you today?"

Jennifer was my biggest competition, according to my mom. She'd recently developed a distaste for Jennifer's mom, and she didn't want me being nice to her daughter.

"Oh, that Jennifer thinks she's the next best thing. And her mom! Don't get me started on her mom. She's so full of herself. She thinks Jennifer is going to be what? The next Elizabeth Manley?" Mom ranted as we drove home from practice.

Mission accomplished.

•

The day of my first competition was a freezing cold Saturday in March 1994. I had received my first skating dress as a gift for my tenth birthday and had been saving it to wear for this occasion. It was a long-sleeved teal dress with pink trim. My hair was pulled back tight into a high bun.

My bangs were curled, and Mom used a hair pick to create a perfect poof. I held my arms crossed over my chest and hunched my shoulders to hide the outline of my bra. Each girl from our group performed the exact same program. I executed both my short and long programs flawlessly. Mom and I were anxious for the results.

Finally, the standings were posted. We ran up to the wall with the swarm of other skaters. I got first place! My body felt electric. I vibrated with excitement and couldn't help but smile ear to ear.

"Yes! You beat Jennifer!" Mom said with excitement.

We skipped back to where Dad was to tell him the good news. We passed Jennifer and her mom along the way. Mom smiled with a smirk and had an extra skip in her step. I was happy that she was happy.

"Dad! I got first!"

I jumped into his arms. He wrapped them around me and picked me up off the ground, squeezing me tight.

"You did?" he asked.

I nodded my head, still smiling as big as ever.

"Of course you did, you were amazing out there! I couldn't be more proud."

Dad put me down and reached over to grab a single red rose wrapped in cellophane with a pink ribbon. I had never received a flower before.

My eyes widened as soon as I saw it. I jumped up for another hug.

"Thank you, thank you, thank you."

"Okay, you two," Mom interrupted.

Dad put me down on the floor and we listened intently as Mom shared the news about Jennifer placing second. For the short program, Jennifer and I were in different flights, and I placed second. Mom didn't seem to mind. She was only focused on the fact that both girls who placed first and third in my division were twice my size and weight. The professional photographer who took the photos with our medals had to change our positions because we looked ridiculous standing side by side. It was a story that Mom loved to tell.

SECRET SHOWER

I walked into the kitchen to find Jason cooking a homemade pizza. It smelled delectable. Jason wasn't known to cook unless he was hungry, but this time he was making pizza for the whole family.

"Pizza!" Mom and Dad came into the kitchen, just as surprised as Chad and I were.

"I can't take another meal of spaghetti and Caesar salad this week," Jason said.

It was the fall of 1994, a year after we moved to Regina. Mom and Dad had recently quit smoking and Mom developed intense cravings for spaghetti and Caesar salad. We were eating it almost every night. We sat down together as a family for dinner, and I immediately inhaled my ham and pineapple pizza. I wondered why it took Jason so long to make this insanely delicious meal. As I reached across the table for another slice, Jason told us that he was moving to Vancouver. Chad and I both stopped mid-bite and looked to Mom and Dad for a reaction.

Mom let out an incredulous gasp.

"Chad, Amber, go to your rooms!" she said.

I could tell she wasn't happy. I stood up with my plate in hand, rattled. We had a rule that we clear our dishes from the table. But I wasn't finished eating. We also had a rule that food wasn't allowed out of the kitchen, so I couldn't take my plate to my bedroom. Instead, I stood there, bewildered with indecision.

"Just leave it!" she said sharply.

I put my plate down on the table and hightailed it to my bedroom. Chad had already gone downstairs to his room. I eavesdropped on the conversation from my bedroom door. I understood how Jason felt. He hated living in Regina. He'd left all his friends in Saskatoon and had become Mom's punching bag when she was stressed out from needing a nicotine fix. He finished upgrading his marks and decided to take a year off and go to Vancouver, a place where he always wanted to live.

•

Mom and Dad weren't happy but Jason left anyway. The house was different without him. It was quieter. Sheena seemed to have a pep in her step, knowing she wouldn't be taunted. I asked Mom if I could move downstairs into Jason's room. It was the biggest room I had ever seen, and I would have my own bathroom. The answer was always no.

I rarely went downstairs before Jason left, unless I had to clean the bathroom, vacuum, or was hanging out with Chad. Now that Jason was gone, I felt like I could venture out more freely. It was a Sunday morning and I had just come back from the skating rink. It was the only time that my age group had lessons on the weekend. I had to clean the bathrooms as soon as I got home. I got to work scrubbing the shower downstairs. I sprinkled Comet, added a little water to create a thick blue paste, and scrubbed every inch of the tub with a scrubber. I still longed to have his room and my own bathroom. I decided I would sneak a shower by myself.

I finished cleaning the bathroom and quietly took my cleaning supplies upstairs and placed them in the linen closet. Dad was working in the garage installing new brake pads on Mom's car while she kept herself busy in her room. I snuck downstairs and locked both doors: the door to Jason's old room and the one to the hallway. I stripped down and hopped in the shower, turning the hot water to a perfect scalding temperature. I knew if I showered or bathed before dinner, I wouldn't need to have a bath with Chad. I shampooed my hair and washed every inch of my small frame. It felt exhilarating but at the same time I was nervous about what Mom would say when she found out. It wasn't like me to defy the rules. Taking an unprompted shower outside of our usual routine was unheard of. Still, it was easier than asking to shower alone and face rejection. When I was done, I went upstairs, wrapped in a towel, my hair drenched.

"Did you just have a shower?" Mom asked as she passed me in the hallway.

"Yes," I said as I lowered my head to the ground.

"Why?" she asked, an eyebrow raised.

"I just felt like I needed one."

"Oh," she muttered.

Later that night, Chad showered alone. And from that point on, so did I.

THE PASTEL COUCH

The four of us moved back to Saskatoon after only fifteen months in Regina. Mom was completely miserable and missed her sisters. She hated working at the hospital in Regina. The women in the dietary department there were "hoity-toity" or at least that's what she told Auntie Beth on the phone. After Jason left, we spent every weekend travelling to Saskatoon to stay with Auntie Beth, so it only made sense to move back. Dad quit his job and found another position working for a food-service company in Saskatoon and Mom resumed her position with the Saskatoon health region, working once again in the dietary department.

They bought a small bungalow on the westside of Saskatoon with three bedrooms upstairs, and one bedroom downstairs. This was our third home in three years, but it felt like we could be here for quite some time. My parents started to invest in making this home their own. My room had the same wallpaper that we had in the previous house because it was still on clearance. The living room was closed off from the rest of the house and had two large windows. It was decorated with one large pastel couch and one matching swivel armchair. The fabric was a blend of blue, pink, and lavender pastel colours in a contemporary pattern. Above the pastel couch were three mountainscape photographs from prior camping trips. A wood coffee table and matching end tables sat atop the dusty rose carpet. The metal blinds on the windows were always adjusted and turned up just so, allowing light through but providing complete privacy.

Chad and I returned to our old elementary school. It was easier than when we moved to Regina and knew no one. We knew the school and the teachers. We had old friends, but they had moved on to make new best friends and it would take some time to work our way back into their circle. I started up immediately with figure skating at the Saskatoon club. I was in awe of the rink because it wasn't a hockey rink. It was designed specifically for figure skating. There were no boards surrounding the ice, no lines, the ice was softer, and the temperature was cool but not frigid like I had become accustomed to. There was a track on the ceiling that connected to a harness to assist in jumps, and a VHS recorder and TV to watch playbacks. It had a wall full of mirrors and bars for stretching. It was the real deal.

By the time summer rolled around, we were all established in our routines. Chad had a paper route, and six mornings a week we both got up early, loaded up our bags, and headed out to deliver *The StarPhoenix*. It was technically his paper route, and he oversaw monthly collections, but Mom told him he had to pay me forty dollars a month for helping. I didn't realize at the time that he was getting paid considerably more. I was working for the equivalent to a $1.50 per day to deliver half of the newspapers in temperatures that reached negative forty-five degrees Celsius.

It was important to our parents that we were raised with a good work ethic starting from a young age. We didn't receive an allowance and chores around the house were exactly that: chores. Jason had a paper route when he was the same age and at that time, when I was seven, Chad and I delivered *The Wednesday Advertiser* and *The Sunday Sun* until we moved to Regina.

The summer months required us to get up and complete our paper route by 7:30 a.m. If we didn't finish by then, we'd get phone calls and complaints from customers and that was not acceptable. We stumbled back home, sweaty and out of breath, empty newspaper sacks dangling over our shoulders. We plopped onto the couch and got comfortable, flipping through channels, usually landing on *Much Music* or *SportsDesk* while Dad got ready for work. The mornings were always ours to do whatever we wanted before Dad came home for lunch. Then we would scramble to get our lists of to-dos done before Mom came home.

Summers in Saskatoon were usually hot and humid. That July was no exception. We had just gotten home from doing our papers. I ran into the living room and hopped onto the couch, grabbing the remote control. I turned on *Once Upon a Hamster*. If I had the remote first, then it was my choice what we watched.

"Hey, do you want to see something?" Chad asked, as he came around the corner into the living room.

I knew he wasn't interested in watching what I had chosen.

"What?" I replied.

"Have you ever seen a boner?"

"What, you mean like an erection?" I asked.

I was eleven years old and my vast knowledge of the male sex was what Chad had shown or told me, plus the time the last year in fifth grade when they separated us into two groups. Boys and girls. The girls discussed breast development and menstruation, and we were all given a sample pad that we tried to discretely hide before the boys came back into the classroom.

Chad came over and sat next to me on the couch. He pulled his erection from his sweatpants. His penis looked different. It had been over a year since we bathed together in Regina. It looked more grown-up this time. He had a full amount of pubic hair, and his penis was thick and veiny.

He looked down at my hand and reached for it. He grabbed my fingers and pulled them toward his penis.

"Feel it," he said, wrapping my hand around himself.

He squeezed my hand forcefully around his penis.

"Doesn't that hurt?" I asked.

I was trying to deflect the situation as I sat there, motionless.

He closed his eyes for a long blink. Then he sat back and exhaled while moving my hand up and down the shaft of his penis. I froze. I had no idea what to say. I couldn't pull my hand away because his hand was wrapped around mine. I hated this moment, but I also felt a strange sense of gratitude. I reminded myself that it could always be worse. It was better than having a bath together. I didn't feel as vulnerable or exposed. I looked up at the ceiling and then down at the dusty rose carpet.

As he strummed his penis with my hand, I noticed a loose strand of fabric from the couch and twisted it with my free hand. The smell of cigarettes escaped the fibres and I thought of my mom. She'd started smoking again that year, and I was reminded that I needed to change over the laundry before she got home. Chad finally let my hand go. There was a small amount of a sticky, clear substance on my thumb and pointer finger. He tucked himself back into his sweatpants. He was still hard, and he wrapped his own hand around himself before grabbing the remote.

I went to the bathroom and pumped three pumps of soap to wash my hands. I rinsed them and then washed them again with three more pumps of soap. I struggled to feel like I was fully clean. Chad stayed in the living room, channels switching rapidly as he tried to find something to watch. I went downstairs and pulled my mom's uniforms out of the dryer. It was important that they were hung up immediately so they wouldn't wrinkle. Ten uniform sets. The pants needed to be hung with a centre crease over the hanger and paired with a matching top. I came back upstairs to a waft of melted cheese and Miracle Whip. Three beeps and Chad was at the microwave pulling out his hot sandwich on a piece of paper towel. He took a bite and cheese dripped from his mouth. He inhaled while he chewed, as it was too hot.

"Want one?" he asked.

"No thanks," I said, shaking my head.

I didn't have much of an appetite.

MATTHEW

Matthew was my first real boyfriend. He wasn't my first kiss, however. When we lived in Regina, I shared my first kiss with a boy named Landon. It happened in a neighbour's garage. Jordan, my neighbour, was a year older than I was. He was tall and lanky and wore glasses. Exactly my type but he was out of my league. Landon was short like me. He had pale skin, green eyes, braces, and dark spiked hair. The jeans he wore had a four-inch rolled up cuff at the bottom and still pooled onto his Converse shoes. We started with awkward conversation and then he leaned in and planted one on me: a quick peck on the lips. I wiped my mouth with the sleeve of my shirt. We smiled awkwardly at each other, lowered our heads in embarrassment, then headed back outside to jump on the trampoline with the rest of the kids.

Matthew was different. He asked me to be his girlfriend. We were in seventh grade, and I was eleven. For picture day I wore a light pink turtleneck under a pink striped cardigan, a matching pink skirt, and pink earrings. Mom picked out my outfit and brought it home for me to wear. My hair was straight, past my shoulders, with bangs that surrounded my sun-bronzed skin. I was an image of purity and innocence. Matthew was tall and skinny. He had light brown hair in a mushroom-cut style and wore baggy jeans and basketball jerseys. We held hands and sat together. We hugged every day after school, and we occasionally pecked on the far side of the school grounds. Matthew was from McNab Park, an area of town that was desolate and impoverished. All the students from there were new to our elementary school that year and had to be bused in because their school had recently closed.

"Amber's got a boyfriend!" Chad said, letting my secret out of the bag.

"Oh?" Mom asked.

"We're just friends!" I said.

"No you're not. You told me he asked you out," Chad said.

That's the last time I tell him anything, I thought.

"What's his name?" Mom asked.

"His name is Matthew. He's nice. He likes basketball. He's tall with mushroom-cut."

"And whereabouts does he live?"

"He lives in McNab Park," I said.

"Oh!" Mom looked up and made eye contact. "You know those kids are poor, right?"

"No, I don't think Matthew is. He has nice clothes."

"No, if he lives in McNab Park, then he's poor, Amber. Is he Native?"

"No, he's white," I said.

I didn't understand why any of this mattered. Matthew was cute, and he was nice to me. He had decent grades, and he liked sports. I continued to go out with Matthew even though Mom didn't care for the idea. I reminded her that we were just friends.

Our school became increasingly strict, and indoor and out-of-school suspensions were enforced by our vice principal, Mr. B. Suspensions were issued for chewing gum, wearing hats indoors, swearing, showing up late, and various other reasons, usually at the whim of our teachers.

I received a two-day indoor suspension for sitting too close to Matthew during recess. It destroyed me. I prided myself with an image of perfection, and I was never one to get in trouble. Mom and Dad didn't seem to mind. Chad had already received many suspensions, and they had a personal vendetta against Mr. B.

Matthew and I casually dated on and off for the rest of that year and some of the next. If we weren't dating, then he was going out with Amy, another girl in my class. She was cooler than I was. She wore tank tops with spaghetti straps and wide-leg cargo pants. She had dark brown hair from a box dye and wore dark brown lipstick and heavy eyeliner. She occasionally smoked cigarettes. We were complete opposites. It was a love triangle that stirred up enough drama for me but never seemed to affect my grades.

THE CHURCH OF CLEAN

Cleaning is part of my DNA. From the age of six, Mom taught me to vacuum and dust. Spraying copious amounts of Pledge, I would take my finger and write my name in it before rubbing it into the wood. Vacuum tracks were executed with precision and symmetry, covering every inch of the rug. The small attachment was used to do the perimeter around the baseboards. Mom never let me forget.

By the age of seven, I knew how to clean the bathrooms and wax the kitchen floors. The first step was to remove all the chairs, rugs, and pet items. The kitchen floors were vacuumed, then washed by hand with a bucket of hot water and Pine-Sol. After it dried completely, two coats of wax were applied by hand with a small cloth. Mom said one coat was enough, but I thought two looked better. Plus, it made it easier to practice my figure skating spins in the kitchen.

The bathrooms were cleaned from top to bottom. Mirrors, counters, toilets, bathtubs, shower doors, and floors. I sprayed additional Windex on all the chrome pieces to make sure they sparkled. I lined up Mom's toiletries in her bathroom like members of a choir: tallest cascading to shortest. I wanted her to be happy with my performance when she came in to check my work. If I missed a spot or did an inadequate job, she would point it out and I would have to redo it.

Cleaning became a big part of my childhood. The bathrooms became my church. I would tend to all three of them every Sunday, before homework or any type of playing. The main bathroom, my parents ensuite, and Jason's full bath downstairs, were all my responsibility.

By the age of ten, I was ironing my dad's work shirts. Starch first, then work your way around the entire shirt on the ironing board, ending with the collar. Mom taught me how to clean windows with newspaper, and walls with Spray Nine. There wasn't an area in the house that I didn't know how to clean. In the grocery store, it was the one aisle where I could pick whatever I wanted. I always knew how much inventory I had, and what was running low. Sometimes my mom would even surprise me with a new bathroom cleaner.

If I was cleaning, then I usually wasn't bothered, unless I was needed for something else. One day, I finished cleaning both bathrooms upstairs and was making my way down to do Jason's bathroom. Auntie Beth had popped over for a visit, and she was sitting with Mom at the kitchen table.

"Hi, Auntie Beth!"

"Hi Am, you cleaning bathrooms again?"

"Yeah, one more to go."

"Hey, how'd you like to pour us another cup of tea while you're up?" Mom asked.

"I'll get it, Marlene," Auntie Beth said.

She furrowed her brows and laughed a little before getting up and making her way to the stove. Mom's teapot always had a crochet cozy over it. I smiled at my aunt. It was her subtle way of standing up for me. She never treated me like a servant. I continued with my cleaning and knew that Mom would be in a good mood for the rest of the day. She had a visit from Auntie Beth and three clean bathrooms.

EROTICA ENCOUNTER

Jason moved back from Vancouver and tensions were high in the house. He gained a sense of freedom while he was away and now that he was twenty, it was difficult to be under Mom and Dad's supervision again. Jason and Mom fought constantly. There was always something wrong. He was out too late, drinking too much, or bringing a girl home that never bothered to stick around and say hi. Chad and I would run to the back door as soon as we woke up.

"Yep, her shoes are still here," we would yell back to Mom and Dad. It was Natalie. She would spend the night and skip out most mornings without saying goodbye, but recently she'd been staying later into the morning. I was intrigued. Jason had never had a girlfriend before, or at least he never introduced us to anyone. When we did get a chance to say hello to Natalie, we all bombarded her before she stepped out the door. She seemed sweet and bubbly. Perfect for Jason.

Mom and Jason made a deal that if he was going to school, he didn't need to pay rent. Jason gave up on the idea of being a physiotherapist and settled for a journeyman's ticket in air conditioning and refrigeration. We didn't see much of him, except on weekends. Even then, he remained in the basement watching TV most of the day. I rarely went down there, and never if he was home. I didn't feel comfortable talking to him. I felt like I was a nuisance to him.

•

It was another hot summer day in August, and my parents and Jason were all at work. I was tucked away in my closet, arranging items on the shelves that Dad had built when we first moved in. Sheena slept on my bed. Sheena was a miniature dachshund. She was red in colour and was my best friend.

"Hey, come here! I need to show you something!" Chad said, suddenly appearing in my doorway.

"What is it?" I asked, intrigued.

Sheena hopped off my bed and trotted alongside me as I followed him downstairs to Jason's room. It was dark, and smelled of sweat. Jason had an old wooden desk in his room and above it was a framed Jerry Rice jersey. Chad opened the bottom desk drawer and pulled out two magazines from underneath a large stack of papers. *Hustler* featured a blonde woman with very large breasts on the cover. The other magazine was *Swank*. Chad flipped through the pages to show me various photos of naked women, including a few photos where men and women were actually having sex. I had only ever seen pictures of breasts before. Chad had managed to buy a deck of playing cards from the corner store by our elementary school. Each card had a different picture of a topless woman. He kept them above his trophy case in his room so our mom wouldn't find them. The magazines were a whole new level of nudity. I sat there dumbfounded as I flipped through the pages. I had never seen a penis inside a vagina before. I wondered why all these girls were spreading their privates apart.

"Look what else I found!" Chad interrupted my thoughts as he grabbed a VHS tape and ran over to the TV.

He pushed the tape into the VCR. Moans immediately escaped the TV and two women with large breasts were kissing a man. One kissed his mouth while one licked his penis. I became nervous and my stomach started to roll. What if Jason found out that we were in his room going through his stuff? He would be furious. What if Dad came home for lunch? There was a loud bang that came from outside.

"What was that?" I asked.

My heart was racing, and my breathing became shallow.

"I think I heard a car door!" I said.

"Quick, run upstairs," Chad said.

He shut off the VCR and ejected the tape to stash it back in Jason's desk. I ran upstairs, Sheena following behind me. We landed on the couch in the living room. The noise wasn't Dad, it was the neighbour's car.

"I better go back down and rewind it," Chad said. "If I don't, then Jason will know for sure we were going through his stuff."

I felt relieved. Chad was right. We needed to cover our tracks.

THE PASTEL ARMCHAIR

Chad and I were frequently left alone during the day in the summer months. Mom left a list of chores for each of us. Chad's list included mowing the lawn and mine usually consisted of weeding the garden, cleaning, and getting dinner ready. Mom worked five days a week from 6:30 a.m. to 2:30 p.m. preparing meals at a long-term care facility. She had recently left the hospital dietary department because the hours were better. She would come home, take a nap, and if I hadn't already started cooking, she would let me know what needed to be prepared for supper.

I was so excited to go back to school. I was heading into the eighth grade. Chad had graduated and was heading into high school. He was attending the same high school that Mom went to, and she was ecstatic. It was the first time that Chad and I would be in separate schools. Matthew and I weren't dating anymore, which was good because by the end of the previous year he reeked of sweat and I couldn't be around him. But my hopes were high that he would soon find out about the invention of deodorant, and we would be reunited. Chad knew I was nervous about boys. I had yet to French kiss one. The thought of it repulsed me. Sticking your tongue in someone's mouth? So gross.

THE OBEDIENT DAUGHTER

We sat together in the living room. Chad was on the couch and I was on the armchair, my legs hanging over the edge. We talked eagerly about what the next year would bring for each of us.

"I'm going to have a lot of girlfriends," Chad said.

"At the same time?" I asked.

That seemed like an impossible idea.

"Nah. Probably like one after the other," he said.

"Yeah."

That made more sense to me, but it still seemed like a lot of work.

"I wonder how long it will take me to lose my virginity? I bet I could finger a girl within the first month," he said.

Chad sat there in deep thought, pondering what his first year of high school would be like. He loved talking about anything related to sex and was always eager to teach me new things. He got up from the couch and went into the kitchen. I could hear him open the pantry door and assumed he was getting something to eat. He came back around the corner into the living room where I was sitting.

"Why don't we try something?" he said.

He pulled out his erect penis and started to wrap it in Saran Wrap that he'd grabbed from the pantry.

"I promise you, it won't even touch you." He continued to wrap his penis in multiple layers. "Stand up."

I stood up beside the pastel armchair. It was a swivel chair and sat directly in front of the window. Chad directed me closer toward him and then pulled down my shorts and panties. He grabbed my shoulders and spun me around.

"Bend over," he said.

I remained silent and was unable to move. It seemed like a weird spot at the time. But being able to see out the window made sense just in case anyone came home. The chair wobbled and the cover over the armrest started to slide as I tried to balance on it while he was behind me. He pushed and his penis abruptly entered me from behind. I could see outside through the cracks in the blinds. There was no one in sight; nothing but stillness and parked cars. The crescent was always quiet. The pain finally hit me, and a scream escaped my mouth. He backed off.

I got up, pulled up my panties and shorts, and quickly went to my room. My room was my safe place and the only place I could ever be alone. There was no lock, and people would enter as they pleased, but it was mine. I laid on my bed, limbs shaking, and felt the burning sensation that lingered in my behind. What had just happened? I didn't want to learn about this stuff anymore. I looked over and saw my Barbie doll house at the end of my bed. I hadn't played with it for almost a year, but it was one of those things that I really cherished from being a little girl. I could create any world that I wanted to with my Barbies. Life seemed simpler back then.

Sheena pushed the door open with her nose and jumped up beside me on my bed. She nuzzled her nose under my arm and scooted closer to me. I laid there a few more minutes, looking down at her soft red coat and white face. She was getting older. I left my room, knowing that I needed to start my chores before Mom got home.

Chad looked at me as I walked down the hall.

"Hey, so you're not going to tell Mom or Dad about this, right?"

I could tell he must have been pacing and waiting for me to come out of my room. I shook my head no and walked past him. I grabbed the vacuum, a pail, a scrub brush, and Pine-Sol. The window screens needed to be taken out and washed. At least if I was cleaning, he wouldn't bother me. I buried this secret deep down, and so did Chad.

THERAPY

Dr. M. leaned back in her chair, notebook sitting on her lap. She took a long breath, exhaling out her mouth. I wondered if she, too, felt anxiety in her chest like I did.

"I'm so sorry that happened to you." She had the same look on her face that everyone did when they found out. A look of dumfounded shock, like she had just heard someone died by suicide.

I took a long breath myself and looked away as a tear fell down my face. I didn't know what to say in response to that. Thank you? She could tell by my expression that I didn't want to hear an apology.

"Does that trigger you? Me saying that?"

"Yes," I said, still looking at the floor.

"Tell me more. What do you feel when I say that?"

"I hate it when people say they are sorry. I'm not a victim, and you yourself have done nothing wrong. This life is all that I've ever known. I'd rather people say 'I'm proud of how far you've come.' Or 'Speaking up takes courage.' I feel like when people say they are sorry they're looking at me with pity. I don't want or need their pity."

"You're right. The fact that you are here doing the work speaks volumes."

She took a sip of her coffee and pulled her notebook to her chest, hugging it tight. I could tell my story, in all its detail, physically affected her.

"I'm proud of you for speaking up," she said.

She leaned forward, her hands clasped and the notebook still close to her chest.

"I'm proud of me, too," I said.

I smiled a small smile, my lips pressed together. My face was still damp, and I knew my eyes were red from crying.

"I want to talk more about your mom, but it will have to wait until next session. I think today was heavy enough, and we are out of time."

It was the reason why I was here. To share and eliminate the emotions attached to my trauma. But she was right. Today was enough, and I needed to get myself freshened up before picking up my daughter from school. What would everyone think if they saw me like this? I packed up all my memories, trauma, and emotions and put them back inside me. Then I carried them with me, as I did every day.

SWEET BUT SHARP

Christmas was my favourite time of the year. The magic, the twinkle of every light, and the excitement of Christmas morning. Mom was exceptional at Christmas time. We shared a mutual love for the season. She would decorate the house, and we would go to Bruce's on 33rd Street every year to pick out a Christmas tree. The smell of fresh pine needles spread throughout the living room. Mom and Dad would spend hours in their room with the door closed, wrapping presents for us all. We would eagerly await the arrival of a parcel from Grandpa and his wife, Evelyn. Each year they sent a large box of presents. Chad and I would shake every present and try to guess the contents before placing it under the tree.

I was twelve years old in December 1996. Mom and I spent the whole day baking, as we did every year. She made all her specialties: butter tarts, shortbread, chocolate haystacks, sugar cookies, and my personal favourite, peanut butter marshmallow cookies. I sat next to her at our oval oak kitchen table. It was a special piece of furniture that Mom cherished. There were three layers on top of the table: a padded cloth that she'd sewed, a light green tablecloth, and a plexiglass top. The table was set with placemats for each person. Scattered across the table were recycled ice cream pails and large margarine containers filled with assorted cookies. Mom pulled the peanut butter marshmallow cookies from the fridge and began pressing them with a large knife, cutting small one-inch squares. She and I were at the kitchen table assembling the boxes when Dad came in from the garage. Mom had been tense all day. Dad hadn't offered to help with the baking and was outside working in the garage. He came in, excited to dig into a freshly baked tray of cookies and was shot a daggered stare from Mom.

"You can carry these containers down to the freezer," she said.

"You bet, I can do that," he said as he took another bite of a warm shortbread cookie.

"You know, you could've spent less time out in the garage and offered to help me inside."

I said nothing and kept my head down. I wasn't sure how much more help she needed. I had been helping her all day. Her cookie cutting started to become more aggressive, and her voice grew more agitated. Dad, in his simplicity, thought he could make it right with a quick fix. He came to the table, asked for the knife, and offered to cut the cookies for her.

"No!" she yelled.

"You think you can come in here while I've been slaving away all day and help at the last minute? I don't think so."

Mom slammed the tray of cookies onto the table. Bits of marshmallow and peanut butter went flying. It caught me off guard, and I scooted my chair over slightly to give them some more space.

"Let me help you!" he said.

Their arguments were nothing out of the norm for us. They always escalated quickly, no matter how hard we tried to make Mom happy or fix the problem. He reached over and tried to grab the knife. Mom pulled away and raised the knife with the blade only centimetres from his throat.

"Marlene!" Dad said, sounding surprised. "Put the knife down! Put it down! What is wrong with you? Give me the knife, Marlene. Let go!"

I sat there frozen, looking up at them. I could see the panic starting to build in my dad's face, and throughout all of it, she barely said anything. She looked at him with a cold, blank stare.

"No! You let go," she screamed back.

They struggled, and Dad grabbed Mom's hand that held the knife.

"Put the fucking knife down!" Dad screamed at the top of his lungs.

He never swore. By this time, I had run into the living room on the other side of the wall, where Chad was. He was in there watching TV the entire time. He ushered me to come toward him. He put his arm around me, and we crouched down. Nestled together, we cried on the floor. This was the moment we were both certain Dad would die from a nine-inch blade. When Mom became enraged, she transformed. A darkness came through her eyes, and she became unrecognizable. She was scary, unstable, and unpredictable. Dad managed to pry the knife out of her rigid hands, and as soon as he did, she took off and left the house.

I went back to the kitchen and finished packing up the cookies, tears running down my face. Dad carried the cookies down to the freezer, and we tidied the kitchen. It would be hours before she returned. There would be no apologies, and we would never speak about it again. It imprinted though, like many other memories.

FEMALE ACCOLADES

It was the winter of 1997, and I could breathe a little easier. I was in eighth grade, and I had just gotten that French kiss that I was so nervous about. It was with Matthew. It happened during the middle of class. Our teacher left the room while we were watching a movie. Our classroom was exceptionally large. It was meant to hold three separate classes, but the other two were empty. Matthew and I snuck behind the dividing wall over to the coat rack. The kiss was beyond gross, much too slobbery, and not at all what I expected. I felt ill prepared, and I didn't understand what the hype was all about. We broke up shortly after that. It was for the best.

Schoolwork and figure skating were my biggest priorities and passions. I was practising three nights a week. It became less of a commitment for my parents because they could drop me off and pick me up when I was finished. As much as it felt like they weren't invested in me, it also provided a sense of relief that I could have conversations with other skaters without being scrutinized for wasting expensive practice time on the ice.

Chad entered ninth grade and was masterfully working his way through sexual experiences. Mom and Dad never sensed anything; they were too focused on him playing football. Jason had also played high school football. He'd been the quarterback, so naturally Chad would do that as well.

Mom loved to talk about Chad's exceptional arm and his broad shoulders. We would watch his reel tape over and over and listen intently to the commentators. "Look at the arm on that kid," they would say. He even took to track and field once football was over and went to the city finals for all the throwing events. Javelin, discus, shot put. He broke city records. Mom printed off 8x10 photos of him in action on the football field. Chad signed them and gave them as gifts to our relatives, thanking them for their support. He seemed to be a living, breathing high school legend in the making.

Chad and I sat up late one Saturday night together. He stretched himself along the couch and flipped to channel 54. We didn't get the channel, but the *Red Shoe Diaries* were on, and he liked to watch it scrambled. He turned the volume down low so our parents couldn't hear the moans.

"Hey, did I tell you what Britt and I did?"

Britney was his most recent girlfriend, and they had been dating a number of weeks.

"No," I said. I was tired but realized the more engaged I was in his sexuality, the less it would involve me.

"We were at her house on Friday night, watching a movie, and I slipped two fingers into her pussy. She was moaning so loud, and her mom was upstairs!"

"Crazy, can you imagine if you got caught?" I said. I couldn't imagine taking a risk like that.

"Yeah, she was super wet, too." He smiled as he reminisced.

I got up and went to bed. Sheena followed behind me. I felt relief knowing that I was off the hook. Chad seemed to have all the girls at school at his disposal. I climbed into bed and pulled the covers up. Sheena hopped up and went straight to the bottom, underneath the covers, as she always did.

MACBETH

The summer before going into ninth grade finally came, as did my period. I was outside, jumping on the trampoline, when I felt something wet in my underwear. I ran inside to find bright red blood in the crotch of my underpants. Mom advised me to wear a pad and change it every time I peed. However, she forgot to mention the floodgate that happened every time you stood up, or the jellyfish that emerged every time you coughed or sneezed.

Summertime always made me nervous, but this year Chad was busy with his part-time job at Superstore. He kept in touch with all his friends from school and girls, of course. Every spare moment he had, Mom told him to practice throwing around the football. I was allowed to attend one week of skating camp, which I was thrilled about. I had never attended summer camp of any kind before. Each morning, I walked four blocks to the bus stop, got on Bus No. 8, transferred downtown to Bus No. 2, and continued all the way to Sutherland, which put me three blocks from the skating rink. It took me an hour to get there and an hour to get home every day, but the freedom was exhilarating.

Chad and I continued to deliver the newspaper each morning and kept busy with yet another season of trash TV shows. Right before school resumed, I made the impulsive decision to cut off all my hair.

My hair went from below the shoulders to a pixie cut. I'm not entirely sure why I decided to do it; perhaps it was to look less feminine or less desirable. I was a small frame of eighty-two pounds, and my shoulders were always hunched over to hide my bulging breasts. My boobs earned me the nickname "socks" at school because everyone thought I stuffed my bra. This was me in ninth grade.

I enjoyed school. I could always produce multiple A's on my report card. The praise I received from my teachers was more than what my mother gave me. Chad, on the other hand, wasn't the smartest kid. He was barely passing most of his classes, except for gym and woodworking.

One day, Mom called me into the kitchen. I was busy working on an English paper about the movie *Mask* when she hollered at me.

"Amber!"

I shuddered as I heard her yell. I came out of my room and saw Mom and Chad sitting at the kitchen table. Mom had just received a call from Mrs. B., Chad's English teacher. He was failing.

"It's clear Mrs. B. has it out for football players. She said Chad needs at least a sixty-five on his paper in order to pass English. If he doesn't pass, he doesn't play football. So, I'm gonna need your help. Whadya say, Am?"

Mom always called me Am when she was in a good mood, or when she was happy with me. Looking back, I realize it was also when she needed something from me as well.

"Sure, you want me to help him write it?"

"No, he doesn't understand *MacBeth*. I want you to write it for him. Think of it as a leg up on next year, you know? You'll be top of your class because you'll have already read it."

I had never been needed in this way before. It felt good.

"Okay, I can do that."

"Great, it's due Monday."

I read Shakespeare's *MacBeth* and wrote his paper for him. He submitted it, and without hesitation, Mrs. B. returned it with a note stating that plagiarism was not acceptable, and he was to resubmit his own work. Mom modified my essay, and he resubmitted it for a passing grade. After this, I was rarely asked to do his homework and when I did, Mom gave it a once over before submitting it. From then on, I stuck to cleaning and helping Chad change the sheets on his bed. I wasn't entirely sure how this became my responsibility, but it was something that Mom assured me Chad couldn't do by himself.

MARIPOSA GIRL

Mom loved to shop and spend money on things we didn't need. I would happily tag along. She taught me to scour the clearance racks and ask store managers for additional discounts on damaged or stained merchandise. We'd spend hours in a Sears or at the mall. It made her happy, so it made me happy. She would take me into her favourite stores to try on clothes. I'd sit holding her purse and wait for her to give some sort of indication as to whether she liked each item so I could agree with her. Sometimes I'd recall existing items or shoes she had in her closet that could be paired together. Mom loved wearing a suit even though she wore uniforms to work. She was always slightly overdressed for any occasion, which I thought showed her sophistication and class. When she dressed up, she had an air of confidence that I admired.

We'd go into Mariposa, and she would pick out clothes for me to try on. She loved it when I wore dresses or skirts. Mom would pick out clothes that I would never pick for myself, but I didn't have the heart to say no. Such a small disagreement would set her off into a tailspin of rage, and our shopping would come to a halt. I never wanted to seem ungrateful, so I happily tried on the clothes, and we purchased whatever she loved the most.

One afternoon at Mariposa, I grabbed a green sweater with a ruffled collar and held it up to my chest.

"I like this one!" I said. "It would go great with the skort that you picked out and it matches my eyes."

"Ha!" She laughed a belly laugh of mockery. "Your eyes aren't green, they're stinky hazel eyes just like mine. That's what my mother used to called them."

I looked back in the mirror with disbelief. I leaned in to take a closer look, my breath fogging up the mirror. She must have been colour blind because her eyes were brown and mine were definitely green.

We carried a pile of clothes to the cashier and placed them on the counter.

"Somebody made out well!" The sales lady was elated to claim the sale as her own even though Mom did all the work.

"She's a Mariposa girl!" Mom said with a smile.

Mom paid for the clothes with her credit card, and we left the store. As we headed to the food court I leaned in, wrapped my arm around her, and gave her a soft kiss on her cheek.

"Thank you for the clothes," I said.

I had previously made the mistake of waiting until we got home to say thank you. Mom became upset immediately and referred to me as an ungrateful little brat, so I learned to say thank you as soon as we left the store, or better yet, at the cash register.

"You're welcome, Amber. Just make sure you wear them. And we don't need to tell your brothers or your father how much they cost. Do you understand?"

"Yes, Mom."

"How about we share a meal. You're not that hungry, are you?"

This was her way of letting me know that I didn't need something. Even though I was starving, I agreed we didn't need to spend more money.

"No, not really. What would you like?"

We walked past Taco Time and New York Fries, some of my favourites. The smell of deep-fried goodness wafted through the air. We headed over to Manchu Wok, a trusted favourite of Mom's, to order the three-item combo, two glasses of water, and a side plate.

We sat together in the food court, eating in silence.

•

When we got home from shopping, she instructed me to try on my clothes to show my dad. She did the same.

"See, look at this, a size ten!" Mom proudly patted her stomach. "And it was on clearance!"

My dad never seemed too phased with her spending.

"It's only money, Am. You can always make more," he said.

Shopping made her happy. He sat patiently on the couch as she walked back and forth to her room, showing him every single outfit. After trying on her new clothes, she hung up each item in the closet. Dad came down the hallway, put his arm around her, and gave her a kiss on the forehead.

"You look beautiful, honey," he said.

TORN

I'd recently switched skating coaches. Mom wasn't happy with my previous coach. She was furious that she was getting billed for my coach's time at competitions.

"Why the hell should I have to pay for her to coach other kids over the weekend?" she asked.

I didn't really mind the switch, to be honest. My new coach, Arthur, seemed to have a more talented roster of students, and I was hopeful that I would be one of the best, too. Arthur asked my parents if I would consider skating full time and getting a tutor to help me with schoolwork, but Mom was adamant that school came first and skating came second. My new program music was from the soundtrack of *Forrest Gump*, and even though my program was good, I still felt like it needed to be tweaked. Arthur advised to play around with it and feel it out. Our club had a specialized choreographer and dance coach. His name was Andre. He was such a beautiful skater, and I thought he was hysterically funny. It was never an option to get lessons from him or book a choreography session. Not because we couldn't afford it, but because Andre was gay. I never had any aversions to people who were gay, but I knew my mom did. I knew skating with Andre for dance testing made her skin crawl. If you ever wanted to get under my mother's skin, then you could make a joke or a statement about marrying someone who was Catholic, or Ukrainian, or, heaven forbid, someone who was not white.

I was entered to compete in a local competition that weekend. I was pushing myself extra hard the week leading up to it, making sure my doubles were hitting every time, and trying to increase the speed of my spins without travelling on the ice.

I hit an edge after landing a double toe loop and fell to the ice. A sharp, stabbing pain in my right ankle hit instantly, and I was unable to stand up. I hobbled off the ice and tried to put weight on my foot but couldn't. The pain was unbearable. A passerby offered to help me get to the changing room, and I carefully took off my skating boot. My ankle started to swell. I took it easy over the next three days, icing it daily and wrapping it. We had an endless supply of vet wrap at home from Chad's injuries. He'd dislocated his pinky finger a while back and Mom insisted that it worked best on swelling.

Saturday came and I was convinced if I wrapped my ankle and took a couple Advil I would be able to compete as normal. I took it easy during the warm-up. I needed to save my strength for the two and a half minutes of my short program. I got on the ice in my bright pink skating dress. The dress was a joint Christmas/birthday gift from Mom, Dad, and Jason. I took my starting pose and waited for my music to begin. I hobbled through the first minute of my program only to realize they'd played the wrong music and I needed to start over. As I skated my program for the second time, the pain in my ankle was too much to bear. I fell on every single jump. I couldn't finish and tears streamed down my face in pain, embarrassment, and disappointment. I placed tenth out of twelve skaters in my flight.

"See? Could've been worse. You could've gotten last!" Mom joked as we left the rink.

We headed directly to the doctor for X-rays, and the doctor gave us the news.

"Well, I've got good news and bad news. Good news is, it's not broken. Bad news is, it looks like you've torn all the ligaments in your ankle on this right side." He pointed to the outside of my ankle bone, where it was swollen and bruised.

He instructed me to keep it elevated, iced, and wrapped with a tensor. He also suggested I use crutches if needed. He instructed Mom to massage the outside of my ankle to help with pain relief and healing.

Mom and I went home, and she set me up on the couch with an ice pack and more Advil.

"Do you think you could massage it like he said?" I asked.

Mom sat at the end of the couch, looking at my ankle and assessing the amount of bruising as she moved around the ice pack.

"No, I think you're going to be fine," she said.

She sent me to school the next day with more vet wrap, two extra Advil, and no crutches. It would take me months of physiotherapy to get my ankle back to its previous state. It was the end of competitive skating as I knew it.

REVENGE SPEND

Mom and I were spending more time together. Each day she arrived at school at 3:15 p.m. and parked in the teacher parking lot facing the field. I would make my way out to the car, and we'd spend the next ninety minutes watching Chad practice football. Every single day. For the entire season. I sat in the backseat while she yelled and scoffed. I would slouch down and do my homework or make up an excuse to go running back through the halls of the school. She never missed a single practice.

The team would go on to win city and provincials that year. She attested their success to her unwavering dedication and loyalty. She celebrated their win and rewarded them with a party at our house. Well over one hundred underage kids showed up with mickeys of hard alcohol or coolers and cases of beer in hand to celebrate their victory. We were never the kids who had parties. We were only allowed one birthday party growing up. It was when we each turned six. The birthday party was an activity like swimming, followed with hot dogs and homemade games and one of Mom's famous money cakes, where she baked coins covered in Saran Wrap in the cake.

Football season made Mom happy. She channelled all her energy into Chad, and she went to every game. She made sure to tape the sports highlights on the news every night, just in case he was mentioned. When the season ended there was a lull, a frigid Saskatchewan monotony of winter. Mom and Dad picked up where they left off with fighting now that Christmas was over and the bills were piling up. If I put my head down, did what she said, occasionally asked if she needed help with anything over and above what I already did, I could steer clear of setting her off.

Tensions between Mom and Dad had always fluctuated. I never understood how she could get so mad at him. He never went on solo trips with friends for fun. He never went to bars. He had minimal friends outside of her and her family. He went to work, brought home a steady paycheque, and by all accounts was a stand-up husband and father. I felt sorry for my dad. Anything could set Mom off. Leaving a blanket unfolded in the living room, a dish on the counter, or a section of the newspaper in the bathroom. She was volatile.

•

One Sunday afternoon, I was trying to study for an upcoming math test. My bedroom door was closed but I could hear her yelling and snide remarks through the walls. She was mad that he hadn't gotten around to putting a door on the laundry room downstairs. She didn't feel like a priority.

"Amber! Pack your bag. We're leaving!" She barged into my room.

I packed my bag in disbelief. Why me? Why was she taking me and not Chad? I thought about every fight that she and my dad had had over my childhood. She had always left alone. When I was seven we went camping, and she and my dad got into a huge argument. She left the campsite and hitchhiked into town where she drained their bank account at an ATM. Dad felt immediate remorse, and we packed up and went looking for her. If it were me, I would have let her go.

"You think you can treat me like shit, well it fucking stops here."

THE OBEDIENT DAUGHTER

I'm done! You're an asshole, and I'm not putting up with your shit anymore," Mom yelled.

I packed my bag with two changes of clothes, pyjamas, and toiletries. I had my bag in my hand, and my backpack slung over my shoulder, but I didn't want to go. I looked at my dad. He looked deflated and hurt. I wanted to stay with him. Maybe that was the reason she was forcing me to go.

"Get in the car, Amber," she instructed.

I walked past my dad and gave him a look that tried to convey *I'm sorry and I love you* to my best ability. We got into the car and headed toward Circle Drive. Overwhelmed by rage and vengeance, she ranted about my dad and how she deserved better. She always vented to me when she was mad.

She stopped at the bank and ran in to withdrawal money. I'd seen this move before a few times. I wasn't sure if it was for revenge spending, or so that no one could tell where she was.

She came back into the car with hundreds of dollars in twenty-dollar bills and a teller receipt.

"You hungry?" She stuffed the money into her large red wallet and then put her purse back on my lap.

"Sure, I guess."

I had no idea what was going on or what the point of leaving was. She was unpredictable at best. We headed across the street to a shady pub and sat down at a table. She ordered a steak sandwich, a beer, and a Clamato. I ordered chicken strips, fries, and a Sprite. The music was loud, and I found it easiest to agree and nod along as she talked herself down from the ledge she was previously on.

"Hey, what do you say we play some slot machines?" she asked.

"I'm pretty sure I'm not allowed to do that?"

I've always been a rule follower.

"Pfft . . . What are they going to do!" She took forty dollars out of her purse and handed it to me.

"Yeah, but can't we get in trouble?"

She scoffed and instructed me to sit down beside her at the next machine. She sparked up a cigarette and walked me through how to work the machine and place a bet. After two hours of playing, I won $160. Mom cashed us out and took back her forty dollars and let me keep the rest. We headed next door to the Travelodge where she booked a standard double room for the night and paid in cash. We sat in silence as we watched TV. I looked over at her sitting on the other bed. I couldn't help but feel pity for her. She wasn't hard done by. My dad wasn't abusive or disrespectful. I could tell that she was replaying the fight in her head. She was lost in her own thoughts. Her hands and lips were moving but there was no sound. Small, slight whispers escaped her lips but nothing more. She was a leading actress in her own silent film. I turned back to continue watching the TV and became lost in my own thoughts about what I could buy with my winnings. I wasn't sure why I was involved in this fight. Mom didn't have any friends other than her sisters. I'm sure they would've been more fun than me. Perhaps this was a lesson in life for how to respond during an argument with your spouse. Whatever the reason, she dropped me off at school in the morning, picked me up at the end of the day, then we went home. We never spoke about our night at the Travelodge or playing the slot machines, but the next weekend, Mom and I hung the door to the laundry room ourselves. She taught me that day that it was important to never need help from a man.

THERAPY

"I want to go back to something you said last session about your bedroom," Dr. M. said as she leaned back in her chair and crossed her legs. "You called it your 'safe space.' Looking back now, did it really feel like your safe space?"

"In some ways yes, but mostly no," I said.

"How so?"

"My mom controlled every square inch of the house. There were numerous times when she went through my things in my room. She found notes that I had kept from school, juvenile things like 'do you like me check yes or no' to a boy from when I was in fifth grade. She scolded me for having them and even showing interest in a boy. When I was older, in high school, she snooped and found a pair of thong underwear that I'd secretly purchased when I was out with friends. She stretched it out and hung it on the brackets of my bookshelf in my room. She was like that. She could fill you with shame and make her presence known, all without saying a word."

"And what would happen if you did say something to her about it?"

"It would always come back to me. I got mad at her for snooping in my room and she told me thong underwear was for sluts."

"How did that make you feel?"

"Shitty, I guess. But it was predictable. She did the same thing when I was in eighth grade and found a Winnie the Pooh underwire bra that I bought from the SAAN store. She told me underwire bras were for girls who wanted to make their boobs look bigger, and those girls were also sluts."

"And looking back now, how do you feel about how she approached all of that? Did you feel like her comments were warranted?"

"Oh, I find it somewhat comical, albeit extremely hypocritical for what she said. She sure had pretty strong morals and expectations of purity for someone who had a teen pregnancy. Maybe it was her way of trying to steer me away from making the same decisions she did, but she had a pretty fucked up way of doing so. I never had the autonomy to make any decisions for myself."

"How would you, as a mother, do things differently?"

"She always preached communication, but she never followed through on it. We never spoke about anything of importance. It was always: 'end of discussion!' I want my girls to be able to talk to me about anything. I would never judge them or their decisions, and if they fall, I will be there to help them back up. They will have the freedom to make their own decisions, carve out their own identity with clothes and style. I will teach them about sex and consent."

"Sex and consent is a topic I would like to understand a bit more from your past experiences. Let's start with that in our next session."

DOLLAR STORE CANDLES

Jake was my first high school boyfriend. He was short and had a slim, muscular frame. He had dark brown hair, green eyes, and a constant flush to his face that looked as if he was just walking in the cold. We were both in tenth grade, but he was seventeen, two years older than I was. He was held back during a lower grade, and I was the youngest in my class. Jake was the only one in our grade who had a car. At the time, I didn't realize that dating him would eventually be the start of my newly developed reputation. According to the student body, I would only date a guy if he drove a nice car. Jake was exceptionally tidy, and if we weren't cleaning out his teal Pontiac Sunfire, then we were cleaning out his dad's Camaro. And because I was small, it only made sense that I would climb in the back and clean out all the small spaces and windows. I'd say it was a typical high school relationship. We didn't really have real dates but enjoyed fast food and watching movies.

  Up until this point, my sexual experiences with boyfriends was nil, and my most advanced relationship consisted of a fling with a hot make-out session at a party. I had a couple sips of a beer and tried to appear sexy by flipping my hair. Somehow, I ended up upside down with my head between the crack of a bed and the wall. My then boyfriend pried me from the trap and tipped me back upright, assuring me that it was "most definitely sexy" and wasn't at all embarrassing.

Jake and I dated three months before the topic of sex came up. We were both still virgins, and he was much more eager than I was. Because he was older and I didn't want to disappoint him, I said I was open to it. We decided we wanted to make it special, romantic even, and settled on an elaborate production with candles. We headed to the mall, and The Dollar Store called us in. My palms were sweaty, and my legs weak. We bought three six-inch pillar candles, $0.99 each, all in a deep red colour. Jake paid for them. He was always such a gentleman. We took the candles back to his house and found his dad was at home. I felt such relief knowing that that day wouldn't be *the* day. I was off the hook and could remain a virgin for another day. We snuck the candles into his room and hid them in the bottom drawer of his dresser. Over the next few months, he would ask me periodically if today was the day. "No, not today, I'm on my rag," I would say with relief. Weekly reminders soon turned into daily reminders, and by the time we'd been dating six months, it had started to become overwhelming and annoying.

What was the big deal anyways? I tried to reason with my conservative self. *Everyone does it.*

By this time, Chad already had at least three people on his list of sexual partners. He had sex with two girls from his grade and one from mine. He still told me everything and boasted about every new notch on his belt.

"Oh man, it's like the best feeling ever, and she fucking bled all over the sheets," he said, as he described losing his virginity. Chad turned into the stereotypical jock, and most girls in my school were pining over him. I couldn't understand why. He had acne and a unibrow.

He was now dating Libby. She was quiet and didn't say much when she came over. She didn't seem like his type. He was usually into jocks, and she didn't play any sports. Jason said that Chad was whipped because Libby would never let him do anything without her. He seemed happy enough, at least until his eyes wandered and he saw some other sparkly creature that piqued his interest.

I finally told Jake that I was ready, and we made plans for that Thursday, when school let out early. We climbed into his car and headed back to his place. We were certain his parents wouldn't be home for at least two hours. My heart pounded as we dropped our backpacks on the floor, locked the side door, and went to his room. I had spent many hours in his room before. He had a TV and a waterbed, and the walls were decorated with various hockey trophies and posters. I placed a towel on his bed and got undressed while he lit the candles and pulled out a condom. The shades were drawn shut to set the mood. I got under the covers, shivering and shaking with nerves. My heart was still pounding, and my breathing intensified. Jake got on top of me, positioned himself between my legs, then inserted himself. I was overwhelmed with a painful, stretching feeling in my genitalia. I tried to think about something else, but the pain was too much. The only thought that entered my mind was how did people think this felt good? As awkward as sex was for a fifteen-year-old virgin, I wasn't prepared for the instability of a waterbed. And to make matters worse, he wasn't circumcised. I'd never seen an unsnipped penis before. I was only familiar with what Chad had taught me. I didn't know what to do with it and frankly, it scared me. He struggled to get a full erection this first time—and the two subsequent times we had sex—and was never able to ejaculate. I couldn't help but think he was in pain through most of it. Our struggles left me confused. Was I so displeasing to him? This was nothing like I had seen in Jason's porn videos, and Chad never explained this either. Wasn't sex what all guys wanted? Why wasn't I succeeding at this? I felt dirty, embarrassed, and unprepared.

My relationship with Jake struggled, and I became isolated in my own shame. I was so unhappy that I'd succumbed to the pressure. I didn't want to be touched. I couldn't be touched. He would try to hold my hand or wrap his arm around my waist, and I would pull away. I was disgusted with myself, and I broke up with him.

As I look back on my teenage self, I can see how much I struggled with this. At the age of fifteen, I did not want to have sex. I was never taught about consent and that you have the choice to say no when it comes to your own body. I lacked confidence and female guidance, and no one was there to tell me that my body is a temple and should be valued alongside my virginity. My experience with Chad led me to believe that this type of sexual activity was normal and acceptable, when in fact, it wasn't. And I was not ready. The dots for me didn't connect at the time: that Chad's "lessons" weren't teachings at all. I can see now that the trauma of what happened with Chad still lingered in my body, resurging each time I gave in sexually to someone else.

WITHOUT A GOODBYE

Sheena was getting older. She was the only dog that I had ever known, and she was fourteen. Her face was now completely white, and her eyes were starting to go, as cataracts covered both of them. Sheena was always my comfort. Her love was constant. I always knew that with a sound of a kiss she would come running. Each night I would summon her from Chad's room into mine. She would come traipsing in, tail wagging, and crawl under the covers to my feet and stay there until morning. She was my everything. I loved that no matter what the day was like, no matter what mood Mom was in, I could pull Sheena into my arms, and she would give me all of her love. The house was always divided by those of us who loved her (Dad, me, and Chad) and those who didn't (Mom and Jason). I never knew why Mom didn't like her. She never picked her up or snuggled with her, and she would always find a reason to yell at her.

Sheena got to the point where she wasn't herself anymore. She had a swollen lump on her leg, and she wasn't eating. Sheena had never been to the vet before. Mom and Dad always thought it was a "waste of money" and that vaccines weren't necessary because she was a "house dog." But since she seemed in pain, they made an appointment to get her checked out.

I was heading out the door for school but stopped to give Sheena a kiss as I always did.

"Mwah, love you," I said, as she let out a small groan. "Mom, you're taking her to get checked out today, right?"

"Yes, I'll take her. She'll be fine, away you go," Mom said, ushering me to head out the door.

•

Chad had track and field practice after school, so I caught a ride home with a friend. Eagerly, I walked in the door and looked at Sheena's bed. We always kept a soft bed for her right beside her kennel in the kitchen. She wasn't there.

"Where is she? Where's Sheena?"

I started to get worried. Mom was on the phone with Auntie Beth. She pulled the phone up away from her mouth but kept it still attached to her ear.

"We had to put her down today," she said.

A life-altering scream came from my mouth. My chest felt heavy, as if I couldn't get enough air. I felt like my world was ending.

"Okay, I'll let you go . . . sure, yep . . . call you later."

She ended her phone call and proceeded to tell me that Sheena had had a tooth that started to rot and was infected. The bacteria travelled to her heart, making it twice the size.

"The doctor said there was nothing more they could do."

"But I never got to say goodbye!"

Tears came streaming down my face at an unbearable rate.

"She was in a lot of pain, Am." Mom put her arm around my shoulders and patted me twice. "She's in a better place now."

The only place she should be was in my arms. I was angry with my mother. How could she do that to me? Sheena was mine. I loved her the most and now I felt more alone than ever.

Mom brought her home in a box and Dad dug a hole, and we

buried her in the backyard under the trees. Up until this point, the idea of loss didn't really exist for me. I had never lost or experienced death before. Sheena was my deepest loss. I felt such sadness that I wasn't there for her in her last moments. I wondered if she was looking for me or if she was scared. I felt like I had abandoned her. I let her down.

GAS STATION CHOCOLATES

Not long after I broke up with Jake, I started dating Derek. He was a popular hockey player at school. Tall, blond hair, and blue eyes. For those who are keeping track, he drove a brand-new black Toyota Celica. I struggled with the idea that I was no longer a virgin. I didn't tell anyone except for Chad. I waited to tell him until after Jake and I broke up. Chad and I had grown apart over the last year. He was busy with Libby and sports, and I'd started cheerleading. Since I wasn't skating anymore, I needed other things to occupy my time. I joined the school dance team, the cheerleading team, track and field, and the canoe club.

"Hey, I've got something to tell you," I said one day after the breakup.

"What's up?" Chad asked.

He was downstairs on the couch. Jason had recently moved into his own house, so naturally Chad claimed the space as his own. I sat down on the adjacent couch. The couches were old, and I refused to sit on the big one. The cushions were gross, and the black fabric was torn.

"So. I sort of lost my virginity," I said.

Chad perked up immediately. "You did? When? With who?"

"With Jake, back when we were dating. It wasn't like a lot. Just a couple times."

"Did you bleed?"

"No," I said. It seemed like a weird question to ask.

"What did you think of it? Did you like it?"

"Not really. It was pretty painful, I suppose."

"Hmm. Cool," he said.

Was it really that big of a deal now? No one had had the conversation with me about the value of my body and what it means to have sex or multiple partners. I figured it didn't matter how many people you slept with after you weren't a virgin anymore. Derek was a prude. He had very little experience and it felt like I was an expert in comparison. We dated for a couple of months. Our dates consisted of going to Burger King and KFC for lunch every day. He always made me pay for the more expensive meals, even though he received a daily per diem from his parents.

We ended up having sex once. It was extremely brief, then it was over. We sat watching a movie at my house, late into the evening after my parents had gone to bed. A small echo of light from the TV screen cascaded an onyx hue over the walls as we kissed on the couch. We had been physical before. Our sessions were heavy in foreplay but always came to an abrupt end.

"We can if you want to," I whispered that night.

"Okay," he said.

We moved to the carpeted floor, and I removed my jeans and panties. Within two minutes he was in and then out. I quickly put my pants back on before anyone upstairs could stir. Derek tucked himself back into his pants, and I noticed tears welling up in his eyes. He was angry and disappointed in himself. I sat there in disbelief. *What the hell is wrong with me?* I wondered. I thought all boys were supposed to be excited about sex. I tried to console him as best as I could. I wasn't exactly sure if he was disappointed in his performance or if he regretted losing his virginity.

He went home and was filled with so much remorse that he told his mom. I knew they were close, but this was a new level of attachment that I had never experienced. She never said a single word to me. Soon after, Derek moved away on his own to play hockey for a WHL team in a small town. We spoke on the phone very little and saw each other even less. One weekend, he invited me to travel with his parents to see him play. I sat in the back of his dad's very large truck. We got to know each other on the drive. I felt like I was making some serious strides with his parents. What was there not to like about me? I was respectful and dressed conservatively. I made good grades. Sure, I deflowered their sweet baby boy but maybe they had forgotten about that.

We watched the game and then went out for supper. Derek was distant, but I thought it was because his parents were there. At the end of dinner, they gave him a hug and a kiss, told him they loved him and that they'd be waiting in the truck. I leaned it to give Derek a hug and he pulled away.

"Hey, so this isn't working. Me being here. You being in Saskatoon. I can't be with you anymore," he said.

I was stunned. This would have been a lot less painful over the phone.

"Is it because we had sex?" It was the only reason I could think of.

"No, not at all. I just don't want a girlfriend right now."

"Oh," I said.

I refused to let myself cry, so I buried my chin into my chest and stared at the ground. Tears started to well and Derek put his arm around me like I was his kid sister. He gave me two pats on the back and then guided me toward his dad's truck.

I got in and tried to conceal my tears. I was completely embarrassed. His parents were very comforting, but I was convinced they facilitated the entire thing. We stopped and filled up for gas before driving the remaining ninety minutes back home. Derek's dad came out of the gas station and handed me a box of chocolates that he'd gotten for free with a fill-up. I guess it wasn't a complete loss.

CHILD THERAPIST

It was a Friday night and Dad and I were curled up watching a movie. Mom was upstairs balancing her chequebook and Chad was out with Libby. It was just the two of us, lying on adjacent couches in the dark basement. I was sixteen. We were watching *The Breakfast Club* for what seemed like the twelfth time, and a commercial for a Hallmark movie came on the TV. It portrayed a perfect family: two parents with three children all sitting together at a supper table, laughing. We never laughed, at least not together as a family.

"Wouldn't that be nice? I always wondered what it would be like to have a family experience like that," Dad said.

I looked at him with sadness in my eyes. My heart knew exactly what he was saying because I, too, had always wished for that perfect family.

"Yeah, that would be nice," I agreed. "But I don't think we will ever have that."

"I don't think so either," he said.

Dad and I shared a love for movies. They became an escape. An opportunity to shut out the world and travel to a different place for a moment in time. We confided in each other. He told me about his relationship with Mom and how she made him feel. I became enmeshed in his marriage, giving what I deemed my best advice when solicited. It was the only time I felt heard and valued. I wanted him to stand up for himself, and if he could learn to do that then perhaps he would also stand up for me. If he could strum up the courage to leave her, then I could go with him. We both could be free. But he was loyal to a fault and never wanted to be like his father. Unfortunately for my dad, she was ruthless in her control.

"Ben!" she yelled from the top of the stairs. I heard her yell my dad's name almost as much as mine. It was always the same. It reminded me of nails scraping a chalkboard.

"Yeah?"

"Aren't you going to shovel the sidewalks?"

It had been snowing for a couple of hours, a light skiff of white scattered the front lawn and driveway. The snow was majestic and weightless and by all accounts Mother Nature wasn't letting up just yet.

"Yeah, I will," he said.

"Well, don't you think you should do it now?"

Dad let out a big sigh and got up off the couch. He went up the stairs, and I could hear her tone. Saying no wasn't an option.

"I was going to get to it," he said.

"Why would you wait to do it later? You're going to hurt your back."

Their voices trailed off and the back door slammed as Dad went outside to shovel.

She controlled the house, and just like that, our time was up.

"Amber!" she yelled from the top of the stairs. I knew I would be next.

"What are you doing right now?"

She knew exactly what I was doing.

"Nothing," I said. I was in the middle of the movie, but I knew what she wanted to hear.

"How'd you like to dye my hair for me?"

Dad and I dyed her hair every six weeks. Her hair started to go grey at the age of eighteen. Her natural colour was now a bright grey-white. It resembled a skunk streak when her hair grew out.

"Sure," I said. I turned off the TV and went upstairs.

She wrapped a towel around her shoulders, and I mixed up the boxed dye. L'Oréal Preference Samantha #64 was her preferred colour. A dark ash brown. She had been using the same colour for years. I pulled on the plastic gloves and shook the bottle. I loved the chemical smell and considered taking a deeper inhale to numb how I felt in that moment.

"Make sure you shake it good," she said.

"I know."

"And try not to get any on my ears this time."

"Okay."

I applied the solution to the centre part of her hair. She had almost an inch of growth that needed to be covered. I massaged it into her scalp and made my way through her hairline and roots. The hair dye made her follicles stand out even more. It took every ounce of restraint I had not to pull one out. I had been pulling out my own hair for quite some time now. It calmed me.

It didn't take long to apply the dye. Then she sat with her hair covered in a plastic disposable shower cap for thirty minutes. After that, I shampooed her in the sink.

It wasn't the usual salon session of gab and gossip. We didn't speak much, and she either read the paper or puffed away on a cigarette.

"Be careful not to make a mess!" she said.

The water splashed around in the sink and small droplets of tainted water sprayed onto the counter. The box of dye came with a deep conditioner that had to sit for fifteen minutes. She usually handled the second rinse herself. In between rinses, she rubbed her forehead and ears frantically with a towel to remove any leftover dye.

Dad had finished shovelling and came back into the house. His face was a sharp red colour, his moustache frosted with snow. It seemed like the moment to finish the movie had passed but he looked over at me and said, "Movie?"

"Sure!" I replied, and we started to make our way downstairs.

"Well, aren't you coming to bed?" Mom interrupted.

"Yep, I'll be there in a minute," he confirmed.

We got settled downstairs once again and watched the last twenty minutes of the movie before he retired to bed as expected.

THERAPY

It was another Wednesday 9:30 a.m. session. Dr. M. was wearing the same long cardigan that she wore the first day I met her.

"Talk to me about the hair pulling." Dr. M. leaned in with intent, her hand resting under her chin.

"When did this start?"

I hadn't told anyone about my hair pulling before. I had no idea it would come with so many questions. I knew it was weird. My face suddenly flushed and felt warm.

"I was young. Not sure exactly how old I was. It seemed to bring me comfort but grew to be an obsession, I guess."

"Where about would you pull hair from?" she asked.

She wrote something in her notebook, and I knew this was a symptom or type of behaviour that she was analyzing.

"I pulled from everywhere. My legs, pubic hair, eyebrows, eyelashes, and hair from my head."

"Did you ever have bald spots on your head?" she asked, continuing to write.

"No. I gave myself limits on how many hairs I could pull from my head at any given time. I only pulled out eyelashes that were out of line with the rest of them."

"Why do you think you pulled out your hair?"

I wanted to say 'you tell me, you're the expert,' but I didn't. I just shrugged and said, "I'm not sure, perhaps anxiety."

"Yes, that's right. It's usually a key indication that you are living in a stressful situation or dealing with anxiety. It's called trichotillomania."

I already knew this. I had googled it several years prior out of fear that I was a complete psycho. She continued to take notes and quickly changed the subject to my dad.

"Let's shift to the conversations you had with your dad. You mentioned that you had become enmeshed with their marriage. How so?"

"We talked about everything. Their fights, how she made him feel, the control she had over him. I began to watch them together, anticipating her every move and what would set her off. Dad and I had similar dreams for what we wished we had in our family. In some ways, I felt like a therapist to him."

"Why did you feel the need to give him advice? Did he ever seek out a therapist?"

"I felt bad for him, I guess. I know now how difficult it is when you're in the thick of it to see clearly. To really see abuse and how someone can be controlling. I was in a constant state of freeze or flight mode. I thought if I supported my dad and convinced him to leave, then we could both be free from her. In a way, hearing his turmoil made me feel less alone with mine. Maybe it was my way of seeking the one person I trusted the most to take me away from all that was happening to me, without actually telling anyone about the abuse. Dad suggested therapy a number of times, but Mom would never allow it."

"And looking back now, how do you feel about being put in that position?"

"Sad, I suppose."

"Tell me more."

"I look back on my entire childhood now and I can see the impossible turmoil that I faced. I was a maid, an emotional dumping ground, a therapist, and my brother's prey. Each person seemingly unaware of the control that they all possessed over me. I didn't have a childhood. My innocence in every aspect was stolen from me."

"I completely agree with you."

She paused, taking a few minutes to jot some scribbles in her notebook. Then she closed the front cover and placed her pen on top of the book.

" Okay, that's our time for today. We can pick this up again next week."

I left her office feeling no better than when I first started seeing her. There had yet to be any healing, but I persisted in hopes of finding some sense of freedom.

NOAH

"Amber! Phone! It's Robert Wallace," Chad bellowed from the kitchen.

It was the name that popped up on the caller display. Wallace? The only Wallace I knew was Noah. We went to school together. He was Derek's best friend. I had no idea why he'd be calling me. Noah was extremely tall at six foot four. He had a slim build with brown hair and dark brown eyes. His hair looked like Freddie Prinze Jr. but he had a more reserved smile. I grabbed the portable phone.

"Hello?"

"Hi Amber, um, this is Noah. Um, Noah Wallace. Uh, I was wondering if you'd ever give me a chance and consider going out, um, with me?" His voice rattled with nervousness.

"You?" I was completely shocked. I had no idea that he even liked me, let alone wanted to go out with me.

"Uh. Okay then . . ."

"No, no. That's not what I meant. I had no idea that you thought of me like that. Yes, I'd like to go out with you!"

"Phew! Okay you scared me for a minute there. I was like *boom and rejected!*"

Noah and I were both sixteen and we immediately became inseparable. He had an infectious way of making everyone around him laugh, and he never took anything too seriously. I hung off every word he said, and it wasn't long before we were head over heels in love with each other. Our young love was like the love in movies. It was safe for me, full of adventures, and carefree. Noah was unlike any other boy I had ever met. He was peculiar in ways that you would never expect. His handwriting was perfect. Every word was written intricately in perfect calligraphy, and he kept a stack of *Reader's Digest* magazines next to his bed because he liked to read the articles. We spent hours together, skating hand in hand at the oval in the winter, and in the summer, we went to a beach on the outskirts of town. We frolicked in the sun with friends and snuck away into the water to cool off as the sexual tension built. We took it slow and waited six months before we had sex. Noah knew that I wasn't a virgin, and I knew that I would be his first. But this time things felt different. There was no pressure, and I could feel that he loved me.

We had early dismissal from school every Thursday. On those days, Noah and I would hop into his Chevrolet Cavalier, blare Matchbox 20 over the speakers, and go to his house. We would head directly downstairs to his room in the basement, have sex, and be sure to be finished and watching TV before one of his brothers came home. Noah was one of four boys in his family, and they were all very nice.

It wasn't long after we'd started having sex that I got a panicked call from Noah.

"Hey, we have to talk," he said.

"Hey, what's up, we are talking. Why are you so upset?"

"My mom was going through my room and she found some condoms!"

My heart started to pound. There was no way she wouldn't tell my parents.

"Oh my god, you're joking? What did she say? What did you say?"

"I told her that they were mine and I . . . practised with them."

"What? What do you mean you practised with them?"

"I practised. You know, like I used them by myself."

"Oh! And she believed you?" I asked.

"I think so?"

We both let out a nervous chuckle.

•

A couple weeks later, Noah told me that his mom wanted to revisit the conversation about sex. She wanted the three of us to meet and sit down together to talk about it. I went over to his house, and we drove in complete silence to the A&W burger joint on 22nd Street.

"Are you guys hungry?" she asked as we sank into the opposite side of the booth.

"No, thank you," I said.

I couldn't imagine trying to eat during this conversation. I was sweating and so close to vomiting, the last thing I needed was to shove onion rings into my mouth. I was terrified. Noah's mom was going to tell my parents. I just knew it. If my parents found out we were having sex, they would forbid me from seeing Noah, and I would be grounded forever. I was spiralling out of control.

Noah's mom sat down with a coffee and two cups of Root Beer.

"Now, I know you guys are having sex . . ." she said.

She wanted to know all the details. How long it had been going on. Why there was no blood from the first time we had sex. Had I really been a virgin? Noah tried to do me a favour by telling her that we were both virgins. He thought telling her about Derek and Jake would only fuel her hatred for me. I proceeded to tell her that I broke my own hymen when I was going into tenth grade when I first used a tampon. It was the truth. Bless my mother's heart, she gave me a box of cardboard applicator tampons and told me to "go read the directions and figure it out." I'm not entirely sure that Noah's mom was convinced. She agreed not to tell my parents and for a moment I was relieved. A week later, she spoke to Derek's mom and found out that he and I also had sex and that I was most definitely not a virgin like we had said. All faith in me was lost. Noah and I tried to explain that it had been just a one-time thing with Derek. But in her eyes, I had a scarlet A on my chest and stood firmly in the position of eleventh grade harlot.

FROM SCHOOLMATE TO SKANK

French was always one of my favourite subjects in school. I liked the way it sounded. I liked knowing a language and being able to speak it at home so no one would know what I was saying. I had two high school French teachers. One was a very large Black man who was extremely kind but also strict. He was my ninth-grade French teacher. He would ask the class: "What would Amber say?" Don't get me wrong, it was mortifying, but it also made me feel special.

My other teacher was Madame E. She was an important mentor in my life that would provide guidance and instill confidence. I worked hard for her approval. She accepted my application to go on a student exchange to France for three weeks with a large group of high school students from across the city. It was a pretty big deal in our house. No one had ever been away for a long period of time, nor had they travelled off the continent. Mom and Dad said they would help me pay for the trip. To make things "fair" for Chad, Mom bought him a new stereo system with a CD player and subwoofer for his car.

At the time, Chad's friend Craig was living with us for the year. He was a football player in twelfth grade. His mom moved away, and my mom offered to take him in, so he could graduate with his class and continue playing football. Craig and I didn't see eye to eye. He called me spoiled when he found out about my trip to France. I didn't understand why he even got a say since he wasn't technically a member of our family, and we were the ones doing him a favour.

There were a number of kids from our high school who went on the student exchange, including Amanda, Tenille, and Meghan. They were part of the popular group at school. They were all beautiful, smart, athletic, and on the student leadership council. They were best friends with Derek and Noah, and since Noah and I were still going strong, our paths crossed.

Our trip to Paris was filled with fun, touristy things. We saw all the highlights: the Eiffel Tower, the Louvre, L'Arc de Triomphe, Champs-Élysées. We ate fresh baguette sandwiches and tasted various treats from the bakery. We soon left Paris and headed to our host families. My host family wasn't quite what I expected. The father was from Cambodia and the mother was French. They had two girls and two boys. I was given a room on the main floor with a pullout couch and some cabinets for storage. I was not allowed to go upstairs where everyone else's bedrooms were located, and when they spoke about me, they called me "correspondent" instead of Amber.

My exchange partner and I did not have much in common. She was a tomboy who loved manga and comic books. She was repulsed that I was a girly-girl and head over heels in love with Noah. I got along well with her older sister who was nineteen and had a driver's licence. I learned that if we ate everything we were served—including sardines and butter on bread—we would be able to go to fun places like the discotheque and shopping.

I was very homesick. I missed my family, and I missed Noah. Three weeks seemed like a lifetime. When I met up with the other exchange students for mandatory activities, they talked about how they were best friends with their host partners, going to places like Disney Paris together. I didn't have a lot to talk about, other than the bug bites all over my chest and stomach. My room was infested with red ants.

On the flight home, the topic of virginity came up. Amanda, Tenille, and Meghan all admitted that they were still virgins. Then it was my turn. I didn't want to ruin our friendship. Amanda was religious and would never forgive me. So, I lied. I told them that I was a virgin, too.

•

A couple of weeks later, I received a note in class. "You better find another ride to gym or you're going to die." The note was from Tenille. We were all in the same gym class and were required to drive off-site to various activities. Since returning from France, I'd been riding with them in Meghan's car. My face fell pale. What had I done to deserve this? I soon found out that Amanda and Derek started dating and he told her of our history. He was back in town and attending school now that hockey was done for the season. He was making my life a living hell. In the eyes of Amanda, Tenille and Meghan, I was a liar and a skank and would never be their friend again.

When I got home that day, Mom could tell there was something wrong.

"What happened? I can see it in your face. Did something happen at school?" Mom wasn't usually this observant.

"I got this note in school today," I said, passing it to her.

"Who sent you this?"

"Tenille."

"A death threat, Amber. What could you have done that was so bad to deserve a death threat?"

I didn't have the strength to tell her about who I really was and what I lied about. Mom preferred my image of innocence and purity. I could not risk her discovering that not only was I not a virgin, but that I'd had sex with three boys. I could only imagine the slut shaming that would accompany the conversation. I couldn't handle any more punches.

"I think Amanda is mad that Derek and I dated because now she's dating him."

"I'm calling the school."

She picked up the phone and dialled the school. She left a message with the receptionist to have the principal call her.

•

The next day, I avoided the trio like the plague. I sourced a new ride to gym class with another girl from the France trip. When I got home, Mom told me that they would be dealt with. She asked me if I wanted them to be forced to give up their positions on the student council.

"What good would that do?"

"Well, it's a punishment. And those catty bitches shouldn't be in that type of position."

"I guess, but no. I don't want to make a huge deal out of this."

I anticipated that it would fuel their fire and they would make it known to the entire school that I was a teen trollop, pretending to be innocent and sweet. From that point on, my relationships with girls and women would forever be different.

NOT JUST ONE, BUT TWO

"Hey Am, you want to come with me to Crappy Tire?" Dad asked.

"Sure!" I never understood how he could spend so much time and money at a store he called crappy, but it was time for just the two of us. We pulled up on a Sunday, and the smell of burgers instantly hit my nose. The parking lot at Canadian Tire always seemed to host barbecue fundraisers for various local sports teams. Cheap, processed burger patties with cheese and grilled onions covered a flat grill at the entrance of the store.

"Hey, should we get a burger?" Dad was always game for a burger, no matter if we had just eaten lunch or if dinner was around the corner.

"Yeah! Sounds good to me!"

It was one of the things that I loved about him, how he said yes to life's simplest things. It cost us six dollars for two burgers and two drinks. We sat there eating together, leaned up against the car with the sun beating down on our faces, completely silent. Bellies full, we walked into Canadian Tire and were hit by their signature smell of rubber tires. We perused through the aisles and picked up the parts, tools, or bottles of whatever Dad needed to fix the car.

"Hey, you want to check out the puppies at Petland before we go home?" I asked.

I always tried to tack on somewhere else to go, or something else to pick up. Anything to delay going home and whatever it took to spend more time with Dad, just the two of us.

"Sure!" he said.

Dad and I shared a special bond and love for dogs. We always have. We searched them out, just to get a fix. They were a drug, an instant boost of serotonin that kept us happy for a few more hours.

We parked the car at Petland, across the street from Canadian Tire. Without hesitation, we walked toward the puppies in the windows. We had been there more times than I could count, usually just the two of us. Mom would always say not today, or perhaps another time.

"Should we ask them to take one out?" he asked.

"Yes!" The biggest smile came over my face and my mouth dropped.

Dad had never made that suggestion before. We asked the salesperson to take out the sweetest little girl, a beagle with no name. They carried her over to the pet-and-play area. We held and kissed her, and started to imagine what our lives would be like with her in it.

"Oh, I just love her. Isn't she the sweetest, Dad?"

"She most certainly is."

He looked at me with such love and adoration in his eyes. I never wondered if my dad loved me. I knew he did. My life at that very moment seemed to be perfect. Just Dad and me and this sweet puppy.

"What do you think Mom would say if we just brought her home?"

"Well, I don't think she'd be too impressed."

Dad assured me that even though we couldn't take her home that day, he would talk to Mom and make a strong argument for getting a new dog. My heart broke as we left the store without our sweet girl, but the hope of a new puppy kept me going.

•

A couple weeks went by without any promise of picking up our new beagle from Petland. I was convinced that we would be too late, and she would already be adopted. I'd just finished a shift at the mall and Dad was there to pick me up. My first real job was working at Ricki's, a women's clothing store.

"Can we stop off at Petland?" I asked as I got into the car.

"No, not today, Am. We need to get back to Jason's house. We've been building the fence all day and we're almost done."

Jason was still living in his fixer-upper in the heart of Westview, where we grew up. Natalie had recently moved in and they'd started to fix it up, installing new flooring and painting the walls. It was slowly coming together but the area had become rougher over the years and made me nervous. We pulled into the alley and hopped out of the car. A number of people were there helping including Chad, Libby, and some of Jason's friends.

"Amber, I have something for you," Mom said.

She walked toward me and handed me a shoebox. Mom wasn't one to buy me random gifts. If she did, it was usually something she thought I needed, not necessarily something I wanted.

I opened the box and sitting inside was the smallest miniature dachshund puppy I had ever seen. It was a girl with big brown eyes, brown-red colouring, and a dark stripe down her back. She shook nervously and looked into my eyes. Tears fled rapidly down my face. I had never experienced happy tears before now. I took her out of the box and snuggled her into my face, smelling her ears and puppy breath as she licked my nose. I was in complete disbelief. Mom went and did this all on her own and surprised everyone.

"Hey, Am," I heard Chad call me from inside the house.

I turned to look over at the screen door. Sitting on the back porch was another miniature dachshund puppy. A boy. If I thought I was in shock before, I was paralyzed with shock now.

"A girl for you and a boy for Chad," Mom said.

We sat down and Mom shared the story of how she travelled to get our little girl in the morning, brought her home and then decided to go back and get another one shortly after.

"Is this why you said no when I asked if we could go to Petland today?" I asked Dad.

"Yeah! Wasn't this a good reason?"

"The best!"

I nuzzled my sweet puppy in my arms and started to think about what to name her. It took sixteen years to experience such an overwhelming happiness. It was love at first sight, and her name was Abby.

GRADUATION

I didn't understand all the hype around graduating from high school. It seemed like something that just needed to be done and an initial requirement before going on to secondary education. No one in my family had previously attended university. My parents never went, and both my brothers went to polytechnic college for trades. I put applications in for scholarships and bursaries with the hope of getting financial aid. I needed all the help I could get.

Mom and I sat down together at the table, the windows open slightly, letting in a steady breeze of fresh spring air. She was the one who informed me that scholarships were available and made sure that I stopped by the guidance counsellor's office to pick up all the applications. One was a merit award for $500. It was based on community merits and doing good deeds for others in your community.

"What should I write down for community support?" I asked.

"Well, go ahead and write about your volunteering experience at the school, write about the award you got for track and field. You were a hostess at the basketball tournament. Write down that you babysat for your cousin while she underwent cancer treatment."

I'd spent every Thursday afternoon that year volunteering in a fourth/fifth grade class. I arranged it with my biology teacher to miss one class a week. I was also a hostess, and I did receive an award for track and field, but I had not babysat for my cousin when she underwent cancer treatment. I babysat her kids a long time prior, but it was well before she had cancer.

"But I didn't babysit," I said.

"Doesn't matter. You used to babysit for her, and now she is going through cancer treatment."

I didn't feel comfortable writing it down. It wasn't true. Mom asked to see my application when I was finished.

"Why didn't you write down the babysitting?"

"I don't know. It just didn't seem right. I don't want to take advantage of her situation."

"Oh, don't be silly. She wouldn't mind. Get the pen. Write it down."

I reluctantly wrote it down and returned the application to the guidance counsellor the next day.

•

In alphabetical order, each one of us dressed in a cap and gown, we walked across the stage and accepted our diplomas. We sat in rows in the auditorium, watching our peers cross the stage. As the afternoon progressed, the scholarships and bursaries were announced. I listened intently, and as I did, I noticed my application details were being read aloud. The mentions of volunteering in a classroom, and my previous accolades. And then they said it. They read aloud that I'd babysat for my cousin while she underwent cancer treatment. My heart raced and I felt disappointed in myself. My aunt Cheryl was sitting in the auditorium with my parents. She was my other godmother and my cousin's mom. She would know that it was a lie. I nervously stepped onto the stage to accept my award. I felt like such a fraud.

I wanted to believe that my accomplishments would have been enough on their own, but Mom knew best. She knew I needed more, that I needed this one additional detail, one last tug on the heart strings to make me worthy. Everyone congratulated me on my accomplishment, but it never sat well with me because of that lie. To top it off, I was a 0.04 percent short of reaching the honour roll average for the year. Each student who made the honour roll received a badge for the year they were recognized. After everything was said and done, Mom called the school and demanded that I receive my fourth-year badge regardless of my average. It was sent in the mail but meant absolutely nothing.

THE BREAKUP

As we started university, Noah and I began to drift apart. We both grew insecure about a newer, bigger world full of people. I was no longer getting straight A's like I had in high school, and the pressure to work at my job in the mall, go to school, and pay for my education was insurmountable. Noah wanted to start a joint savings account so we could save for a vacation. It scared me to death. I would never be allowed to go away with him, so what was the point? I wasn't allowed to go camping with him and a bunch of friends during the summer after highschool. The idea of us heading to Mexico for spring break seemed somewhat laughable. It would be stressful to save money to begin with, and I feared I would lose it in the end. We had been struggling since our last year in high school, primarily because he'd remained friends with the girls who loathed me. I didn't understand how someone who loved you could leave you to spend time with people who hated you.

We both attended the University of Saskatchewan in hopes of receiving our Bachelor of Education degrees. We set up our schedules to be similar and enrolled ourselves in some of the same classes. Our university was in Saskatoon, so it made sense that we lived at home while we attended. I made the university cheerleading team. I'd cheered for three years in high school: the first two years as a flyer and the last as a base. This team gave me a sense of belonging, a purpose. Being a first-year university athlete, I needed to prove myself in order to cement a placement on the team, especially as a flyer. I was determined to do that.

I was busy with school, cheerleading, and work. Noah attended classes and kept a steady paying job. Mom had liked Noah initially, but that year she'd become more involved with our relationship. She meddled so much that she made it clear that he wasn't right for me, that I was young and needed to "spread my wings." I hadn't realized it yet, but my mom had a way of celebrating my losses and exacerbating my wins. Noah was actually good for me. He was liked by everyone and was on my side. Although naive, he didn't quite understand the potency of Marlene.

One day in late May, Mom and I sat at the kitchen table. I was upset that Noah had gone to visit Amanda and Tenille. I offloaded my grievances about the savings account and his loyalty to my nemeses.

"You're really going to let him go hang out with those little scritches?" she asked.

That was her polite way of referring to girls as bitches. I'd just needed to vent, but Mom didn't see it like that. Everything was black and white to her. She was never a neutral party, willing to listen. She was taking a side and would never waver.

"I want you to get everything he has ever given you, every piece of his clothing that you have, and get a bag. You get a bag and put it all in there for when he gets here, Amber."

Mom sat at the kitchen table with a cigarette in hand. It seemed too harsh in my opinion, but I did what she said.

"You don't need to be controlled like this. He is not a nice person. You don't need this in your life right now."

If only she knew what she was saying. He was freedom. And that was a threat to her control. So, she eliminated him.

As the evening approached, the sun was still shining. I invited

Noah to come over after his shift at work. I packed his white hoodie that I loved. It smelled of Curve cologne, and I wore it when I missed him. I had a couple of his CDs and a pair of socks. Mom told me to put the ring and watch that he had given me in the grocery bag as well, but I couldn't. They meant too much to me, and I knew he wouldn't accept them anyway.

He arrived at the door with his usual bubbly smile. Mom sat still at the table and instructed him to sit down. The three of us sat at the table and I broke up with him. I could tell he hadn't seen it coming. The look on his face and the hurt in his eyes. He was broken.

"I'm sorry, Noah." I tried to soften the blow.

"We can work this out, I'm sorry." He pleaded with me to change my mind.

But I sat there, lifeless, with my head lowered and fingers strumming the placemats. I didn't want to break up with him.

"No, this is what she wants, Noah. You can take your things and go," Mom interrupted.

Noah got up, grabbed the grocery bag and stormed out the door. I started to cry as soon as he left, and Mom offered up a hug.

"It's okay, Amber. It's for the best. It was just young love."

I trusted my mom knew more than I did. I assumed she could see things that I couldn't and would use her years of experience as a guide to help me make the right choices. I was wrong. I regretted breaking up with him, and it took me years to get over him. Still the damage was done and that would be the end of our story.

CHI-TOWN SHANE

It was my second year of university. I was still trying to get over Noah, and nothing and no one seemed to do the trick. I met Shane at Fairweather, where I was working. It was a women's clothing store in the mall that had recently transitioned from a classy establishment with black marble floors and countertops to a cheap discount store that had bright-coloured signs on top of every single rack. He entered the store and I decided to introduce myself. He was the opposite of Noah. He was short, with dark hair and blue eyes. He spoke with an accent, so I knew he wasn't from Saskatoon.

"Where are you from?" I asked.

"Chicago, but I was born here. I'm home for the holidays," he explained.

"Oh wow, what do you do there?" I was instantly intrigued. Another person who was born and raised here and had managed to get the hell out.

"I am an investment banker. I've been there for ten years. I went to school at DePaul University."

Silently, I did what every woman does when she meets a potential prospect: I ran through the checklist of attributes: educated, has a job, no wedding ring, attractive, doesn't live here. Check, check, check.

"Can I help you find anythings specific?" I asked.

I'd been working at Fairweather for two years, so I had it on autopilot. It was Christmas season, and this usually was the only time you'd see men enter the store. They were always looking for last-minute Christmas gifts.

"I'm looking for a gift for my mom, actually."

I mentally added "respects his mother" to my checklist. I helped him select a couple sweaters for his mom and checked him out at the till.

"I'm Shane, by the way. Thanks for your help," he said, smiling.

"I'm Amber, and you're welcome."

There was an obvious attraction between us, but he left the store without any attempt to exchange numbers.

A month later, a spitting image of him walked into the store. I knew right away that it was his mother. She had the same eyes and rosy cheeks.

"Hi, I'm here to return these sweaters," she said as she approached the counter. "My son bought them for me for Christmas but the sizes are off."

"Would your son's name be Shane by any chance?"

She looked at me with a sparkle and a smile and said, "You must be Amber?"

"I am," I said excitedly.

My first thought was that he must have mentioned me to his mother. I didn't, however, think that she may have just read my name tag. I helped her return the two sweaters. She wasn't interested in seeing anything else and accepted a credit note for future spending. Before she left, she handed me a piece of paper with Shane's email address.

I was nervous to contact him. What if he didn't remember me or thought I was a lunatic? I sat down one Sunday afternoon at the family computer in the basement. Mom had purchased a refurbished desktop computer, monitor, and keyboard from a used computer store. I used it primarily for school or ICQ, and Chad liked it for downloading music on Napster and rating girls on hotornot.com.

I started typing. *Dear Shane. I'm not sure if you remember me. I'm the girl from the clothing store.*

Delete. Delete. That sounded ridiculous. *Dear Shane, my name is Amber. Your mom gave me your email address.* Delete. Delete. I eventually mustered up a random email, convinced he wouldn't write back.

Click. Send.

Two months went by and finally, there in my inbox, was an email from Shane. He remembered me. We spent the next few months communicating over MSN Messenger and on the phone. Our relationship was more of a friendship than a romance. He would call me randomly at 3 a.m. I was sure to keep the portable phone next to my bed and answer it on the first ring so my parents wouldn't hear it.

"Hello?" I whispered in a groggy voice.

"A-love! Baby, you got to hear this sick beat!"

He was always at a rave, high on ecstasy, and feeling every bit of the night.

"P! It's Amber, come say hi to her," Shane said in the background.

P was short for Patty, which was short for Patricia. She was one of Shane's best friends and always out with him on the weekends. We spoke briefly about nothing of substance. My care factor for the *latest beat being laid by the tightest new talent* in Chi-town was extremely low, especially considering I was half asleep. What I really valued was a sober, daytime conversation, just the two of us. And this was not it.

When school started in the fall, I called Shane in between classes from campus. Our friendship had become more romantic but was still solely based on email, MSN Messenger, and phone calls.

You need to come to Chi-town for a visit. I will take you out, show you the town, he wrote.

I really want to but I just can't with school, I said, lying. I actually wanted to go but knew two reasons would prevent that from ever happening. One, I couldn't afford it. A plane ticket was almost $1,000. At this point, I was paying for my tuition, books, food, gas, insurance, cell phone, and all my own toiletries and clothes. I was only making $8.25 an hour. The second reason was really the biggest reason. My mom would never allow it. If cheerleading wasn't a team sport, she probably wouldn't let me travel to out-of-town competitions. I remembered one time during the summer after high school graduation, a few friends were planning a weekend camping trip. She said no, even though Chad had done the exact same thing the year before. I had camped with the same group of friends during our four years of Nor'Westers canoeing club in high school, but because this trip was unsupervised, it was not acceptable. "You need to stay and work," she said. This was an excuse; her word was the only word that mattered.

"I have a friend who is driving down from Saskatoon. He is staying a week. Why don't you catch a ride with him?" Shane suggested.

The idea of travelling and seeing a new city was exciting, and Shane was just a bonus. He was a reason for a trip. An excuse. Most of my friends travelled during spring break or reading week. Some even went backpacking in Europe. I felt so sheltered and deprived. Bound by invisible barriers and control that no one could see from the outside. It made me look pathetic and immature. My parents knew of Shane. They referred to him as "Chi-town" but didn't think much of it since he lived so far away. I floated the idea of visiting him past them, but Mom said no. "Do you have any idea how dangerous it is in Chicago? You do not need to be traipsing down there for some guy."

I left it at that and decided I needed to facilitate my own plan to freedom. I knew if I didn't show up at home one day, they'd think I was abducted, or in danger. So, I planned a mid-night exit. I packed my suitcase the night before and wrote a letter:

Dear Mom and Dad,

I am sorry to have to write this to you in a letter. I have been feeling extremely exhausted and stressed and - to spend some time soul searching. Please don't worry. I am fine. I'll be back soon.

I love you,
Amber

    I set my alarm for 5:30 a.m., placed the letter on the kitchen table, and snuck out. I could feel my heart racing, and my hands begin to shake, but I was invested now. I put my suitcase into my car and headed to Hailey's house.

    Hey, I'm here, I texted.

    I'd pre-arranged with Hailey that I would come to her house and give her the keys to my car.

    "I can't believe you're doing this!" she said.

    "I know, me neither!"

    I was as shocked as she was, but something had to break the chains that surrounded me. We headed inside. I showered, and we got ready for the day. Hailey and I drove to the university in her car, and she dropped me off in the parking lot of Place Riel to meet Shane's friend.

    "Have you ever met this guy before? Do you even know what he looks like?"

    Hailey seemed nervous. She was always the one keeping me safe and out of trouble. Hailey had an enviable family dynamic. Two loving parents and a younger brother. She was close to her brother, and her parents were beyond supportive. They came to every university football game just to watch her cheer on the sidelines. They always stayed for the entire game and passed out Twizzler liquorice when we were done. This type of love and support was foreign to me. My parents came to one university football game during my first year. After that, Mom said it didn't make sense to sit through a whole football game to watch me cheer. And they never came back.

    Hailey and I looked around and waited in the parking lot. I began to think about the possibility of him not showing up. What would I do then? Just go home after school? Suddenly a navy-blue Hyundai

Tiburon pulled up and a tall, pale man with ginger-coloured hair stepped out. Hailey leaned over and gave me a hug.

"Am, are you sure about this?" she asked.

"No, but it'll be okay," I said, nervously trying to convince myself. "He's a paramedic, and he looks like he's more likely to be a gamer or larper than a serial killer."

We both laughed, said we loved each other, and I stepped out to meet Lance.

"What do I do if your parents ask where you are?" Hailey asked before I closed the door.

"Tell them you don't know anything."

•

Lance and I drove for two days. We spent one night in Winnipeg, at a friend's house. We rolled into Chicago late on the second day and met Shane and his roommates. Before we could say hi, Shane rushed over and fumbled his words.

"Hey, A-love, your dad signed into your MSN Messenger account, and, well, I thought it was you."

My heart stopped. "What did you say?"

"I thought it was you, so I asked where you were and why weren't you on your way with Lancer?"

"Fuck."

"You didn't tell your parents you were coming?"

Instantly, I felt like a child again. I was eighteen but unable to make any decisions without my parents' approval.

"No, I didn't. I left early in the morning and left them a note."

"You left them a note?" Shane was completely shocked.

He didn't understand my family dynamics. He was twenty-eight and living his best life.

"Yeah, it was just easier that way," I said, trying to sound independent and mature.

"Well, fuck. Am I going to have cops show up looking for you or what?"

"No," I said with a laugh.

I tried to act like that would be an extreme reaction, but I knew full well that it was a possibility.

"Well, we better get a drink into you tonight because I told your dad I'd get you to call him tomorrow."

He mixed me a drink of vodka and flavoured water. I drank to numb the anticipated dread of tomorrow's phone call. It hit me a lot harder than I thought. The legal drinking age in Canada was nineteen, and I had yet to build up any sort of tolerance. I was introduced to Patty and Shane's three roommates: Dom, Demario, and Chris. All of them were athletes and extremely good looking. Chris had impeccable teeth. They were straight and white, almost veneer-like. He had green eyes like me and stared deep into mine. He reminded me of Noah.

Shane started up his turntable to spin some music. He grabbed two vinyl records and placed them on the table. I didn't have much knowledge or appreciation for his music or mixing skills. The music was fine, but it wasn't worth writing home about. I went to fill up my drink and came across Chris. He was with Dom and Demario. We started talking and it soon felt like Shane didn't even exist. Chris was in his fourth year at DePaul, majoring in commerce.

"Why are you with Shane? I know I shouldn't be saying this, but I'm infatuated with you. You're so confident and sexy," he said.

He was coming on strong, and I knew full well that it was lust, not love, but it was more attention than I'd received from Shane since I arrived there. He leaned in and kissed me. The effects of the vodka were enough for me to linger longer than I should have.

"I shouldn't," I said.

I pulled away, letting my moral code direct me to do what was right, not what I actually wanted to do, which was to continue kissing him.

"We don't need to tell Shane, okay?"

"Okay," I agreed and left to go find everyone else.

We all sat in the living room with our drinks, and I couldn't help but think of that kiss. Shane took half a pill of ecstasy and was feeling every beat that he was laying down, or so he said. Somehow, he found out about the kiss with Chris. Maybe Chris's conscience got the best of him and he confessed.

"I thought you were here to see me?" Shane asked.

"I am," I replied.

It was enough reassurance for him to pull me close and kiss me. He grabbed my hand and pulled me into his room. We started to have sex until he fell asleep. That was a first for me. I felt embarrassed and unwanted while he snored.

•

The next morning, Shane woke up and had zero memory of anything that had transpired the night before, including falling asleep on me. He apologized, went to work, and left Lance and me to venture out into the city for the day.

Before we left, I decided to get the call over with. The invisible control my parents had over me was palpable. I loved my dad very much and didn't want him to be disappointed in me. I knew I needed to call so I called him right away, hoping my mom would still be asleep. I sat down on the couch, flipped open my cell phone, and dialled home.

"You have a collect call from . . . Amber."

"Hello, Amber," Dad said.

I could hear the disappointment in his voice.

"How is your time decompressing and soul searching going in Chicago with your boyfriend Shane?" he asked.

I never wanted to hurt him, and it hit me suddenly that I had hurt him in a big way.

"It's okay," was all I could say before I was interrupted by my mom in the background.

"You tell that little bitch to get her scrawny ass back here right fucking now."

I immediately wanted to hang up, but I kept the phone to my ear. I had never hung up on my dad before. He knew if he handed the phone to her that I might never come back, and he was right. He went on to tell me how he reached out to the police and the US border control, but because I was eighteen there wasn't anything they could do for him. My parents went to various lengths to find out where I was, including searching my room for my passport and anything else they could find. They went to the bank to see if I took out any money or picked up a recent credit card, which I had. They called my cheerleading coach and friends, including Hailey. They asked Chad for my password to my MSN Messenger account, which he handed over willingly. Traitor.

"You need to get on a plane immediately and get back here," Dad demanded.

"Okay, Dad."

I dug my nails into my leg, scraping myself from calf to my thigh. It helped pull me out of the moment. Mom was still yelling in the background. She scared me and this was the first time that I had ever done anything bad. I couldn't imagine what type of punishment I was going to receive.

"I love you, Dad," I said, hopeful he would say it back.

"Goodbye, Amber."

He hung up the phone and my heart felt instantly heavy in my chest. It was the first time in my life that he hadn't said he loved me back.

THE GREATEST PUNISHMENT

Lance and I left for the day to explore the city. I was determined to see some of the tourist attractions before I had to face reality and go home. We saw everything from the Sears Tower to Navy Pier to Buckingham Fountain. I fell in love with Chicago. It was not at all like how my mom had described it. It was big and beautiful and clean. We met up with Shane for lunch, and he helped me find a travel agency to book a flight home for the next day. I was thankful I picked up the emergency credit card before I left. I used it to pay for my flight, which was almost four hundred US dollars. We spent the rest of the day touring Chicago and shopping on the Magnificent Mile. I wanted to get Hailey something for everything she did for me and settled on rugby shirts for the two of us from Old Navy.

I couldn't fully embrace my time away because the phone call with my dad wasn't sitting right with me. This was the first time I had done anything that went against their rules. I remembered once when Jason was caught drinking underage. They made him drink a number of shots, a few beers, and a bottle of wine until he puked. They did the same with Chad when he was caught smoking. They made him smoke a pack of cigarettes and a cigar all at once at the kitchen table while they watched. I thought volunteering at the cancer ward would be much more effective. I couldn't imagine what Mom would say when I got home. My dad's obvious disappointment and hurt were more than enough punishment. I would regret making this choice for the rest of my life.

•

The next day, I boarded a flight home. When I landed at the airport, I took a cab directly to cheerleading practice. I saw the disappointment in my coach's eyes. I had lied to her and told her I would miss the game on Saturday because I was going to visit my grandma. Vacations weren't allowed, especially during the season. My mom had called her and told her what I did. I was pulled out of every stunt for the rest of the football season and was only used as a last resort. My mom knew it would affect my position on the team and that was the deepest cut she could make.

"Hey," I said sheepishly to Hailey.

"Hi."

I could tell she was pissed.

"You okay?"

"We can talk about it later," she said.

"Okay."

I felt like my world was caving in. The people and things that mattered most were no longer there. I managed to scorch them all by being selfish in my decisions. After practice, I asked Hailey for a ride home and reluctantly she said yes. I grabbed my suitcase and wheeled it to her car. We sat in silence until she pulled out onto the road. I was nervous, and I hated that she was upset with me.

"Hey, what's the matter?" I asked.

She turned down the radio and exhaled.

"This whole situation was fucked up and unfair to me. Your dad called me and demanded to know everything. They came and got the keys to take your car. I felt like you left and dumped it all on me."

I didn't realize the effect it would have on her. She was right, and for some reason I hadn't considered that it might play out this way. Part of me thought they wouldn't look for me at all. I've always been pretty good about playing out situations and anticipating scenarios. I had gotten used to doing that with Mom. But this time, I didn't. I can see now, being a parent myself, how truly terrifying this was for my parents. But I can also see how even the slightest bit of freedom can be liberating and life changing.

"I'm so sorry, H. You're right. I never meant for any of that to happen. Thank you for helping me, supporting me, and being there for me. I brought you a gift!"

I pulled the yellow-and-purple striped rugby shirt out of my bag. I could tell by the look on her face that a shirt wasn't going to make it up to her. We pulled up to the front of my house. I leaned over and gave her a hug.

"I'm so sorry. I love you, Hailey."

"I love you too, Am. Good luck, okay?"

I could sense the nervousness in her voice.

"Thanks."

I carried my suitcase up the driveway and into the house. My mom was sitting at the table in her usual spot at the end.

"Sit down!" Her brown eyes had turned black. She held a cigarette between her two fingers, with her thumb pressing into the side of her cheek.

"Did you have fun galivanting all over the place?"

She had a snide tone that she used when she was mad.

"Do you feel less stressed now that you've had some 'time to yourself'?" she said, quoting the letter that I left them. "Go look at the fridge and read what is taped up there."

I went over and grabbed a note. She had placed it on the fridge while I was gone. In her handwriting it read: *The choices we make dictate the lives we lead.*

"Read it out loud," she said sternly.

I read it again, aloud this time.

"That's right. You make these choices, you have to live with the consequences, and it will dictate the life you have. Now get to bed."

I was beyond shocked. That was the least amount of rage she had ever shown me. In fact, she'd shown much more fury over far less of a transgression. I knew that my dad had probably gotten the brunt end of her rage over the last two days.

My dad came into my room later that night as I was unpacking my suitcase.

"Hi, Dad," I said with a solemn look.

"Nice to see you're home safe."

"I'm so sorry, Dad."

"I was worried sick about you."

"I know. I could tell how mad you were when you didn't say you loved me back on the phone." Tears started to well up in my eyes.

"You know I will always love you, Amber."

"I love you, too."

Dad wrapped his arms around me and gave me a hug.

"Did you have fun?"

I nodded but kept most of the details to myself.

The next morning, I sat on the floor behind my door applying my makeup for school. Chad pushed the door open as far as it could go before hitting my knee. He pushed his head through the opening and looked down at me.

"Hey, how was the trip?"

I gave him a look of chagrin and discontent.

"Why did you give Mom and Dad my MSN password?"

"Cause they were freaking out! What did you expect? You left them a note, Amber!"

I rolled my eyes. Who was he to lecture me for making shitty decisions? He was notorious for making a comment that would ignite a spark. It sparked and fuelled Mom's rage. He would then sit back to watch the warfare.

The decision to go to Chicago was one that shocked everyone. It would never be forgotten by anyone in my family. It changed my relationship with my mother, and she became slightly less strict throughout my remaining years at university. My curfew was extended from 12:30 a.m. to 2:30 a.m. when I turned nineteen, and she never asked about any guys that called. I believe it was that one act of disobedience that showed my mother I wasn't scared. That I could break free if I wanted to.

EXIT PLAN

It was term two of my second year of university. By this time, I'd declared French as my major and kinesiology as my minor. I was getting all my prerequisite classes to get into the college of education. I wanted to become an elementary French teacher. I attended classes on Mondays, Wednesdays, and Fridays. On Tuesdays and Thursdays, I worked at my dad's office helping with reception. I worked evenings and weekends at my job at the mall and had cheerleading practice Thursday and Sunday nights. I needed to work to pay for my tuition. Student loans were never an option because the government said my parents made too much money, although not enough to help out, according to Mom. Dad co-signed a student line of credit for $10,000 and if I maxed it out, I wouldn't be able to finish school. I needed to constantly pay it down to have enough money for the next semester's tuition and books.

    I was exhausted and Mom could see that. We had been fighting more and more since I started university. I wasn't having much luck with dating. Dates ranged in extremes from a guy serenading me with an original song while sitting in my car, to a guy calling me at three in the morning to masturbate to the sound of my voice while I was half asleep. Then there was Jesse, a football player who was only interested in sex and not looking for a commitment, until he upgraded to one of my coworkers. There was Aaron, who was ten years my senior. He was a friend with benefits and after six months, he still had no idea what my last name was. And there was Theo, the guy who bought me a belly button piercing for my birthday. I never gave him the impression that I wanted one. I felt like I couldn't refuse the gift, so I pierced it even though I didn't want to.

I was at a low point. It was a Sunday night and I had just gotten home from cheerleading practice and taken a shower. I tiptoed to my room with my hair dripping wet, a towel wrapped around my body.

"Amber!" my mother wailed from the living room.

I assumed she needed a cup of tea or more smokes. I cringed in my towel. It was the way she yelled my name every time. I hated it. I hated the sound of my own name because of her.

I made the mistake of responding with "what?"

"Don't you 'what' me!"

This was her most common dagger and I should have known better. The acceptable response was *yes* or *yes, Mom*. She barged down the hall and pressed her bodyweight into my bedroom door, trying to pry her way into my room. She wanted a fight.

"You think you're better than everyone else because you're going to university; well, you're not!"

"I never said I was!"

"You don't have to say it, is how you act. Your brother doesn't act like that! All you care about is yourself! You're a piece of work. A real selfish bitch who thinks they're better than everyone else!"

"Leave me alone! We all know he's your favourite," I said.

I tried pushing her out of my room and shutting the door. She barged back in and threw a punch that landed on my jaw. She had given me spankings as a child, but this was the first time she hit me as an adult.

"Don't you dare say that, you're just jealous of him. I treat you all the same."

We pushed back and forth on the door. I was convinced it was going to break. Exhausted and defeated, with tears running down my face, I pleaded with her.

"Get out. Please. I don't understand why we are this way. We need therapy," I said.

I was able to push her out enough that the door closed. I sat on the floor, my back pressed up against the bottom of my door, still in my towel. "I hate you," I said under my breath. It was the truth, and I knew she felt the same.

She continued yelling, reminding me again that she would never pay a stranger to listen to our problems. Eventually, she marched down the hallway and back to the kitchen table. I could hear her lighter click as she lit a cigarette. She took a drag and then let out a long exhale. My dad was in the garage, and I knew she would call him in and tell him everything. There was never a quick end to our fights. She created a hostile environment, and she would stay mad for a number of days afterwards. I never understood that. Holding onto the anger and inflicting tension on other people for that long.

I laid down on the floor in the fetal position, completely exhausted in every possible sense. Tears streamed down my face, and my hair was dripping onto my back. I just wanted it to end. Hopeless feelings of defeat ran through my head: *How did my life become like this? Why does she hate me so much? I don't want this life.* Then thoughts of suicide ran through my head. Killing myself seemed to be the only option, the only way to make it all stop. How could I do it? I could hang myself in the closet? Or jump off the train bridge? Or drive my car into something? I knew I didn't want to hurt anyone else, just myself. I silently considered my options and without hesitation picked up the phone and called Anna, one of my best friends.

"Hey," I said as tears still poured down my face.

"Hey, Ambs, what's up?"

She could tell I was overwhelmed and distraught.

"My mom and I just got into a huge fight."

"Shit, you okay?"

"No. I want to kill myself," I said, struggling to get in enough air.

Anna was silent for a long moment.

"Ambs, you can't. I know it seems unbearable right now, but it'll get better. I promise. You can't let her get to you. What if you move out?"

Anna lived on her own in a small condo. She was right, maybe I should just move out. I earned enough money to try and make it work. Anything would be better than this.

I cried myself to sleep that night and went to school in the morning. Face puffy and eyes swollen, I walked through lower Place Riel and saw a sign for the student wellness centre. It froze me in my tracks. I stood there, debating whether I should go in. My palms were clammy, and my legs felt weak. I knew I needed help, but I risked being committed to a psych facility if I told anyone that I wanted to kill myself. And the backlash I would receive from my mom would be even worse. I quickly remembered an instance in high school when my cousin ended up in the hospital. She took an excessive amount of Advil to end her life and needed to have her stomach pumped. "She's always doing things for attention. This is just another one of her stunts," my mom said.

I chose to forgo receiving help and kept walking.

•

A couple days later, Mom finally started speaking to me again. Small, short sentences or requests at first. I apologized for what I said and how I acted. She stayed stoic and unmoved. I asked her how she felt about me moving out.

"Why would you waste your money when you have a perfectly good place to live here?"

"I don't know. We seem to be fighting a lot . . ."

"And whose fault is that?"

"Both of ours," I said.

"Ha!" She laughed at the idea of being even partially to blame.

"You hit me in the face!"

"Pfft! I barely even touched you."

"You did. And I think a little space could benefit us."

"No. You won't be moving anywhere. You've got school to pay for, and that student line of credit is tied to your dad's name. It needs to be paid off. End of discussion!"

I knew I couldn't bring it up again. "End of discussion" was always Mom's way of saying it was over and we weren't going to talk about it again. She always had the final say.

AN OMBRE OCCASION

It was an incredibly hot Sunday in August when Mom popped into Fairweather. I was working as many shifts as I could that summer. I needed every cent I could make. At the end of the prior semester, I'd been plugging the parking metres with dimes and collecting multiple parking tickets each week. Since I was working so much, Mom and I didn't have much time to spend together, and her shopping trips had become solo adventures.

"Hey, what are you doing here?" I smiled and greeted her as she walked into the store. Any visitor was a nice break in the day.

"Oh, just thought I'd come down and see how your day was going."

"What's in the bag?"

She opened the top of the bag, revealing two pairs of men's dress pants.

"Just some pants for Dad."

Mom always bought Dad's clothes. She bought him everything he needed and even some things he didn't. She dressed him older than what he was, with pleated khakis and button-up shirts. He never seemed to mind and wore whatever she chose for him. He had complete trust in her choices.

She walked slowly through the store, making her way to the back where the long dresses were located. Fairweather's leftover graduation dresses and the summer's collection of bridesmaid dresses hung on various racks.

"Have you thought about what you're wearing to the wedding?" she asked.

Jason and Natalie were getting married in a few weeks.

"Yes! I have, actually. I was thinking about this dress here," I said.

I pulled the dress from a rack to show her. It was a navy-blue sleeveless column dress with a high neckline.

"I've got my size set aside in the back room. I was going to try it on after work."

"Oh. It's nice."

I could tell that she was unimpressed with my choice.

"What about this one?" she asked, pulling a dress from the rack.

It was an ombre halter dress with a low back. A sparkly graduation dress that had yet to sell.

"Seems like a bit much, don't you think?"

"Well, if you aren't going to be a bridesmaid, then don't you think you should have something that stands out? You *are* doing a reading!"

Mom was upset that I hadn't been asked to be a bridesmaid. Chad was Jason's best man, and I could tell that doing a reading was their way of making me feel included. I was a little disappointed, but Natalie and I weren't close.

I needed to wait until my shift ended before I could try on the dresses. Mom stuck around and browsed for the last fifteen minutes, and I skirted off the floor at 5 p.m. sharp.

"Here take this one, too," Mom said, handing me the blue ombre gown.

I tried on the conservative navy dress first and came out smiling. It hugged my curves and was modest.

"Too plain. Try the sparkly one."

I headed back to the dressing room. I was never one to pick a dress that was backless; my boobs were too big, and I was not comfortable going braless. I stepped out while holding onto the sides of the dress. I turned my back toward Mom so she could lace up the back.

"Now that's a dress!" she said. "Don't you think, Am?"

I looked in the three-way mirror and it shimmered against the light. I looked like a disco ball, and it seemed inappropriate for a wedding.

"I guess . . ."

"I'll buy it for you!" Mom offered.

It was on sale for $150, double the price of the navy dress I'd planned to pay for myself. And even that was more money than I wanted to spend on something I'd never wear again. I knew if I said no, she would be mad, so reluctantly I agreed.

•

The day before the wedding, Mom came barging into my room. I was on my bed studying flash cards for a class on the architecture and artwork of the French Revolution.

"Amber, I need your help."

I put my cards down and sat up.

"What's up?

"Chad hasn't written his best man speech."

Before I could say anything, she interrupted me.

"I need you to write it for him."

The request to do something for Chad was all too familiar. I had less than twenty-four hours to write a speech. I turned on the computer and started to type. I had no idea how to write a best man speech. So, I did what I knew how to do and channelled what I wished I had. I wrote an emotional speech about how loving and supportive Jason was as an older brother. The bond that the two of them shared and how Jason was such a role model to Chad. I printed it off and handed it over to him.

"Thanks, Am."

The next day was Jason and Natalie's wedding. It was the long weekend in September of 2003. The morning seemed calm and quiet in our house. The sun was shining, and Jason and Chad got ready in their rented tuxedos. Mom wore a navy sleeveless dress with a high neckline and matching blazer, and Dad wore a suit and tie. I came home from the hair salon after spending the morning getting my bleach-blonde hair styled in an updo. A dress like mine couldn't be worn with a ponytail.

We all drove to the wedding together. When it came time, I made my way to the podium for my reading. I could feel the stares and I started to tremble. I spoke the original words that I wrote about marriage and what it meant to build a foundation of love and trust. I was a nineteen-year-old girl speaking from a place of no experience. I had never seen love or a marriage like that, so I channelled my Hallmark family and spoke from what I hoped I would have one day. I started to cry as I spoke, and so did the entire congregation.

Natalie never said anything about my dress. She was too kind for that, and I'm not sure it really mattered to her. I received a few side-eye glances from other women, but I had a couple of drinks and it no longer mattered by then. The rest of the speeches took place after a hot buffet meal, each person standing up and toasting to the couple. When it was Chad's turn, he stood up and fumbled through his speech. It was more eloquent than he was capable of, and he hadn't bothered to practice. He started to cry, and everyone was in such awe with his words. My words. When he finished his speech, Jason stood up and gave him a hug. I'm sure it was the first time Chad had ever expressed any type of gratitude or appreciation for Jason.

LUCAS

In year three of university, my dreams of becoming a teacher started dwindling. I applied twice to get into the college of education and was rejected both times. I was considering applying to the University of Alberta and to Western University, but Mom said no. I chose to receive a bachelor of arts and science instead with a double major in sociology/French and a minor in kinesiology.

Cheerleading was what kept me going. I loved the sport and the feeling of closeness with my teammates. I loved pushing myself to try new skills. I was fearless, and I felt more valued as a member of my team, than a member of my family. Lucas, my stunting partner, was one of my best friends. I trusted him wholeheartedly, and he became my safest space. He was Mormon, didn't drink, was still a virgin, and by all accounts was the most innocent person I had ever met. I envied him. His life seemed uncomplicated. He came from a large family with three boys and three girls. His parents seemed so accepting and kind. Lucas caught me every time I fell, in every aspect of my life.

My first Pap test results came back with precancerous cells. It was pretty serious, and I needed a cone biopsy and a LEEP procedure done right away. I was told that I contracted Human Papillomavirus or HPV and that's how my cells became precancerous. Lucas was the first person I told.

"I have no idea what any of that means. What can I do to help?" he asked.

I needed to have someone drive me to the hospital for my procedure. He pleaded to accompany me to the doctor's office, but it felt weird. I didn't want people in the waiting room thinking he was my boyfriend and I was at some Planned Parenthood-type appointment. That just wasn't me. I told Lucas that my mom knew and insisted on taking me. Three days later, Mom and I arrived at the hospital, which was connected to my university. My only thought was *Dear God, please don't let me run into anyone I know*. Mom and I sat together in the waiting room, thumbing through old editions of *People* magazine from the spring of 2001.

"Amber?" A petite nurse with brown hair and glasses called my name.

Mom and I both stood up. Startled, I looked at her and said, "I'm good." She resumed her position in the large blue chair and continued to flip the pages of her magazine.

I followed the nurse and was ushered into a small room. She handed me a paper dressing gown and told me to undress from the waist down.

"Go ahead and hop up on the table and put your feet in the stirrups when you're ready."

She left the room and allowed me some privacy to get undressed.

A knock came at the door.

"Hello?" I said.

One doctor, two nurses, and seven students with clipboards came barging into the room.

"Were you aware that we are a teaching hospital?" the doctor asked as she lifted the sheet up to my knees.

With my vulva in full view, I replied, "Um, I am now."

"Can I get you to scooch down a little more?" she asked. «Okay, and a little more. Knees to the side."

I tried to distract myself with my thoughts, wondering why each time a gynecologist was examining you they had to use the term "scooch." She grabbed a remote and turned on the large TV that was mounted on the wall. A closeup of a vulva appeared on the screen. At first I thought it was a video to detail the procedure for the medical residents. As a hand came onto the screen and started to insert a speculum, I realized it was *my* vulva on the screen! A small camera was now broadcasting my vagina and cervix onto a 42" screen. I felt like fainting. My face turned instantly red. I was mortified. I listened and watched as she meticulously explained her every move while burning a portion of my cervix. One of the nurses was so kind to hold my hand and ask me questions. She wiped away a tear that fell down my cheekbone. The smell of burning skin was something I had never experienced and now would be embedded in my mind forever. The residents asked the doctor a few questions and within an instant, the entourage was gone, and I was left to get dressed. I sat up from the table feeling violated. My abdomen was cramping already. I got dressed and forced a nonchalant expression on my face to greet my mom in the waiting room.

She got up from her chair and before we could get into the elevator, she started to pry.

"Amber, do you want to tell me why this happened?"

"I'm not sure. What do you mean?" I said, convinced she'd rummaged through all the HPV and LEEP procedure pamphlets while she waited.

"Well, are you having sex? This doesn't happen to girls that aren't having sex, you know."

I paused for a minute. I was nineteen years old and had been on birth control for almost two years. There had been some instances of sexual assault on campus a couple years prior, and it seemed like the perfect time to bring it up and suggest to Mom that I should be on birth control just to be safe. Mom had attended all my doctor appointments since I was born.

"No, Mom, I'm not having sex." The lie left my mouth.

She couldn't prove anything, and I wasn't in any condition to fight with her. We sat in silence on the way home. The cramping was becoming more intense.

"You know, your Aunt Beth had a similar procedure done when she was younger. You should ask her about it. It's probably hereditary," Mom said.

Normally, I wouldn't have hesitated to correct her, but I replied, "I didn't know that; I will ask her about it. You're probably right."

A small smile came across her face from the satisfaction of hearing she was right.

•

A couple days later, the cramps were excruciating, and I was still bleeding. I couldn't get the experience out of my head. Lucas invited me over to his house that evening.

"Amber, how are you feeling?" he asked.

"Honestly? It felt like I was raped."

The words left my mouth without any hesitation. My childhood experiences with Chad never even entered my mind during this time, but looking back now I can see why this experience was so traumatic for me.

"I felt completely violated with everyone watching me."

I walked him through every step of my experience and shared that, once again, I felt like I couldn't be touched.

"Would it help at all if I gave you a back massage? I can be someone safe for you, and you know that I have no expectations."

Lucas was beyond sweet, and I trusted him wholeheartedly.

"Okay," I said.

This was Lucas's way of "getting back on the horse" after a traumatizing experience. He left the room so I could undress my top half and cover myself with a blanket on the floor. He knocked before he entered and came in with a bottle of lotion. He warmed his hands and gently started slowly massaging my shoulders.

"How's this?" he asked. "Does this feel okay?"

"Yes," I said.

He massaged down the middle of my back and continued to check in with me as he progressed toward my lower back.

"Are you still okay? Would you like me to stop?"

I assured him I was okay, even though I'd started to cry. Lucas introduced me to consent for the first time. He finished massaging my back and left the room to allow me to get dressed. He gave me a big hug when he came back, and we instantly changed the subject to computer coding and income tax. Lucas mentioned he'd just received some money from his parents from their income tax returns.

"What do you mean? They gave you money?" I inquired.

"Well, they claimed my tuition on their tax return and gave me the money to pay off my student loans."

"Really?" I was shocked.

"Yeah, since you are still living at home, your parents can use your tuition as a tax deduction to pay down your student debt," he said.

Mom always did everyone's tax returns. She would gather our T4 slips and sit at the kitchen table for hours while she calculated and tallied our earnings. Tirelessly, she would fill out each box and mail paper copies. I never understood why she had yet to move over to online filing. Each year she asked me to log into my student account and print off the form that would allow me to transfer my tuition over to my parents to claim on their income tax.

"My mom told me I didn't make enough money to claim it on my taxes, and that's why I transferred it over to her," I told Lucas.

"And you never received any money from them to put toward your tuition?"

"Nope," I said, dumbfounded.

A look of shock and disappointment came over Lucas's face as he explained to me that it wasn't right. I left his house that night having forgotten about my violated feelings and cramps. I was newly fixated on this revelation. How had I been so easily duped?

•

I ended up confronting my mom about the tuition deduction that she'd claimed for the past three years. She denied that it made much of a difference on their taxes and said that it didn't give them a refund. Her explanation was that it simply allowed my dad to keep more of his money that he earned instead of paying it to the government. I was told to think of it as covering my living expenses and rent.

THE PURPLE DRESS

It was an exceptionally cold winter. It was my fourth year of university, and I was excited to be done with school. Although it was bittersweet as it was my last year of cheerleading.

It was goulash night at home. Ground beef, two cans of mushroom soup, mashed potatoes and one can of creamed corn. On my plate, they were all separate. I ate one item at a time. I finished my supper and quickly did the dishes.

"C'mon, Dad, hurry up," I said.

Dad and I had been going to the gym nightly at the Cosmo Civic Centre.

"I'm coming, I'm coming . . ."

Dad grabbed his gym bag and water bottle, then put his jacket and toque on. It was the first time that Dad and I'd spent a consistent amount of time together, just the two of us.

We arrived in the parking lot, the tires crunching through a fresh snowfall. We ran down the ramp with our gym bags in hand. The air was frigid, and it took our breath away. I loved seeing my dad run; he looked so young and playful.

The gym there was tiny, with the bare minimum of equipment. The average age of the clientele was sixty-five years old and usually, late at night, no one was there. We got on the treadmills, which were side by side. A slow jog turned into a full sprint, and we leaned forward, pretending we were crossing the finish line in an Olympic race.

"I won!" I screamed.

"As if, guy! Booyah!"

We erupted in full belly laughter together. My dad has a perfect laugh. His eyes disappear, his teeth shine ear to ear, and his shoulders shrug up to his ears. We lifted weights and finished off with crunches. This was the happiest I'd felt in years. I felt confident and strong, and so did my dad.

It felt great to get in another workout before the university athletic banquet, a special night with sports awards for all the sports teams. Technically, cheerleading wasn't an official sport at the university, but they graced us with an invite each year, and we graced everyone with our presence.

•

I knew Damian would be at the banquet. He was a hockey player. I had never spoken to him before and had only seen him in the halls or in the campus newspaper. He was tall with shaggy blonde hair, and blue eyes. I'd recently purchased a new dress and had every intention of looking as incredible as I felt. Hair straightened, shoulders back, I walked into the kitchen to show my mom my new halter dress. My bust was spilling out, but I had never felt better.

"Mom, what do you think?" I asked.

She glanced at me, peering over her glasses. She was sitting at the kitchen table, fixated on balancing her cheque book.

"What colour is that? Is that burgundy?" she asked.

"No, it's purple."

"Oh. Is it stretchy?"

"Yeah, pretty stretchy."

"Well, you better go show your dad what you're wearing."

Dad was in the living room, stretched out on the small loveseat, legs up over the side. I walked in, knowing full well that he had been listening to our conversation.

"Well, what do you think, Dad?"

"Where do you think you're going dressed like that?" he joked. "Just kidding. You look beautiful, Am. You remember that, okay?"

"Okay, Dad, I will."

•

I drove over to Amy's house. She was a friend and fellow cheerleader, and we went to the banquet together in her car. We walked into the ballroom feeling like we had it all. We won "Best of the West" that year and had a huge trophy on display amongst all the other sports teams. I scanned the room from our dinner table and made eye contact with Damian. He stood up immediately and walked toward us with a teammate.

"Hi, I'm Damian. This is Kyle. We play on the hockey team."

I knew that but acted casual. "I'm Amber, this is Hailey and Amy. We are cheerleaders."

"Cool," Damian said.

The conversation started to stall. I fumbled slightly with my words and nerves came over me.

"Did you see what happened to our trophy? Someone dumped mashed potatoes all over it," I said. My comment felt like a burst of verbal IBS.

Amy quickly chimed in. "We know it was the women's hockey team. They hate us! We can't help it if we're prettier than they are!" She fluttered her eyelashes and placed her hand on her hip.

"Bitches!" Hailey added.

The five of us danced the night away and drank more than we should have. Damian leaned in at the end of the night and kissed me. He invited me to meet him the next day at school, after he was done coaching a youth hockey camp. I said yes, gave him my number, and we all went our separate ways for the night.

THERAPY

"I want to go back to your graduation for a minute. Let's talk some more about the award that you won and the patch, or badge, I think you called it, after you graduated. Why do you think your mother involved herself in your application form and with the school for your badge?"

"I suppose it could have been a number of reasons. I'm not sure she was convinced that I could win from my efforts alone. Perhaps she wanted me to win to make her look good. Who knows."

"Do you think she may have done it for your own happiness and success?"

The thought had never crossed my mind. She usually celebrated my failures. "Normally I'd say no, but she knew how much my fourth-year badge meant to me, so maybe."

"Have you ever thought how you, as a mother, would do that exact situation differently?"

Damn it. This felt like a classic therapist question. *Think, Amber.*

"I would never ask my girls to lie on a form or inflate their accomplishments. I would never ask them to take advantage of someone else's situation for their own personal gain. If they didn't win a scholarship, then it would be a hard lesson that someone else was more deserving. I think the badge is a bit tougher. I can see where my mom was coming from, but I would be more discreet about it, or at least make them feel worthy of it."

"Okay. Now, let's talk for a minute about your suicidal thoughts. I have to ask: At this point do you still have suicidal tendencies or have feelings of hurting yourself or someone else?"

"No."

"Okay."

She sat silently scribbling a note at the top corner of her notebook. Therapy was supposed to help, but in that moment I felt vulnerable. Exposed even. Did therapists not understand that their notetaking and their mm-hmm sounds felt judgmental? I reminded myself that she was there to help, and that I shouldn't fear being judged. She was not my mother and that is just my past trauma surfacing in this moment.

"I can't imagine feeling that way and then thinking that you would be worse off if you did reach out to someone for help. Were these types of thoughts something you felt often, or was this a one-time occurrence?"

She sat straight up and reached for her coffee cup to take a sip before putting it back down onto the side table.

"I had numerous flashes of instances where I thought about driving into oncoming traffic, but nothing like that night."

"Did you ever find a way out of her control?"

"I did, eventually. It was with Damian."

DAMIAN

Our relationship moved fast. Damian soon became a way for me to escape my home. School was coming to an end, and my parents were starting to question what I was going to do with myself. After applying for convocation, I learned that I was two classes short of my sociology major. I didn't have a degree. How could I have let this happen? I decided not to tell my parents, at least not right then. It was my life. I was paying for my education, and I needed a break. Damian didn't have a job but worked for a hockey camp each summer. His tuition and rent were covered by his parents. He was from a small town in southern Saskatchewan and was the youngest of two. His older sister was married, with a son and another on the way. He played junior hockey in the WHL for four years while he was in high school. He moved away to another small town and lived with a host family while attending school and playing hockey. He still had dreams and hopes to make it further in his hockey career.

 That summer, we travelled three hours south, to Damian's hometown. It was a small desolate town with a few houses and one main street with a pub, post office, gas station, and a small grocery store. It was isolating there. Land as far as you could see. Crops of wheat, canola, and mustard. They had a small, older house, but it was nicely renovated on the inside. I was meeting his family for the first time. His mom, Lynn, was a petite woman with short brown hair. She had glasses and was soft-spoken. She was never one to start up a conversation or boast about anything, but she had kind eyes that sparkled when she smiled.

David was his father. He spoke with a boisterous voice that came off angry at times. He had a full head of grey hair that skimmed the nape of his neck and a matching, burly beard. He walked slightly hunched over and scowled every time he couldn't hear something. He was intimidating. We were headed to Damian's hometown so he could help his dad with a neighbour's cattle. The idea of a branding repulsed me.

"Do you know what they do with the testicles once they cut them out?" David asked eagerly with a smile on his face.

"No," I said. I presumed they threw them out or used them in fertilizer.

"They fry them up in butter and garlic and eat them! We call them prairie oysters!"

The thought of eating calf testicles made me want to vomit. I raised my eyebrows and gave a sarcastic "yum!" in response.

•

The next day, Damian and his dad went off to the branding, leaving me home alone with his mother. She puttered around and eventually sat down to read in her chair by the window.

"Can I help with anything? Is there something I can do to prep for dinner?" I asked, trying to come across as respectful and polite.

Mom had always instilled in me that a good wife is supposed to cook, clean, and take care of her husband and family.

"Nope," she replied and smiled.

We sat there for hours without saying another word.

When David and Damian came home later that day, we had

steak, potatoes, and vegetables for dinner. David loved to barbecue and considered himself quite the foodie.

"How do you like your steak?" he asked me.

Growing up, we only ever had meat that was well done. That was the way Mom liked it, and she wouldn't eat it any other way.

"Well done, please," I said.

"Not in this house we don't," David said. "You'll have it medium rare. That's the only way we eat steak here. You'll love it."

I didn't have the courage to say no or object to him.

The next day, Lynn and I spent the morning keeping ourselves busy around the house, doing the dishes from breakfast, then showering before heading over to the branding. We pulled up to a large farm and found more than twenty people helping, including a tall cowboy with a rope and another man wrestling a small calf. Lynn and I watched as this small calf was roped and turned on its back. It was sliced with a knife and its testicles were pulled from its underside and dropped into a bucket. Another man came over and branded the calf's leg, burning a number into them. The calf got up and limped away, and they moved on to the next one. The sight and smell made me completely nauseated. These helpless animals, everything seemed so inhumane. Lynn and I stuck around until the end of the branding. I was introduced to numerous friends and townies. They made small talk and told old stories.

"Here, give this a try," David came over to me, his overalls covered in mud and a little blood.

In his hand was a small, deep-fried piece of meat.

"What is it?" I asked, suddenly squeamish.

"It's a prairie oyster!"

"No thanks." I shook my head.

"I knew it! I knew you wouldn't have the guts to try it. Come on, just try one!"

He kept pushing and wouldn't let up. I received less pressure to drink absinth throughout my four years of university.

"Fine, give it here." I succumbed to his coercion and popped the calf testicle in my mouth.

It resembled the texture of a deep fried eyeball. It had a crunchy coating, but the inside was squishy. I swallowed it almost whole and from that point on he approved of me.

EMBRACING THE RED FLAGS

I was working at Mark's Work Wearhouse that summer, taking every shift that I could. Damian would visit me on my lunch break and then busy himself until my shift ended, usually around 9:45 p.m. My parents agreed that he could sleep over as long as we slept in the basement spare room. As the summer blossomed, Mom suggested that Damian move in. We had been together for only a couple of months, but she developed compassion for him and didn't think he should have to pay rent for a place he was never at.

I felt myself so hopelessly wanting this to work out that I started to search for signs that it was meant to be. Damian's real first name was Benjamin, like my dad, which was also the name of my maternal grandfather. My favourite cousin's name was Damian and we had always been close. Oh, and there was the fact that we had matching scars on our thumbs, both caused by a nail. Sure, mine was a fingernail and his was an actual nail, but it had to mean something, right?

Damian was offered a position on the Las Vegas AHL team. He was moving, and he wanted me to go with him.

"One year tops," he said. "Just to say that I did it, then we can come back, get married, find jobs, have kids, all of it. They will set us up in a big townhouse on a private golf course with a pool. They will find you a job and give you a work visa. It'll be great. What do you say?"

How could I say no to that! It was the perfect break that I was looking for. September through to April seemed like such a short time and I loved Vegas. The past year, my cheer team had gone to the USA Cheer Nationals, and it had been a riot.

I approached the subject with my parents. I sat them down at the table on a Sunday when Damian was busy coaching.

"Mom, Dad. Damian is moving to Las Vegas, and he wants me to go with him."

"Pardon me?" Mom said.

Mom always used this phrase even though she heard you just fine. I repeated myself.

"You want to what?" Mom's voice rose as she spoke. "Why the hell would you move away with some guy you just met and give up using your degree and finding a job?"

She made a good point but at the time all I could say was "He's the one, Mom."

Dad sat there quietly, as usual.

"Ben! Aren't you going to say something?"

"What can I say, she's going to do what she wants. She's an adult now," Dad said.

Dad very rarely disagreed with my mom. This wasn't necessarily his way of disagreeing, but it was his way of throwing his arms up and saying I can't stop you. I'm sure memories of Chicago flashed through their minds as they realized I'd go with or without their permission.

*

The next month was spent planning and packing, visiting friends, and getting excited for the move. By this point, Damian had moved into my parents' house. One night while I was working, he went out to spend time with friends.

Hey, I'm getting off work soon. What time are you coming home? I sent him a text while he was out. I had been so busy that I had yet to get a key made for him, and Mom would never let me go to bed with the door unlocked.

Won't be that long. 12:30 maybe, he texted.

I went home, got into my pyjamas, and curled up on the couch to watch TV. I waited until 12:30 a.m. and sent him another message.

Hey, just checking in.

No response.

1:00 a.m. came. Then 1:30 a.m. Still no message.

He had done this before, not responding to my messages. But those other times, he'd come home when he said he would.

At 2:00 a.m. I called him.

No answer.

I started to worry. What if something had happened to him? At 2:30 a.m. I called again. Straight to voicemail. Was he blocking my calls? I went upstairs and grabbed my dad's phone. I called, expecting it to go straight to voicemail, but he picked up on the first ring.

"Hello?" he said, sounding confused.

He hadn't recognized my dad's number. I stood there steaming and in shock.

"Hi, it's me. I've been trying to get ahold of you," I said, the hostility in my voice projecting into the phone.

"Oh, hey, I didn't get your messages. My cell was on silent. I'm leaving here soon. We're at Kyle's place playing cards."

I wasn't entirely sure I believed him.

"I'll leave the door open. Make sure you lock it."

I went to bed fuming and within an hour, he was home. I pretended to be asleep. The next morning, he stuck to his story of not seeing my messages or my calls.

HIS NUMBER

A couple nights before he left for Vegas, we sat downstairs, cuddled up on the couch talking.

"I really wish you didn't have to go down early," I said.

Damian was going down for a month to start practice and set up the house.

"It'll go by fast, and I need to get us moved into the condo, plus I'll be doing two-a-day practices and workouts. You won't be missing anything."

"Have they mentioned anything about the work visa?" I asked.

"No, not yet. But I'll work on it when I'm down there."

We changed the subject and managed to start talking about our past relationships.

"So you've really only been with thirteen girls?" I asked.

We had discussed this earlier in our relationship. Initially, he'd said it was only three. He could tell that I didn't believe him and quickly retracted his response and said it was actually thirteen. Damian was five years older than I was but something in my gut told me he wasn't telling the truth.

"Well, about that. Don't be mad, but I sort of reversed the numbers. It's actually thirty-one."

I don't know if I was more in shock because of the number or that he'd lied to me. Damian had been in one long relationship with a girl while he played hockey in the WHL. It was long distance and he said that it was extremely difficult, but they made it work for seven years: five years in the WHL and then two more years while he played in Europe before heading to university back in Canada.

"So if you dated your girlfriend for seven years, how did you sleep with thirty-one girls?" I asked the question that I needed to ask, but deep down was beyond scared to hear the answer.

"My host family didn't really like her. She was controlling, so they would let me sneak out at night and on weekends to go hook up with girls. They said I was young and needed to have fun, so I did. Then it just sort of continued when I went overseas. She came to visit, but we weren't meant to be."

I was completely flabbergasted. Who would promote that kind of behaviour to a teenager? And secondly, this felt like a form of extortion. If I decided not to go with him to Vegas, we would end up the same way.

He interrupted my thoughts. "But I would never cheat on you, honey; you're going to be my wife. I love you." He said it so confidently as he ran his fingers through his long blonde hair.

He tried to comfort me as he could see how unsure I was in that moment.

"You promise?"

"Absolutely. Would I be bringing you to Vegas if I didn't want to marry you and spend my life with you?"

"I suppose not."

The conversation ended and we went back to watching TV.

The next morning, he packed up his hockey equipment, some stereo equipment, a few personal belongings, and every single item of clothing he owned. He was gone.

100 CANDLES

Now that Damian was gone, I had a month to get my life in order. I had to finish working, figure out which clothes to pack, and get enough birth control for at least ten months. I was making a list of everything I needed to do when Chad came into the room.

"Hey Am, what's up?"

"Just making myself a list."

Since Damian had been living at the house for the past month, Chad and Libby had made themselves scarce. Space was limited and we claimed the basement. I really hadn't seen him much over the summer, between both of us working and dating.

"Can I ask you a favour?" Chad said.

"Depends." I figured he wanted to borrow money.

"I'm going to propose to Libby and I need some help setting it up."

I was shocked. They had been dating since high school but broke up for a few months and recently had gotten back together at the start of summer.

"You want to ask her to marry you?" My eyebrows reached their maximum height.

"Whatever, Amber. You and Damian have been talking about getting engaged for months now. What's the difference?"

The difference was that Damian was five years older than I was, he had a job, and a degree. We were moving in together in a couple of weeks in our new home, in a different country. Chad was twenty-two, an apprentice in a machine shop, and Libby was working as a receptionist.

"Okay, I'll help. Do you have a ring?" I asked.

"Yep, it's right here." He pulled out a Peoples Jewellers box with a cluster diamond ring and matching wedding band. "It came as a set," he said with pride.

"What do you have in mind for a proposal?"

He started to go into elaborate detail about his plans for the proposal.

"I'm going to bring Libby over and we will be in the hot tub . . ."

Occasionally, my parents would rent a hot tub for a week in the summertime.

He continued. "While we are in the hot tub, I want you to set up a blanket in the living room, with a bottle of champagne on ice, and rose petals here," he said, pointing to the spot he picked out just in front of the fireplace.

"I want you to hide the ring right here, then sprinkle roses all the way over to the patio door. I need you to light all these candles in an aisle toward this spot," he said.

I looked down at his hand and he was holding a pack of one hundred tea lights.

"You want me to light one hundred candles?" I asked, surprised.

It seemed a little over the top but this was his plan, so I went along with it.

"Yeah, make a pathway of candles with rose petals in the middle. Put candles here and here, alongside here . . ." he trailed off, pointing to every available spot in the living room. "When you're done, come outside and tell us that you're leaving, okay?"

"Where am I supposed to go?"

"I don't care. Go downstairs or to Hailey's house. Just come and say that so I know everything is ready, okay?"

I agreed and the next day the plan fell into motion. Libby arrived, and they headed outside to the hot tub. I quickly took out the champagne and ice and put it into a bowl on the coffee table. I hid the ring, laid out the blanket, and scattered rose petals. I meticulously placed every single tea light around the room. I could only thank God that Mom and Dad were camping for the weekend. Mom would lose her shit if she saw rose petals and candles on the rug.

I lit all the candles, then let them know I was "leaving." I went downstairs quietly and watched a movie, keeping the volume low. I guess the proposal went off without a hitch because within ten minutes they were having sex and Libby's moans were cascading throughout the house. Ew. I turned up the volume to drown out the sound. I didn't care if she knew I was downstairs.

Mom and Dad came back the next morning. The big news escaped Chad's lips and he explained how I helped him with this romantic proposal. They beamed with pride and excitement and wanted to know every detail.

"What's this?" Mom asked as Chad walked them through the living room.

"It looks like wax from one of the tea lights," Chad said.

"Amber!" Mom yelled.

I was in the kitchen, finishing my breakfast. I could hear every word.

"What?" I replied, annoyed with a mouthful of Cheerios.

"Don't you *what* me!" she said. "You can help your brother get all of this wax off the rug. I want it all gone; do you understand me?"

That was another one of her key phrases: *do you understand me*. Of course I do; I'm not an idiot.

"Yep," I replied. I found it easier to say less.

"Then you can clean all the bathrooms," she said.

I lowered my head and continued to slowly eat my cereal. I couldn't help but think that it wouldn't be much longer until I could get the hell out of there.

ONE-WAY TICKET TO FREEDOM

While Chad and Libby were still glowing from their newly engaged bliss, I shared some of my own wedding plans with Libby. It would be in August or September. Red, orange, and yellow flowers. Roses and some gerbera daisies. Two days before I was to leave for Vegas, I asked Libby about her upcoming nuptials.

"So Libby, do you have any details planned yet for the big day?"

Part of me was wondering if I'd have to fly back for this before the end of the hockey year, and the other part was hoping they'd elope.

"We want a September wedding, at the church on thirty-third street, and we're thinking the legion hall where Jason and Natalie got married."

"Oh, that sounds nice. What about colours?" I asked.

I was genuinely curious. Damian promised me that we would be getting engaged this year and that we would have a wedding next summer. That would mean two family weddings in one year. I wanted my wedding to be nicer than Chad and Libby's.

"Well I want burgundy as a main colour, with orange and yellow gerbera daisies for the flowers."

She stood there looking spitefully into my eyes with a smirk on her face. She knew this would make me mad.

"Well, that sounds almost exactly like what we want for our wedding. You don't remember me saying that?" I was furious.

"What are you even talking about? You don't even have a ring, Amber! You are planning this made-up wedding that you are creating in your own head."

This was the most she had ever spoken to me since I had known her. And most certainly the most emotion she had ever shown toward any member in my family. I felt such spite toward her. She showed no appreciation or gratitude for my involvement in her proposal, not a single thank you. She was just another girl who got what she wanted and now couldn't care less about anyone else.

My mom came storming into the room and interrupted our argument. Finally, someone to come and support me.

"Hey, hey, hey," she yelled. "What is going on here?"

I explained the situation, and to my surprise, she took Libby's side.

"You know, Amber, Libby is right. You don't have a ring; you are not engaged. Libby can choose whatever she wants for her wedding and when you get engaged, you can decide then. You need to concentrate on getting to Vegas and finding a job."

What had just happened? My own mother. Up until then, she'd had nothing good to say about Libby. She used to rant about how she controlled her son, how she only cared about her family and not ours, and how she never had more than two words ever to say to us when she was around. I needed to get as far away from here as possible.

•

The day finally arrived: I was moving to Las Vegas. I packed two extremely large suitcases and bought myself a one-way ticket. My parents drove me to the airport, and Mom didn't seem too fussed. I checked my bags, and we arrived at the security entrance. Dad had tears in his eyes, as I knew he would. Seeing his emotion brought tears to my eyes, too. Mom had a straight face. No tears, no emotion. It was just another thing she needed to check off on her to-do list for that day. I gave them both a hug and a kiss and told them I loved them. I waved goodbye and turned into the security area. They started to walk away. Dad turned as he always did and waved a second time before we went out of view.

I boarded the plane and connected in Calgary. I would have a short layover and go through US Customs. I was nervous as I stepped up to the customs officer.

"Where are you headed?" he asked.

"Las Vegas," I said as I handed him my passport.

"What's in Vegas?" he asked.

"Um, a bachelorette party," I nervously lied. I was told that US Immigration was cracking down on visitors hoping to move into the country.

"Why only a one-way ticket? How long are you planning to stay?"

"Just four days or so. I'm going to drive back with a friend."

He could tell I was nervous.

"That's a lot of baggage for four days, miss."

"Ah yep . . . girls you know!"

All of me was wishing that this pathetic excuse was going to be enough for him to just say "Oh right, yes girls! Silly me, go on through and have a great time." But he didn't.

"I'm going to need you to come with me," he said, expressionless.

I was taken to a small room where I was drilled with questions for two hours. My entire suitcase was torn apart. They read my journal and my emails. They called my boss. I had never been more fearful in my life. I didn't know it at the time, but apparently the fall was a common time for women to travel from Canada to the US to stay with their hockey player boyfriends and husbands. I walked right into their trap. After two hours of questioning, they gave me a two-week B-2 visa. They advised me that if I didn't cross back over before my visa expired, I would be considered an illegal immigrant and would be banned from entering the US for ten years.

Scared shitless, I gathered my things, got on the plane, and arrived in Vegas to meet Damian as scheduled. I could smell the filtered air and hear the clanging of the slot machines as soon as I got off the plane. Digital ads and lights lit up the airport, advertising shows along the strip. I was greeted by Damian, and he gave me a big hug. I told him immediately about how I was questioned and how my passport was stamped with a visitor visa. I was terrified of getting in trouble.

"Ah, who cares. What are they going to do, arrest you and deport you?"

"Maybe?" I said, still shaken up.

"Whatever. We will figure it out."

He didn't seem too fussed. We both carried a suitcase and located his Jeep in the parking lot. The air was warm and dry. The sky was lit up with all shades of lights along the Las Vegas Strip. We got into the Jeep and drove twenty minutes west, weaving through cars at a rapid speed to get to our new home.

It wasn't the home at Rhodes Ranch golf course that he promised but rather a small one-bedroom condo on West Flamingo Road. The complex was nice yet slightly worn. It had a pool, an office area with a public computer, and a shaded car park. The practice rink was a few blocks away. I got myself settled, unpacked my suitcases, and put my clothes away. Damian took up two-thirds of the closet and half the drawers with his clothes. Since I only brought two suitcases, I filled the rest of the closet and drawers with room to spare.

·

I confirmed shortly thereafter that I needed to cross back over the Canadian border and go through immigration prior to the two-week deadline. I booked a one-way flight to Edmonton, Alberta, and stayed one night with Hailey who was living there after being accepted into the College of Education at the University of Alberta. It was so good to see her. I missed her. In true Hailey fashion, she laughed at me nervously as I explained my recent immigration troubles and my plans to get back into the United States. I booked a return ticket from Edmonton to Las Vegas, staying only four days. Hailey dropped me off at the airport the next day.

"Love you, A," she said.

"Love you too, H."

We hugged and then I was off. I returned back to the US with no issues or restraints.

MIA

Damian and I settled into a routine. He spent his mornings at hockey practice, followed by time spent on the bike. Game days were a practice followed by a long nap and a carb-loaded pasta for dinner. My days were much quieter. I spent time by the pool, baking in the sun, and getting to know the other girls.

On home game days, we would get ready and head down to the arena. We sat together, and in between the periods, we visited the bar and grill for drinks. After each game we'd meet the guys down by the dressing room, where fans would be waiting for them to sign autographs. You never knew who was going to show up to meet them. Usually, it was families with kids but on occasion you'd see a number of scantily clad girls requesting an autograph on a breast or a portion of their underwear.

By November, I cemented a few close friendships, but others were surface-level relationships. My closest friend was Mia. She was unlike any of the other girls. She had red curly hair and wore little makeup. She was small in stature with small breasts, and she wore large glasses. Her life didn't revolve around her boyfriend and his hockey schedule, which I admired. She worked several different jobs and always had interesting stories to tell.

"Hey, do you want to work a job with me this afternoon?" she asked me one day. "It's a grand opening of a clothing boutique, and they need girls to serve champagne."

"I'd love to but I don't have a work visa and I'm Canadian, remember?"

"Shit, that don't matter," Mia said. "I'll text you the address. Meet me at four?"

"I would, but I don't know how to drive the Jeep. It's a stick."

"Are you serious? What do you do while the guys are away?"

"I usually just stay home, or I walk to the grocery store if I need to get food. Damian said he was going to teach me, but he hasn't yet," I said.

It had already been two months.

"Fuck that. Okay, I'll pick you up today and when we're done, you're coming back here and I'll teach you how to drive a stick."

Relieved and excited, I agreed.

Dressed head to toe in black, we went to work. Silver trays were topped with tall glasses of champagne, which I was not accustomed to carrying. I felt more comfortable selling clothes than holding trays of drinks. I shuffled carefully across the glossy, checkered floor. I held the tray with two hands so that nothing spilled or dropped. I watched Mia as she interacted with the guests, the owners, and moved flawlessly with her tray in one hand. A pianist played a beautiful melody at a grand piano while guests flocked toward the hors d'oeuvre station. It was the nicest clothing store I had ever been to.

Later that day, we found ourselves back at the condos taking the Jeep for a drive. Mia got in and explained each pedal and each gear and at what speed I was to shift. She drove for the first twenty minutes and then I gave it a shot. Within thirty minutes, I felt like I had been given the gift of freedom.

It seemed each time the guys were away, Mia offered me a new job. I worked at an Italian steakhouse where she was the bartender. I bused tables, polished silverware, and folded napkins. Everyone was nice at the restaurant, and they always offered to feed me at the end of the night.

The team was away for almost two weeks, the longest trip that they had taken. They had a stint of games up in Alaska and along the West Coast before they were to come back home. Mia and I were spending the entire day cleaning a house.

"So what's the story with this house?" I asked.

We walked through a large two-story house completely empty but in rough shape. I noticed stains on the walls, ceilings, and carpets. Every bathroom was considerably soiled. I could never let a bathroom get this dirty. But if there was one thing I knew how to do, it was clean.

"Was this a bank repo or something?" I inquired again.

Each time my family moved, we cleaned the house prior to handing over possession to the new owners, so this type of situation was completely unknown to me.

"Jesus, there are clothes still in the washing machine."

I held up a pair of black pants and showed Mia.

"Yeah, an older couple lived in this home, and they were killed in a car accident. Their kids came in and sold off everything and now they are going to sell the house once we clean it."

Completely shocked, all I could say was a solemn "oh."

We spent the next eight hours working silently together, cleaning the house from top to bottom. I wasn't the most confident at serving champagne or pouring water or clearing tables, but this was a job I could do. As I scrubbed every bathroom with a small brush, I tried to piece together who this couple might have been. I could tell they were an elderly Black couple by the hair I pulled from the drain. I imagined that they had two, maybe three kids from the number of bedrooms they had. All of whom were older now, of course. Instantly, I was saddened by the loss of this couple I did not even know. I kept working, hoping they would be proud of the job I was doing.

Later that night, we drove home in silence, our young bodies achy from a long day of work. It was dark but the air was still very warm, a feeling that was still new to me. Mia pulled into the complex to drop me off. She didn't live there; she had her own place with a roommate. Before she left, she leaned over to say something to me.

"Hey, thanks for helping me today," she said. "Um, I need to tell you something."

"Yeah, sure, what's up?" I replied.

"I hate to be the one to tell you this, but Brad told me that Damian is cheating on you. I just thought you should know."

LOVE BOMB

I sat dumfounded and frozen in Mia's car.

"What? How does Brad know that? When would he even have time to cheat?"

My head was spinning, and my heart suddenly sank in my chest.

"He told me that Damian cheats when he's on the road. Groupies maybe? You seem so set on getting married to him, and I just don't want to see you get hurt. You're a nice girl and you could do so much better."

"Okay . . . thanks for letting me know."

I opened the car door, got out, and walked up the short walk to our apartment. I dropped my purse and my keys on the counter and headed straight for the beige couch. I stared down at the beige rug that connected to the beige tile that surrounded the beige walls. A cockroach skirted across the floor, but I didn't have the energy to kill it.

I had never felt more alone. I couldn't call my parents because they'd say come home or I told you so. I called Damian. I considered texting but my fingers hurt and I wouldn't be able to decipher if he was lying. I pushed his contact on speed dial, and the phone began to ring. I laid back onto the couch and pulled my legs up behind me.

"Hello?" Damian answered.

"Hey, how are you?"

"Fuck, pretty shitty. We're zero for three here, what about you? What did you get up to today?"

"Not much. Mia and I cleaned a house. I made a hundred and twenty dollars," I said.

"How long did you work?"

"Almost nine hours."

"Why would you work that long to get paid only a hundred and twenty dollars?"

"Well, it's better than nothing, isn't it?"

Damian was only making $450 per week, and we were barely getting by.

"Not really."

Annoyed, I sat straight up, my body now tense. I mustered up the strength to ask him about Mia's confession.

"Hey, so I need to ask you something. Mia told me today that Brad told her that you are cheating on me. Is that true?"

"How could you even ask me that? I fucking hate that guy, everyone does. He's such a loser. I don't want you spending time with Mia anymore. She's a liar, and it's Brad that cheats on Mia . . ."

He continued ranting without taking a pause for a single breath, then turned things on me.

"How do I know that you're not cheating on me?" he asked. "When I'm away and you're spending time with all the guys at the restaurant, who knows what you're doing. This is fucking bullshit, Amber! I can't believe you would even think that!"

"You didn't really answer the question, though," I said.

"Amber, you know I love you. Why would I invite you to come here and spend our lives together and talk about getting married if I was going to cheat on you? That is just Brad making shit up. I'll talk to him. Clearly, we can't trust anyone here. It needs to be just you and me, okay?"

"Okay," I said.

We said goodnight and ended our call. My knees throbbed and my back was sore and now I was emotionally spent from this last argument. Perhaps I should have just kept it to myself or waited to see if it actually made sense. I got into bed and cried myself to sleep. I couldn't help but wonder if what Mia had said was true. What if Damian was cheating? Could I be that naive? The signs were clear, but I was stuck in a fog of disbelief.

•

Two days later, the guys returned home from their trip. In walked Damian to the condo.

"I have a surprise for you!" he said excitedly.

Clearly, he felt bad about our argument or maybe he missed me. He handed me a small flyer of engagement rings from Fred Meyer Jewelers.

"We were at the grocery store and I saw this and picked it up. I thought we could look at engagement rings!"

"The grocery store?"

"Yeah, they have a jewellery store that is connected to the grocery store, so a couple of the guys and I stopped and took a look."

It wasn't the surprise I was expecting, but I guess it was nice that he was looking at rings. It must have meant he was serious about an engagement. It was just enough to distract me from the cheating accusations. From that point on, the narrative was that Brad was deflecting from his own relationship issues and we needed to be careful who we trusted. I wasn't to be friends with Mia anymore.

SOPHIE

As I pulled away from the other girlfriends and drama of the team gossip, Damian and I fell more in love. He was exceptional with Christmas coming up and wanted to make sure it was special, as it would be the first time I was away from my family for the holidays. We had been talking about getting a puppy to keep me company when he was on the road. My heart was set on a Frenchie or a beagle, but Damian wanted an Akita or Shiba Inu. One afternoon, we stopped off at a pet store that was close to our condo. A small, red fuzzball with pointed fluttering ears and squinty eyes looked up at us as we approached her kennel.

"Aw, she is smiling at us," Damian said. "Can we take her out?"

The salesperson came over and told us a little bit about the puppy.

"She is a purebred, eight-week-old female Shiba Inu, which is like an Akita breed but smaller. They tend to shed, but they generally don't bark."

"I love that about this breed. I hate yappy dogs like your parents' dogs," Damian said.

"They're not yappy," I said defensively.

"Abby is!"

Abby had developed a high-pitched bark and sure, some would

describe her as yappy, but she was mine and it didn't matter to me. I had asked my parents if I could bring her with me to Las Vegas, but Mom said no, the dogs couldn't be separated. I offered to take both of them, but she said absolutely not. I knew at that point that Abby wasn't truly mine, and I set out to find a new fur baby just for me.

I brought up getting a dachshund when we first started discussing a dog, but Damian immediately shut it down with an abrupt no. I loved all dogs and was just grateful that he was going to allow it. We picked up this small red fluffball of a pup. She showed little emotion toward us, but I figured it was because she was alone most of the time and was sad. She had tiny eyes and pointy ears and a small cinnamon bun for a tail. She was sweet.

"How much is she?" Damian inquired.

"Eight hundred," the salesperson said.

"Would you take $650?"

I hated it when Damian tried to negotiate the price. Most of the time it didn't work, and I always felt embarrassed that it made us look cheap. She advised that the price wasn't negotiable, and we put down a $200 deposit to come get her at the end of the week, once Damian received his paycheque from the team.

We picked her up on the Friday after we cashed Damian's cheque and put all of it toward paying for her, a new bed, leash, collar, food, and toys. She sat in my lap and fell asleep on the way home. She was perfect and I named her Sophie.

A DESERT CHRISTMAS

It would be my first Christmas away from home. The team didn't get much time off, we had Sophie, and given my visitor visa issues, I decided to stay put. I went to Walmart to buy Christmas decorations. I bought a six-foot artificial tree, a tree skirt, a star topper, and some rainbow-coloured Christmas lights to hang in the windows. I loved the look of white lights, but Damian wanted the coloured ones, or Mexican lights, as he called them. I stopped off at CVS to get a few additional decorative items. I came home to unload everything and start decorating.

"Let me put on some Boney M.," Damian said.

"Okay, I'm just going to call my mom first," I said.

I made a conscious effort of only calling her when I was in a good mood. If I was sad or depressed, she made it worse. I sat down in the big armchair with Sophie on my lap. I flipped open my cell phone and scoured the directory until their home number popped up. I hadn't yet told her of my plan to stay in Vegas, and I knew she wasn't going to be happy. The phone rang, and I sat in silence while Damian flipped through the albums of CDs.

"Hi, Mom," I said.

"Hello, Amber. What have you been up to?"

I kept it short and sweet and used my recent shopping trip for Christmas decor as a segue to explaining my choice to stay put for the holidays.

"You promised me when you were a teenager that you would never miss a Christmas. You said that. Do you remember that?"

Mom was mad. Toward me, she was never sad or crushed. Just irrefutable anger.

"I do, Mom. I know and I'm sorry. I want to be there, but I don't want to get stuck and not be able to come back."

She scoffed. I wasn't sure that she really cared about me physically being home for Christmas, but the public perception that I would choose to not come home would be a harder pill for her to swallow.

"Well, I guess I'll have to pack up your gifts and send them to you."

"Oh wow, thank you, Mom. I would really love that. Would you be able to wrap the jackets for me?"

"I suppose," she said.

Before I moved down to Las Vegas, I bought plaid Mac jackets for every member of my family from Mark's Work Wearhouse. Mom had always bought my dad and the boys one for fishing and camping, but she never had one for herself. She could never find her size. I knew she would love it.

After the call, Damian and I decorated the house and hung up the lights. We nestled together on the couch with a new Redbox DVD rental.

·

Later that week, a large box arrived with a few presents for both Damian and me, a couple of things for Sophie, some homemade Christmas cookies, and a few Canadian things to remind us of home, like ketchup chips and maple cookies. My mom even added some new tea towels and dishcloths to help pad the box and tossed in some oddities like Advil Cold and Sinus and Robax Platinum, which weren't sold in the US.

I loved receiving gifts; it's my love language. Damian didn't disappoint, either. On Christmas Day, the tree was filled with presents for me from him and Sophie. A blazer, home decor, and a promise ring. I'd had high hopes for an engagement ring, but I knew Damian couldn't afford it yet. Eighteen presents to be exact and a full stocking. I don't think I'd ever felt that lucky before.

A WEEKEND WAR

By January, I'd started a job working for a local company doing cold calls. My work visa never came through as promised, so I was still working under the table. It was for a computer software company that sponsored the team, a family company that I was grateful to be a part of. I worked full days while Damian practised before coming home to take care of Sophie. I loved working and feeling a sense of purpose. I didn't make as much money as Damian, but it was still mine and it was better than nothing now that Mia and I had grown apart.

On the weekends or when Damian was away, I kept busy decorating the house and cleaning. I used some of my money for personal touches. I found a few photos to hang on the walls, some faux flower arrangements, and I swapped out the shower curtain for a patterned one. It was starting to feel and look like a home. I bought a new vacuum to help with Sophie's shedding, and I took simple pleasure in waxing all the floors and tile. Living in Las Vegas was lonely.

Mom and Dad made their way down for a weekend shortly after Christmas. The team was away for a longer stretch in Idaho, so it worked out well that I could take them to a Cirque du Soleil show and show them around the city. We spent a day shopping, and they bought me some clothes for work. Dad was appalled when he saw the amount of clothes that Damian had compared to me, and he wasn't going to leave knowing that I had nothing to wear.

"How long do you think you're going to be down here playing house for?" Mom asked.

She was much more blunt when Damian wasn't around.

"Just for the season, Mom. Then we're coming back, getting jobs, and starting in the real world."

"Good. I'd hate to think that you got a degree in cheerleading for nothing."

I tried to let it go, but she got under my skin. Why did it always have to end this way? She always had to get a jab in.

"Why do you always say that? A degree in cheerleading?" I was fuming.

"Well, it's true, isn't it?"

"Ugh!" I let out a huffy annoyed sound. "Why is it never easy with you?"

I was getting tired of our relationship. I thought my being away for five months she might have missed me, but she didn't.

"You sure know how to treat me like shit. I don't deserve this, Amber."

She accused me of being ungrateful and unwelcoming. They returned to Canada, and I knew they wouldn't make another trip to visit.

•

Damian's parents were much more proactive when it came to booking visits and coming down. They came down a number of times during the season to watch him play. They were always very kind and took us out to dinners and to Costco for groceries. At one point, while I was at work, they even went to a home goods store and bought a lamp, a couple pieces of artwork, and a throw pillow. I came home to a newly decorated condo and all my original artwork or pictures on the walls were nicely lowered six inches to the "proper" height. It was difficult standing up to them. Damian's dad enveloped every inch of space with his personality and boisterous presence. The smaller I made myself, the more invisible I was. If I was nonexistent, or insignificant, then I was less likely to be a target or conversation of ridicule.

I tried to take advantage of every day that we had left in the season. This was our only year, so I needed to make it worthwhile. We spent the last couple of months seeing as many shows as we could, eating out at fancy restaurants, and living up the Vegas life before we packed up all our belongings into a small U-Haul and said our goodbyes.

CANADIAN SUMMER

We returned to Canada, driving a total of twenty-four hours. We stopped at the border, and they did a full check of the U-Haul we were towing. They asked for Sophie's papers and that was it; we were through and on our way home. We pulled up to my parents' house and planned on staying for a couple of weeks until we could find our own rental.

"Hey, where is my car?" I asked.

It was a three-tone brown 1986 Pontiac Acadian with a front hood and fender from a Chevette. Mom and Dad had bought it for me for my eighteenth birthday, and it was an eyesore. It had a rusted-out floor, and the heat didn't work. It also wouldn't accelerate over seventy kilometres per hour until you brought it back down below thirty kilometres per hour, which made for a laugh on the freeway as I puttered along on the shoulder until I could merge back into traffic.

"We sold it," Mom replied.

"What? Who would buy that?" I said jokingly, although somewhat serious.

"Yeah, for three hundred and fifty dollars," Mom said. "And no, you don't get the money!"

She could see the look on my face swirling with optimism.

"What? Why not? It was *my* birthday present!"

"You didn't appreciate that car, so why should you get the money for it? You hated it, and you didn't want it anyways. It's my money!"

I looked over at Dad for any kind of support, but he stayed silent as usual. This was the first glimpse of living with my mom again and being under her control.

Damian and I stayed two weeks until we found an old bungalow on the east side of town. We had the upper floor, and another tenant had the basement. The grass in the back stood almost knee-high and surrounded a cracked cement pad that housed two broken lawn chairs. It was freshly painted and had new laminate flooring throughout. A few of the windows opened but the majority did not, keeping the interior at a sweltering twenty-eight degrees Celsius. There was no dishwasher and no air conditioning.

We moved all our belongings in, most of which were items I'd received for Christmas and birthday gifts when I was in high school. I remember when my friends were getting CD players and Mavi Jeans, I was getting mixing bowls, a microwave, sets of towels, and food storage containers. Mom wasn't the best gift giver, but she thought practical was better than something you wanted, so she gave what she thought you needed. She usually gifted Natalie, Libby, and me the same things. Chad and Jason usually received tools of some kind or sports equipment. Mom kept everything for me over the years packed away in boxes, and she was finally relieved to be getting rid of it all. We moved in one bed and a couple of dressers I had in my childhood room, plus a couch and loveseat that we had downstairs in our house that used to belong to Noah's family and a small wooden table and chairs that we found at a garage sale.

Damian and I set out to find jobs, applying everywhere we could. He started working for a friend, helping him build mobile homes, and I signed up with a temp agency, trying to get my foot in the door doing office work. I was excited to be back home with friends and family and was eager to continue with my life plan. I wanted to finish my degree, start a career, be married by the time I was twenty-five, and have two kids by the time I was thirty.

One night, Damian and I got home from work and the house was sweltering. We opened both doors and let a light breeze filter through the screens. Our usual routine was to prepare dinner, usually Hamburger Helper, and sit down to watch *So You Think You Can Dance*. But today was different. He showered and then sat in our room on the bed. It was dimly lit, with red sheets on the windows. He leaned over and looked at me with heartbreak in his eyes.

"We need to talk."

I was completely confused. We had just moved in. Was he breaking up with me?

"Okay, you're making me nervous. What's wrong?"

Tears welled up, and he lowered his head.

I had never seen him cry before and immediately thought someone had passed away.

"I can't do it. I want to go back. I need to."

I knew exactly what he was asking. He wanted to go back to Las Vegas for a second year.

"But you said only one year."

"I know I did, but if I don't do it, I will always wonder. I'm not ready to give up on my dream of heading to the NHL. I still have so much more that I want to do. What do you say?"

"I told you how I felt about this. I don't want to go back. I won't go back, not without a commitment."

"What, like an engagement?" he said, somewhat perturbed.

"Yes. I'm not wasting my time following you back and forth to Vegas if you're not serious about us."

"I am. I promise. You will have your commitment before we go back in the fall."

He wiped a tear away from his face and said thank you. I couldn't help but feel slightly defeated. We'd just moved everything into this house, and in six weeks we'd have to pack it all up and move again. Mom and Dad were going to be pissed. I had no degree, no job, a shitty rental, and I was following my boyfriend back to the States to pursue his dreams. I knew this life wasn't the life they imagined for me. And frankly, it wasn't the one I dreamt for myself either.

BORROWED ROMANCE

As the fall approached, I knew that an engagement was pending. It was my only caveat that stood in the way of his second season. By this time, I was working a three-week stint as a receptionist for a trucking company. I was sitting at my desk on a Thursday morning in August, entering driver expenses in the system, when my cell phone rang. It was my bank.

"Hello, ma'am, I'm lookin' for a Miss Amber Nicole?"

I could tell she was from the southern US by her accent.

"This is she," I responded.

"Miss, are you aware of a forty-two-hundred-dollar charge on your credit card from a Fred Meyer in Anchorage, Alaska?"

I paused. I almost said no, until it hit me. Damian had used my credit card to pay for my engagement ring.

"Yep, that charge is correct."

"Okay, miss, thank you for verifying that information. We appreciate your continued business. You have yourself a nice day now."

Click. She hung up the phone.

I sat at my desk with so many emotions. I was excited to be getting engaged, but it wasn't at all what I expected. Damian had told me since our first year in Vegas that he had been saving, but it seemed like I'd just paid for my own engagement ring. I continued to work for the remainder of the day before mentioning it to Damian. When I got home, I couldn't hold it in any longer.

"Hey, so I got a call from the bank today."

"Oh? What about?"

"Well, it seems that someone used my credit card for a rather large purchase in Alaska?"

He laughed sheepishly and finally admitted that he was waiting for several paycheques.

"I wanted to make sure it would make it here in time. Actually, would you mind reaching out to Danielle about it to make sure that it gets shipped properly? You know, give her our address and whatever else. You're just so good with that type of thing."

Danielle was one of the other girlfriends whose boyfriend played last season and they lived in Anchorage. Alaska was Damian's choice of state for purchasing because it had no sales tax. This didn't make a lot of sense considering import taxes were still applicable.

The next day, I reached out to Danielle. I purchased additional insurance and a shipping label, and the ring arrived three days later. I signed for the package, paid the additional $400 in taxes and duties, and put the package aside for Damian when he got home.

He arrived after work and immediately opened the box.

"Ugh, you'd think for three grand that it would look a lot better."

He held it up to the light to get a better look at the diamond. It was a three-quarter carat diamond solitaire with three small diamonds on each side.

"Maybe it'll look better outside."

He stormed outside, letting the metal screen door slam shut as he stepped onto the deck. I still hadn't seen it but already felt disheartened by just watching Damian.

"Can I see it?"

"Isn't that bad luck or something?"

I thought since I'd technically paid for it and arranged for it to be shipped, at least I could see it.

Reluctantly, he showed me the ring. Sure, it was slightly yellow in colour, but it was still beautiful. He hid the ring in the house and told me not to bother trying to find it. He would propose on his terms and when the time was right.

ST. JOHN'S CATHEDRAL

Knowing that the ring was here, I knew that a proposal was imminent. I just didn't expect Damian to take a couple of weeks to make it happen. He advised me to go ahead and book a church and a venue, and we decided on August 18 the following year. We set out to have the same legion hall for the reception as both Jason and Natalie and Chad and Libby. I had hopes for a golf course or perhaps a ballroom at a fancy hotel, but those options were too expensive, and I didn't want my mom to think I was too good for the legion hall or better than everyone else.

As a little girl, I would ride along the river with my parents to see the large cathedral churches. They were so grand. The Anglican church was St. John's Cathedral. It had the longest single aisle out of all the churches, a long red carpet that flowed like red wine toward the altar. Peaks of stained-glass windows adorned every side of the church, and a large organ stretched to the ceiling. It was beyond grandiose, and it was the one thing I had always dreamt of having for my wedding. So, we booked it.

I had two days remaining in my three-week contract working for the truck company. I looked up as Damian walked through the door.

"Hey, what are you doing here?"

"Just dropping these off."

He handed me a sheer bag of letter-shaped chocolates.

"Don't open them until you get home though, okay?"

"Okay."

I was convinced this was his big proposal, so I did as he asked and let him carry it out the way he intended. I came home after work to a bouquet of a dozen red roses and another bag of chocolate letters.

"You can't open them up yet."

"Maybe we should put these in the fridge," I said.

The chocolates on the table were starting to sweat from the heat.

I was told to get dressed because we were heading out for dinner. One of our favourite restaurants was a cave-like restaurant on the outskirts of town. We ate a very large dinner with multiple courses that spanned over two hours. My mind was constantly stirring throughout the entire dinner. I thought of the dessert tray with a hidden ring, or a champagne glass with a ring at the bottom. But it never happened. We left the restaurant, and it was almost 10 p.m. I was exhausted.

"Hey, should we stop off at the cathedral and just take a look?" Damian suggested.

It was late and I didn't want to go, but I agreed. We pulled into the dimly lit parking lot of the church and parked the car. The streetlamps were the only light, as the sun had gone down.

"Let's get out," he said.

I followed him to the small set of steps at the side of the cathedral. He got down on one knee and pulled the ring out of his pocket and asked me to marry him. I said yes, and we quickly got back into the car and called our families. My parents were already in bed and from what I could tell, they were moderately happy for us.

We got back to the house and Damian gave me a third small bag of chocolate letters. I spread all the letters out on the table and unscrambled them to spell *will you marry me?* We both took a few nibbles and then headed off to get ready for bed.

I stood in front of my dresser mirror admiring my newly adorned hand. It sparkled as I moved my fingers back and forth. Damian came up behind me and started to kiss my neck. He wrapped his hands around my waist and then slowly moved them down toward my thighs. With the twist of a button, he opened his pants and pulled out his erection. He grabbed my dress, lifting it up to my waist, and pulled my panties to the side. He pushed me over the dresser and aggressively forced himself in and out of me repeatedly. I didn't have the courage to look at him in the mirror. It was one thing to feel it, and another to see it. I stared down at the dresser. It was the same one that was in my childhood bedroom. I had inherited it when my great aunt passed away.

This wasn't the type of sex that I envisioned after getting engaged. It wasn't making love. There was no intimacy or feeling that we were overwhelmed by the love we shared. I felt like he was having his way with me. He had given me a ring, and now he owned me. He finished and crawled into bed. I curled up in bed on my side, facing away from him. I felt overcome by feelings of deep sadness. When I was a little girl, I had always dreamt of these moments, but they looked different. In my dreams, I didn't buy my own ring, it didn't come with strings attached, and I wouldn't have felt like I'd been raped.

I pulled up the top sheet and hugged it tight under my chin. It was the closest I could get to a hug in that moment. My limbs were trembling, and I felt scared. I had no idea what I had just agreed to. Damian was already fast asleep next to me. It didn't register at the time, but the position and experience was similar to when I was twelve. The same position. The lack of consent. The frozen feeling that overcame me as I was no longer a person, only an orifice providing pleasure for someone else.

I wiped a tear and pushed down the desire to vomit, along with every uncomfortable feeling that was starting to resurface. I tried convincing myself that my expectations were too high and that my childhood dreams were just that: dreams. I needed to distract myself, so I imagined what kind of wedding dress I would wear until I fell into a deep slumber.

YEAR TWO

The second year in Las Vegas was tame, all things considered. I enrolled in two classes through University of Saskatchewan's distance studies program to finish my degree in sociology. I knew the routine of away games and the regiment that occurred on home game days. I had our dog, Sophie, to keep me company, and when I wasn't studying, I was planning the wedding. I called my parents with updates, but most of our conversations ended in screaming matches with one of us hanging up on the other. I had "unrealistic expectations" for our wedding because I wanted to get married in the cathedral. Mom thought it was an unnecessary waste of money and called it hoity-toity, but toward the end of the season, she came around and actually spent time helping the minister fix the screen on the exterior door and requested they hold space in the columbarium for her ashes.

Chad and Libby came down for a visit over Halloween, which went quite well. We dressed up in costumes, went shopping, and gambled in the casinos. They were still in their newlywed bliss phase, having married shortly before I left Canada. They had a simple wedding and Libby and I seemed to mend our relationship, but I was never asked to be a bridesmaid or do a reading.

Damian arranged for me to take a full-time nanny position for a ten-week-old boy, whose family were fans of the hockey team. I always felt I was good with babies, but this took on a whole new level of caregiving. Four days a week, his parents dropped him off at 7:30 a.m. and picked him up at 4:30 p.m. He spent most of the hockey season in my care. The baby and I would leave the condo when Damian needed a nap on game day. We went walking, swimming, and shopping. Damian was good with him, but he made it clear that the baby was my responsibility.

Las Vegas had a way of bringing out your biggest insecurities, both personally and with your relationship. Your breasts were never big enough, teeth not straight or white enough, skin not tan enough. I was bombarded with constant advertising for plastic surgery and strip clubs. With every home game, there seemed to be a new group of young women trying to take my place. Strip clubs always hit a nerve with me. It felt like cheating. Maybe I wasn't a fan because my relationship lacked a strong, sturdy foundation of trust. Treasures was one of the "finest" strip clubs in Vegas, and they were now a team sponsor. Big-breasted women in tight white crop tops bounced up and down in between periods while handing out T-shirts to the crowd. The wives and girlfriends, me included, thought it was entirely unnecessary, as were the fines the players received for various violations.

Within our first month back in Vegas, we had a huge blow up about the strip club. Damian lied and told me he was dropping off some of the guys, but as the night went on, he stopped responding to my text messages. He came home late and confessed that he had to go in with the rest of his team or else he'd be fined $100 by his coach.

"A hundred dollars? Who cares? Am I not worth a hundred dollars of respect?" I yelled.

"Why are you so insecure? You're so consumed with me cheating on you. I gave you a fucking ring!"

The fight escalated and we were both volatile. I threw the remote control across the room and it left a big dent in the wall. He blocked the condo door, so I headed for the balcony to escape through the only door I could. I jumped over the patio railing and ran down the side, over an eight-foot drop to the road. I needed space. I needed to be alone. I never understood how he could spin around a valid concern of mine leaving me feeling utterly insane. It was suddenly my fault, and it was my own insecurities that were causing this friction and these feelings of loneliness. Damian was infamous for gaslighting me in every argument, even though I didn't realize it at the time.

At the next "mandatory" strip club event, I tagged along with a few other girlfriends. We each told our boyfriends to pay the fine of $100 to the coach for being present. We watched several of the players get lap dances, and some were led back into the private area. It was my first time at a strip club, and I felt sorry for the women working there. They were sexual objects that men groped and treated like meat. This type of "team bonding" and sponsor support went too far for my moral compass. At this point, I began to realize that hockey players can have, and do, whatever they want.

As the season ended, we had a few days left before we needed to pack up our U-Haul and make the twenty-three-hour drive back to Saskatoon. This was officially our last year. We were saying goodbye to Vegas for good this time and heading back to start our life together as a married couple. We made plans for the ladies and guys to have separate dinners and then meet up later for drinks. One of the girls got us a table at Tao, and we took to the strip in our best dresses. I didn't have a reason to buy a new dress, so I wore the same plum dress I'd worn the night Damian and I met. The same accessories and shoes, and I even tried to replicate my hair from that night. As we walked into Tao, I immediately recognized the hallway of bathtubs that lined the walkway. The previous year, Mia had asked if I wanted to work there as a bathtub girl. The job required being topless and making out with another woman for the night. It paid $100 per hour, but for me, it crossed the line of infidelity. We sat down and ordered more than enough food for the ten of us. We took turns grabbing small portions and putting them on our plates. We discussed our upcoming weddings and all the trivial details that kept us occupied over the last few months. Then we proceeded to the dance floor before leaving to meet up with the guys.

We took cabs down the strip to the Wynn Hotel. I was slightly buzzed by this time and enjoying the night. I saw Damian from across the mezzanine and ran up to him. My heels clicked on the tile floor and the inexpensive spandex fabric of my dress bounced.

"Hey! You guys are here!" I said.

"Why are you wearing that?" Damian demanded.

"What, this? Why not?"

"You look like a slut," he said, stone-faced and looking directly into my eyes.

Perhaps it was the vodka taking action in my system, but I slapped him across the face. He grabbed my wrists and stormed me out of the casino. There were now unwritten rules I wasn't privy to, one being the engagement ring and what it symbolized: I belonged to him. What I thought was a new level of commitment that warranted love and respect was instead a muzzle and handcuffs. And it came with a pre-approved wardrobe.

BARN DANCES AND BOOZE

Damian, Sophie, and I made the long trek back to Canada once again. This time we were stopped at the border for an extended period while authorities conducted a complete search of our U-Haul. They tore it apart and charged us duty and taxes on the items they thought we purchased in the US. Some items were justified, such as our wedding favours, but other items, including a pair of earrings that were a gift from my mom, were not.

We stopped to visit Damian's parents and stayed for a couple nights. The town was holding its summer kickoff event with a parade and barn dance. I dressed in my cutest denim skirt and tank top to show off my Las Vegas tan, and we headed down to the festivities. Damian and I drank beer, and anything premixed in a bottle, then we hit up the dance floor, two-stepping to every classic 90's country song.

We stumbled our way back to his parents' house toward the end of the party. We crossed through town and through a large park, Damian's arm around my waist to keep me upright. Living in Las Vegas, I thought my alcohol tolerance was quite high, but for some reason, on that night, it hit me with additional force. We stopped at a picnic table for a breather, and he leaned in and kissed my lips, working his way down to my neck. He pushed me back onto a picnic table, spread my legs, and pushed himself inside me. I laid there and just stared up at the sky above me. It was lit by thousands of stars scattered throughout the darkness. I felt catatonic, and my skin was covered in goosebumps from the cool summer night breeze.

"Hey, miss, are you okay?" a voice came from afar. It was a couple walking home from the same party.

"Uh, yeah," Damian said. He pulled out of me and picked me up off the table. "It's okay, she's my fiancée."

We powered back home. When we got in the door, he led me to the bathroom and propped me up on the counter. He intended to finish what he'd started. I came to a little more but was still too intoxicated to notice everything happening to me. He transitioned me down to the bathroom floor.

"Don't you dare go to sleep on me," he said.

It wasn't until the morning that I completely understood what had happened the night before. I sat on the toilet in pain, dabbing at small amounts of blood, and realized what had transpired. Damian had had anal sex with me. The instant pain I felt in my rear end triggered memories of when I was twelve. It all came flooding back, and I was reminded that this wasn't my first time. I hated that this had happened again. And I hated that it didn't come with consent or a gentle approach, like it deserved. Because of my past trauma this is something that I would have never consented to. I felt overwhelmed with shame. I did the only thing I knew how to do: I buried my memories and feelings down deeper than they were before.

LEO GETZ

Since we returned from Las Vegas, I'd been working at an orthodontist's office. On Fridays, we closed the office early to catch up on dictation, patient files, and treatment plans. One Friday in July, after I finished all my tasks, I decided to log into Damian's email account. My trust had been shaken since our first year in Las Vegas, but I had not found any evidence that he was cheating. I scrolled through his emails to discover that he had recently created a Facebook account. Damian wasn't on social media. He told me he didn't like it, so this came as a surprise. I quickly clicked on the link to his profile. I scrolled down the page to confirm this was, in fact, his account.

Who the fuck is Leo Getz? I asked myself. *And why would Damian put that as his profile name?* I was completely perplexed. I looked through his profile photos. One hockey headshot, one hockey action shot, and one of him and Sophie. None of us together. I looked for his friend list and didn't recognize any of them. He had five female friends. No male friends. No teammates. I looked through his messages and saw that he started up conversations with four of the women. All the chats were casual and most included plans to get together in the summer or fall. He was fishing and had yet to catch a bite.

Damian was picking me up from work, and he pulled up outside just as I signed out of his account. I locked the office door and hopped into the Jeep. As we drove home, I was silent. I did not understand why he created a Facebook account under a fake name, why he was only friends with women, and why I wasn't one of them. Was his plan to get in touch with his past flames through an alias Facebook account? The fury boiled inside me.

"Is there anything you haven't told me?" I blurted out.

"What are you talking about?" Damian said with an unpleasant tone.

I realized how vague that question sounded and from his standpoint, I'm sure there were a plethora of things he had not told me.

"Why do you have a Facebook account with only girls as friends. And why the hell did you say your name was Leo Getz?"

"No reason. I just created it," he said nonchalantly, as if to imply that he hadn't gotten around to adding me or anyone else.

"And what's with the name?"

"Because Leo Getz what Leo wants," he said.

I couldn't help but think this was an avenue to cheating, but I decided to let go of Leo Getz. Damian agreed to change the name to his actual name and add me as his fiancée. A couple of days later, we were Facebook official.

•

I can see now that that discovery should have been enough of a red flag to high tail it out of my engagement. But Damian still remained the lesser of two evils. My alternative would have been to move back in with my parents, get a job and start to save towards moving out on my own. I wasn't willing to put myself back under the control of Marlene. I still had hopes that Damian would be exactly who I had envisioned that he could be.

THE CALM BEFORE THE STORM

Our wedding day finally arrived: August 18, 2007. We'd moved into our townhome earlier that month, but the night before the wedding, I slept at my parents' house for the last time. I felt like there was something so traditional about sleeping apart the night before the wedding. My three bridesmaids slept downstairs, and I slept in my childhood room. I woke in the morning, having barely slept, but felt unbothered by it. We took turns showering and then, running on adrenalin and coffee, headed to the hair salon. My hair was perfectly set in a French twist with a small bouffant on top, and I had an ivory veil cascading to my elbows. We headed to The Bay for our makeup appointments at the MAC makeup counter. We all opted for natural makeup that would enhance our wise age of twenty-three years, an age that I can clearly see now was too young to be getting married.

Back at the house, we needed to quickly get dressed and head to the church. I stepped into my dress. It was beautiful, but it wasn't the dress I'd wanted. I'd always imagined a form-fitting wedding dress. The day we went shopping, Mom picked out a dress and placed it in my dressing room. I was trying on anything that had a sweetheart neckline. The dress she selected was ivory, with the requested neckline, decorated in beads and crystals on top, and a lace-up back. I stepped out of the change room and Mom's eyes welled with tears.

"Oh, Am, it's beautiful! Don't you think?"

I didn't want to disagree with her; after all, she and Dad offered to pay for my dress.

"Yeah, it's pretty," I said.

"Oh, I think that's the one. Don't you?"

"It could be."

"That's the one I picked out!" Mom told everyone at the store. "Let's call Dad and have him come and take a look, what do you say?"

"Okay, sure."

"Can we get a veil to match?" Mom asked the saleslady who was helping us. "Should we add a tiara?"

I quickly said no. Mom had a way of snowballing when it came to the accessories. Images of my high school graduation came flooding back to me. I had chosen a simple baby blue strapless dress, but my mom thought I needed a tiara, silk gloves that went past my elbows, and a shawl that covered my shoulders. It was all too much and not me at all. Once again, I didn't have the heart to say no to Mom and shatter her excitement.

Over the course of the year, we travelled to the dress shop numerous times to show my dress to my dad, my grandma, and anyone else who visited. Mom lit up and made sure everyone knew that she was the one who had picked it out.

The morning of the wedding, I stepped into my dress and my bridesmaids helped to lace up the back.

"Can it go any tighter?" I asked.

My dress seemed too big. I stepped on the scale that morning and weighed ninety-seven pounds. I had lost six pounds since I'd ordered the dress. We'd lived with my parents that summer before we got possession of our townhouse. The house environment felt toxic, and it only felt right to stay downstairs and out of her space. This meant that after meals, we retreated to our quarters in the basement and never resurfaced until morning.

We pulled my corset as tight as it could go and then I stuffed Kleenex into my cups to lift my breasts. We piled into a Hummer H3, borrowed from a friend of Damian's, and headed to St. John's Cathedral.

Damian and his family were already there. We weren't late but just barely on time. Dad and I stood together at the side door where Damian had proposed, waiting for our cue to walk down the aisle. An overwhelming calm and warmth flooded through my body, like I had been drugged. It was the first time in my life that I'd experienced such a powerful feeling. It was almost as if a spirit or some higher power was guiding me to go through with this marriage. The clarity I realized in that moment was that this wouldn't be my only marriage but to trust and go ahead with it.

Dad leaned over and looked me in the eyes. "Are you sure you're ready for this?"

"It's a bit late to back out now!" I said. I thought a joke would make it more palatable for him. I was, after all, his last child to get married and his only daughter.

"Nope, it's never too late!" He pretended to bolt toward the doors.

We laughed out loud.

"I know, Dad. I'm good. I promise."

I didn't share the palpable feeling of tranquility that I was experiencing, nor the notion that this wouldn't be my only wedding. I simply took his arm, put one foot in front of the other, and walked down the aisle to Damian.

We said I do, and in that moment, I became Mrs. Damian Shrover.

GOOD MOURNING

On a Saturday morning in October 2007, the phone rang. It was Mom.

"Hi," I said quietly.

"Grandma passed away earlier this morning. I'm heading down to Auntie Lynn's house to see her. Do you want to come?"

Grandma was my mom's mother. The two of them had a fraught relationship and didn't always get along. There were more than one hundred of us on Mom's side of the family—aunts, uncles, cousins, and first cousins once removed—so being "close" felt like a relatively foreign concept to me.

It took me a minute to process everything she'd just said. First, that Grandma had passed, and second, that she was still at home, and third, that my mother wanted me to go see her.

"Amber?" she said, interrupting my thoughts. "Are you coming?"

"Are you going?"

"Yes. I'm heading out the door now. You should leave now, too."

Feeling her sense of urgency, I got dressed and headed to my aunt's house. Auntie Lynn was the youngest of my mom's sisters. She was one of my favourite aunts. She was a teacher, and she had a beautiful, bubbly soul that always made me feel welcomed.

I parked my car down the street from my aunt's house, in the only available spot. I walked up to the house and found the door was already open. Inside, my aunts were buzzing around, tears streaming down their faces and sharing embraces. I saw Mom and went over to say hi.

"Grandma's in there. Go give her a kiss and say your goodbyes," she said with a stoic expression.

We stood at the doorway to my grandma's bedroom. The room was dimly lit by a table lamp. She was in bed, lifeless and stiff. Her mouth hung open and her teeth were missing.

"Go on in," my mom said, pushing me to enter the room.

I had never seen a dead body before. She looked nothing like herself. I reluctantly bent down and gave her a kiss on her forehead. Her skin was cold and clammy. She smelled funny.

"Bye, Grandma, I love you," I said as I started to back slowly out of her room.

I overheard a commotion in another room. The sisters were insisting they put her teeth in.

"Her teeth? Why do they have to put her teeth in?" I looked at my mom for an answer.

"Rigor mortis is setting in and if they don't do it now, then they will have to break her jaw."

I was completely stunned. Completely motionless. It all seemed so impersonal and pragmatic. The sisters ran into Grandma's room, teeth in hand and pushed them into her mouth. Chad walked in and gave Mom a hug.

"Hey, Mom, I'm sorry," he said, offering condolences as he kept his arm around her.

"Thanks, Chad. Grandma's in there if you want to go and say your goodbyes and give her a kiss."

"No thanks" he replied.

"Okay, suit yourself."

My eyes widened with shock. *No thanks?* I thought. *Did he seriously just say no thanks and she didn't flip or lose her shit? Meanwhile, here I am kissing a dead lady. What the actual F?*

I passed on my condolences again and as the coroner arrived, we all shuffled out of Auntie Lynn's house and back to our weekend plans. There was a viewing a few days later in which Grandma looked more like her usual self. Teeth in, makeup done, her hair coiffed just so. The funeral was held a short time after, and she was buried in the cemetery alongside her husband who had passed shortly before my parents were married.

BRACE FACE BUNDY

I completed one last credit during the fall after we were married and graduated that January with a bachelor of arts in sociology and French. I decided not to attend my university graduation because it didn't seem worth celebrating at that point. Damian was working as a territory manager for a Fortune 500 consumer packaged goods company. He felt comfortable with the title and the pay and was valued as an employee because of his vast experience in hockey. I applied with a similar company as a food-service rep. I had lots of experience working in food service at my dad's company, so it seemed like the perfect fit. I nailed the interview, dressed in a knee-length pencil skirt and a grey sweater, with a black belt hugging my waist. It was my best "corporate" workwear outfit but looking back, it was more Peggy Bundy than Michelle Obama.

"Are you sure you should take a different job while you're wearing braces?" Damian asked.

I didn't think it would be a big deal. I decided to get braces shortly after our wedding. My boss at the orthodontist office offered to do them for free. He was extremely generous and even offered to pay for dental assistant college. Starting school again after finally finishing my degree felt like a waste of time, so I declined his offer.

"I think it'll be okay," I said. I didn't want to be a receptionist forever, and I only had five months left in my treatment plan.

"Yeah, but you'll be an adult with braces!"

Damian reminded me that I was still a "brace face," and I felt like I was thirteen years old again.

"Whatever," I replied.

I was determined to get a job with my degree and prove that I could make it in the corporate world. I wanted to prove to my parents that I could get a real job that paid a salary worth mentioning. I'd been promising them for two years that I would do this.

I accepted the food-service job and started climbing the corporate ladder. Damian constantly reminded me that he was a "manager" and I was just a sales rep, even though I was the one who helped him prepare for his interview. I was the only female who worked in my office building, aside from the two receptionists. It was unheard of that a female would occupy an actual office, let alone have a position with influence.

FROM A FRIEND

I was working long hours and trying to prove to my boss and everyone in our office that I had what it takes to move up in our company. It had been four months since I'd started. Damian and I became more competitive with each other, taking note of who got more awards and recognition and who was up for a possible promotion. I had just gotten back from Regina. I was there working Summer Invasion, a wakeboard festival that my company sponsored. I came home late and was faced with a cold, angry husband. I wondered if I had done something wrong, or if he'd had a bad day at work.

"What's up? You seem upset," I said.

I grabbed a bowl of leftover supper and put it in the microwave. He hadn't spoken more than two words to me since I walked in the door. I'd learned to watch people well and anticipate their moods. I knew Damian was mad at me.

"Yeah, well, I received this letter at work and it seems as though you are having an affair with Michael. Someone thought they should warn me about it," he said.

"What? That's insane," I said.

He handed me a typed letter and an envelope. I read the letter, which detailed nothing of real substance but was full of accusations and assumptions. It mentioned that Michael and I went out for lunch and talked a lot behind closed office doors. It was signed "from an anonymous friend" who was looking out for him.

"This is ridiculous," I said.

Michael was one of two friends I had at the office, and both were male. I tried to assure Damian that it wasn't true.

"Mike and I are just friends. He has a girlfriend. She's the mother of his child!"

I could tell by the expression on Damian's face that he wasn't convinced. I was reminded of what he used to say to me in Las Vegas: *If I ever find out you are cheating, you'll be boots to the sky out in the desert.* I was scared, but I knew I wasn't having an affair. Damian and I were struggling. We slept in separate beds because he snored, and it had been six months or more since we'd been intimate.

He thought the letter was written by someone from my office, or a friend at my company who was friends with one of his sales reps.

"It's like that movie *Disclosure*, where they get a letter signed 'from a friend' warning that a spouse hasn't been faithful."

I had no idea what he was saying and at that moment I wondered if, perhaps, Damian wrote the letter himself. I sat on the letter for a couple of days and eventually told Michael about it. He was just as shocked as I was, and we had no idea who could have sent it. Eventually, I went into sleuth mode and looked at the envelopes in my office. I couldn't find a match. The stamps were a generic Canada post stamp, so that wasn't of any help, but the postal code could be. I googled the postal code where it was mailed from, and it showed up as the mailbox down the street from Damian's office. I was even more convinced now he was the one who sent the letter.

TWENTY-FIVE

Dad texted me after my mom got out of her hysterectomy surgery. He said everything went as well as expected and that she would be available for visitors soon.

"Can I bring her anything?"

"She's hungry, but I'm not sure she should be eating anything just yet."

I rushed out of work, picked up A&W Teen burgers and fries and then headed to the hospital. I also stopped to grab flowers and a couple magazines for her to read as she recovered.

"Hi, Mom," I said as I walked into the room. I kept the food hidden but the familiar smell of processed meat and onions arrived with me. "I brought you some food!"

Her eyes lit up and she dived into the bag, grabbing a Teen burger and taking a satisfying bite. We sat there and visited for a couple of hours, just the three of us. A rare occurrence.

"Well, this was nice and unexpected," she said, smiling. "Must be because you're now twenty-five and finally matured," she said with a laugh.

I forced a smile and said, "Yeah, maybe. It only took twenty-five years!"

I was the same person, she just never noticed. I visited her at home several times after that to see how she was healing. I brought her food and sat and watched TV with her. I felt a responsibility to take care of her; maybe that was how she raised me, or maybe, deep down I really did care for her. Both Jason and Chad had young children at home, each of them raising a daughter. They didn't have the time like I did. I just had my career.

She was back to her usual self in no time, but she would always speak of when I was twenty-five.

FALLING HEAD OVER HEELS

I worked insanely long hours. From 7:30 a.m. to 5:30 p.m., I visited customers and then continued logging calls and returning emails at home until 9:30 p.m. It was all part of my strategy to get ahead and be noticed. And it seemed to be working. I was given the opportunity to present to our VPGM who happened to be coming to town. He was from Vancouver and rarely made visits to the smaller locations like Saskatoon.

My presentation was a huge success. Our VPGM and management team marvelled at my ideas and the success I'd already achieved with my health-care accounts. I felt unstoppable. By the end of the day, I was depleted but still on a high. I sent a couple of last-minute emails before closing my office door and going home. Our management team had left a few moments earlier to take our VPGM out for dinner.

I went down the stairs and within a flash, I was falling. From the top of the stairs, I fell head over heels, crashing down to the bottom. Seventeen stairs to be exact. I hit the bottom of the stairs and felt a blow to my face as it smashed the cement platform. My head throbbed. My whole body hurt. But humiliation trumped my pain. I sat up after coming to and started to collect myself and my belongings. My purse spilled out and all its contents scattered across the stairs: tampons and pantyliners, makeup and mints. I was missing a shoe, and my pants were ripped. A foreman from the warehouse came running in; he had heard me fall over the muffle of his noise-cancelling headphones.

"Oh my god, are you okay?" he asked.

He started to pick up the contents of my purse. I crawled up the stairs like a chimpanzee to recover my other shoe. The stiletto heal was caught in the torn rug at the top of the stairs.

"Yeah, I'm fine." All I could think about was my professional reputation.

"Are you sure? I think I should call you an ambulance."

"No, it's okay. I'll be fine. I can drive."

I retrieved my things from his hands, my head still throbbing. My left wrist was raging with heat, and a lump the size of a golf ball appeared. I wasn't sure if my wrist was broken. I had never broken a bone before. I left and sat in the driver's seat of my Hyundai Santa Fe, legs dangling over the side of the seat with the door open wide. I took a deep inhale of fresh air and tried to collect my thoughts. My head was hazy and confused. Michael came running over and asked if I was okay. I had no idea he was still in the building.

"Yeah, I fell down the stairs. I got to get this checked out at the hospital."

He looked down at my wrist and told me it was definitely broken.

"Do you have someone you can call? You can't drive."

I called Damian to see if he could come get me. It went straight to voicemail. Then I called my mom. She was always the best in situations of crisis or emergency. I recalled every situation with Chad, and the time my cousin slipped on a jacket and crashed into the glass China cabinet when we were young. A sharp piece of glass cut right through her knee and blood sprayed everywhere. Mom was more than composed, she was calm. She thrived in traumatic situations. Dad and I used to say she should have been an ER nurse. Taking care of people in crisis was her forte.

"Hello?" she said.

I was relieved to hear her voice.

"Hey, Mom. I had an accident at work. I fell down the stairs. I think my wrist is broken. And Damian's not answering his phone." I kept trailing my words, spinning in circles at the same rate as my head.

"Where are you?"

"At work."

"I'm on my way!" she said and hung up the phone.

Within fifteen minutes she showed up in her car with a twelve-inch square tile. She handed it to me along with an ice pack and a dish towel.

"What is this for?"

"It's to hold and put your wrist on it."

I never would have thought of a tile as a thing to bring, but she was right. It was heavy and cold and exactly what I needed to keep my wrist from moving. We arrived at the emergency room, and I was ushered through the doors in a wheelchair. I felt strung out.

"She has a broken wrist," my mom said to the nurse. "She fell down a flight of stairs and her wrist is broken."

"Did you hit your head at all?" the nurse asked.

"Amber. Amber. The nurse is asking if you hit your head," Mom said, trying to rouse me to answer the question.

"No, I don't think so."

I could only force a groan at this point as my eyes felt heavy. I just wanted to sleep. It was obvious that I had hit my head. My left eye was swollen and bruised. I was taken for X-rays, and they confirmed that my wrist was broken in two places. The nurse wheeled me into a small room, and I received an IV in my right arm. She inserted a small syringe of white fluid into the catheter line.

"Okay, sweetheart, I'm going to get you to count backward from ten for me."

My eyes were already half closed, but I began to count.

"Ten. Uh. Nine. Eight."

And I was asleep.

I woke up to find Damian sitting beside me. I did not know how long I had been out.

"Ugh, this is taking forever," he complained.

I was given a few days' worth of hydromorphone to help with the pain and told to come back in two weeks for a new cast and an X-ray to determine whether I would need surgery.

Damian and I drove home, and he helped me into my bed.

"Need anything?" he asked.

I shook my head no. I crawled into bed and fell into a deep medicated slumber.

A FRESH START

The day after my fall, the doorbell rang. I fumbled to get off the couch, drowsy from the heavy painkillers, and answered the door. It was Mom. She had flowers and lunch from Tim Hortons. I was so happy to see her. We sat at the kitchen table eating our soup. She took out a fresh roll and spread butter on it for me.

"Should we watch a movie after?"

"Sure," I said, nodding my head.

She helped me back to the couch and gave me another dose of hydromorphone. She took another look at my wrist and the bruises on my face. She caressed my temple softly with her fingers and moved a wisp of hair from my face. I fell asleep halfway through the movie, and she slipped out to go home.

It was the second time in my life that I could remember her taking care of me. The first time was when I was seven and had chicken pox. Chad got it first and had a mild case, but my bout was more severe. I had hundreds of pox marks and a bad fever that lasted two weeks.

It felt surreal to have her take care of me. If it weren't for her, I'm not sure how I would have gotten by. I took three weeks off from work to heal after my accident. I had a concussion, short-term memory loss, and a broken wrist. I returned to work for a few hours per day, still on pain medication. Plans were already in motion to have the stairs removed and replaced, as they were obviously unsafe. One month later, my boss called to offer me a promotion, one that would require moving to Calgary. I was thrilled; this was exactly what I wanted.

I was nervous to tell Damian. He'd showed little sympathy or care for me after my accident. I felt like an imposition to him. I thought that Calgary would be a fresh start for us. A new city to experience. We could find our love again. We would have no one else to depend on but each other.

"Hey, guess what?" I said as I barreled through the door of our townhouse.

"What?" Damian was already home and sitting on the couch flipping channels on the TV.

"I got offered a promotion! They want me to move to Calgary!"

"You mean us? They want us to move."

"Right, yeah, us. It's for the analyst position."

I could tell Damian was miffed. He wanted to be the one transferred and promoted. I showed him the offer letter, which included my moving package and new salary. It was more than what he currently made.

"What's good for the goose is good for the team, right?" I said.

"That doesn't make any sense," he said, as he shook his head.

"Whatever, you know what I mean." I was determined not to let his mood affect this glorious moment that I'd worked tirelessly for.

•

We visited Calgary in December to shop for houses. We found a large home in the Deep South with four bedrooms upstairs and an unfinished basement. It was more than we wanted to spend but the timing was tight, and we needed something. Damian was set on having a house that we could grow into. He'd wanted children as soon as we'd gotten married, but I was eager to create a foundation for our family that was financially secure.

I started my new role as the sales analyst for western Canada in January of 2010. I was excited to leave a customer-facing role. I had several customers in Saskatoon who were offensive, including one in particular who tried to woo me with pictures of his house in Greece and an invitation to dinner. The next day he required my urgent attention and, to my surprise, when I stepped into his office, he was standing there wearing leather chaps with his foot on a chair and his legs splayed wide open.

We dove headfirst into our new jobs. Damian's role and territory were created for him to ensure that he had a job in Calgary. He would be doing the same thing as he did in Saskatoon. I immersed myself in Excel spreadsheets and formulas with some help from YouTube tutorials. Within two months of starting my new job, I was offered another promotion as an account manager for a set of key customers. I was given a three-level bump, a pay increase, and an office with a view. It was a view of the parking lot, but it was a really big window.

A WEEKEND TO REMEMBER

In early September, Damian and I attended our first work event together: a corporate golf tournament. The event was hosted by my company for their annual employee appreciation day. I liked golf but was by no means proficient. I'd only played a few rounds with Damian and his parents during summer visits. Every single stance, swing, grip, and ball placement had been over corrected and criticized by both Damian and his father. I'd become frustrated and furious that it always fell on deaf ears that it was supposed to be fun. Having someone micromanage my every move was all too familiar to me.

I had high hopes for this tournament, though. Hailey was in town visiting and was coming with us. I was positive that Damian would be on his best behaviour and would pretend to be loving and caring toward me. As we rounded the fourth hole, Damian poked fun of my golf skills to the foursome in front of us. Hailey and I were familiar with comments such as this. We both loathed baseball, and in high school gym class, we sat together at the back of the bench, ushering everyone to go ahead of us so we wouldn't have to swing, miss, and eventually strike out. Baseball was never our thing.

But it felt different coming from my husband and in front of my friend and colleagues.

"Oh, no need to rush for her, she will be here hacking away until the sun goes down!" he said with a chuckle and reassured the group ahead of us that we wouldn't need to play ahead of them.

I kept quiet. I didn't want to make a scene. Normally, the insults would come at restaurants when I asked for a side of sour cream, or in line for a sub sandwich when I asked for a little extra mayo. I didn't care; I'd never see them again.

The insults continued for the rest of the round and when it was finally over, I was beyond relieved to go home. Damian and I sat upstairs in our TV room. Sophie laid herself along my legs, and I scratched the spot under her cinnamon bun tail. Hailey went out for the night to visit a friend, and I couldn't hold back any longer.

"You know the comments you kept making on the golf course today weren't very nice."

"Oh relax, you're so sensitive."

"No, I'm serious. I felt embarrassed, and you were putting me down in front of my coworkers."

"Oh fuck, whatever, Amber. I was joking. Learn how to take a joke and have fun for once."

"I would if you actually cared about me and showed me that you loved me. I feel so alone here."

"Yeah, why is that? Because you don't have Mikey here to keep you company?"

"That's a low blow, Damian. I'm serious. I think we need therapy."

By this time, things had escalated to yelling as they usually did. Hailey slipped back into the house and went immediately to her room, which was adjacent to the TV room.

"Would you keep your voice down?" I said, signalling for him to notice that Hailey was back in the house.

"I don't give a fuck about her! And there's no way I'm going to see a therapist. What a fucking waste of money and time."

"Would you rather sign a separation agreement than go to a marriage counsellor?"

"Yeah, tell me when and where, and I'll sign it."

It was the first time I'd thrown out a test to see if Damian was willing to fight for me and our marriage. He wasn't. I had felt for over a year by then that he didn't love me anymore. When I looked at him, he didn't look back at me. He looked through me.

Damian left the house and Hailey came out of her room. I was still in the TV room, curled up in a ball with tears streaming down my face. She sat down beside me and put her arm around my shoulders.

"He won't go to therapy with me Hails, he'd rather be separated."

"I know, A. I heard. I'm so sorry." She paused for a few minutes, rubbing my back, trying to think of what to say next. "But fuck him. His loss. You are young and beautiful. Fuck him, okay?"

"Okay."

She was right. Fuck him.

SILENCED

We let tensions relax for a few days after Hailey left, but the idea of Damian choosing to separate rather than try therapy still boggled my mind and caused a deep emotional scar. It was a scar that I can see now was a wound that started when I was a child. A feeling of not being chosen. Hailey was the only one who knew about the entire conversation, and I was determined to keep it that way.

Damian and I got back into the work routine, and I chose to put my head down and work as hard as I could. He would call me on my office line when I was working late to confirm that I was actually at work, and he would occasionally accuse me of cheating. Damian and I hadn't had sex in two years by this point. It wasn't because I was interested in someone else or having an affair, it was because sex had become an act of submission and disassociation for me. I simply couldn't give myself voluntarily to someone who didn't love me.

If he wasn't accusing me of having an affair, I was suspicious of him. One day, I reached over and saw his phone sitting on the armchair. Damian was outside giving the lawn one last cut before the leaves started to fall. I read his text messages and discovered he'd been sending out feelers to his female colleagues. *I want to see your tits.*

Classy, I thought.

He came back in, and I made a snide comment about him wanting to see his coworkers breasts, and we spiralled into a huge argument. He followed me into the master bedroom, pushing me further into an unavoidable conversation.

"Why don't you just have a kid and give it to me?" he yelled at the top of his lungs.

It was a sore spot for him in our marriage. He wanted kids, and I wasn't ready. We were still barely making ends meet with the mortgage on our new house. We had two new cars and barely any furniture to our names. How could we possibly support a baby on one income?

"That's one hell of a gift, don't you think?" I clapped back.

Damian told me multiple times over the years that if I ever got pregnant and tried to leave him, he would chain me up to the water heater, wait until I gave birth, and take my baby. He said he was joking, but I still felt threatened by it. It was the main reason why I would not have a child with him. I could not take the risk of putting my baby in harm. So, I decided as long as I was with him, I didn't want kids.

"I've decided I don't want kids. I love my job and want to focus on my career."

"Well, don't you think that would have been important information when we got married? You are so fucking selfish."

I immediately pushed him in the chest. He grabbed my wrists and threw me onto the bed. I stood up quickly and charged after him. He pushed me into the closet, down onto the floor, and shut the door. He held it tight, so I couldn't open it. I banged my fists on the door repeatedly and grabbed onto the handle, pulling with all my weight.

"Fuck you!" I screamed.

The door didn't budge. My feet kept slipping on the carpeted flooring. I wasn't strong enough.

"You can fucking stay in there, you selfish bitch. You don't get to touch me."

I slid down the door and crumbled onto the floor. I knew at that moment he would never give in. I pulled my knees to my chest. My heart was pounding in my chest, and I struggled to catch my breath. I was hysterical with rage and sadness. I sat lifeless in the dark closet and bent down, placing my cheek on the carpet. I could see his feet on the other side. This was not the life I wanted for myself. I needed to find a way out.

ISLAND CLARITY

I stepped off the plane and was instantly swallowed in a wave of humidity. I was in Maui. I made my way to the luggage carousel and there they were standing side by side: my parents.

"Hey, Mom! Hey, Dad!"

"Hi, Am! Welcome to Maui!"

They greeted me with a warm embrace and a kiss on the cheek. They smelled like plumeria and coconut. Their skin was tacky to the touch and sun-kissed all over. I could tell Mom was in a good mood. They had been coming to Maui every year for the last three years. This was her favourite place.

I sat in the backseat of their rented Toyota Camry. I had never been anywhere like this before. It was serene, even in the dark. We arrived at their condo rental. It was their favourite spot to stay in Maui. They always stayed at a beach-front condo in between Kameole 1 and 2 beaches. The condo was on the ground floor and had a large lanai. There were two bedrooms, one master and a second room with two twin beds. They had been there a week already and were already adjusted to the time change.

In the early hours of the next morning, I was roused before sunrise by the birds outside my window. They were singing at an incredible decibel. It wasn't just a few birds; it sounded like thousands. I was officially awake.

The three of us sat on the lanai, each with a hot cup of tea in hand. I knew I couldn't avoid the inevitable for much longer.

"So, how come Damian didn't want to come?" Mom asked.

They weren't privy to the state of our marriage at this point. I had learned from my relationship with Noah just to keep things to myself.

"Things between us haven't been that great lately," I said.

"What do you mean? Did you even ask him to come?" she asked.

I did ask him to come, but when he found out it would be with my parents, he gave a resounding no.

"Yeah, I did. I don't know, we've just grown apart. We've been fighting a lot. I don't think he loves the idea that I've got a bigger job than he does now."

Mom interrupted. "Well, tough shit!"

Dad nodded along and agreed that all success is for the greater good.

"If it weren't for my salary when you kids were younger, we wouldn't have had half of what we had!" Mom's brow furrowed as she spoke.

Dad and I exchanged a side glance at each other, knowing that we were both thinking the same thing. Dad was clearly the breadwinner in our family. He worked extremely hard and was a very good provider for our family. Mom worked hard too, but she made maybe $30,000 a year and it was barely enough to pay for our extracurricular activities and sports. Still, we'd never tell her that we disagreed with her for fear of setting her off. We both nodded in agreement.

I told them about our recent argument and that I was considering seeing a therapist myself. I knew I needed to work on my self-confidence. I felt on top of the world at work, but at home with Damian, I felt shrivelled and weak.

"Yeah, sure, do what you've got to do," Dad said while Mom stayed silent.

I could tell her thoughts were spinning. Therapy was foreign to our family. We didn't ask for help, and we most certainly didn't share our problems with complete strangers. We sat together in silence, sipping our tea as the sun rose. It lit up the horizon and glistened against the water. The view was heavenly.

The trip was filled with various excursions to their favourite places around the island, and most of it went off without a hitch except for the two days when Mom was upset with something that Dad did or said.

I left Maui after a week, fully bronzed and rejuvenated. I took a cab so as to not inconvenience Damian. I returned home to our empty, dark home. I felt alone even though I wasn't.

"Did you have a good time?" Damian asked after I walked through the door.

"I did, actually. It's a beautiful place."

"Yeah, I had friends reach out to me and ask how I was enjoying myself there because they saw your photo on Facebook. I told them you went alone."

There was blame in between each word he spoke.

"It was your choice not to go," I said. It was too early for this, and I had just been on a red-eye flight.

"I know, but you chose to go alone," he said. "I'm just letting you know what people are saying."

"That makes zero sense. I'm going to bed," I said. I felt a sudden burst of confidence, having been away from him for a week.

The next day, I returned to work feeling better than I had in a long time. My coworkers complimented my dark tan and for the first time in a long while, I had a fragment of self-confidence. I made an appointment with a therapist that was recommended through our company. I made sure not to tell anyone for fear it would get back to Damian.

A few days later, I left the office early for my therapy appointment. I had to account for the time of the actual appointment, plus the time to get back home at a reasonable hour. I tried to cover all my bases. I made sure to drive the speed limit and to pay extra parking so I wouldn't get a parking ticket. I had never snuck around before, and I felt immense guilt.

The next six weeks would be filled with weekly therapy sessions, suggested readings, and work to build my self-confidence. In order to tell Damian that I wanted a divorce, I needed to feel stronger and more capable. I was determined to leave unscathed.

BREAKING FREE

Damian and I went back to Saskatoon for Christmas and stayed with my parents for a few days. They could tell that our marriage was at the brink of destruction by how we spoke to each other. We were short with one another, snapping comments back and forth. We had lost all respect and every ounce of love that had once been there. We stayed until December 26 and then returned home to Calgary. My work was closed for the rest of the week, but I went in anyway. My job felt like the only stable, predictable part of my life, and it was also a chance for me to look for a condo.

I was the only one in the office. The silence was deafening. I sat in my office chair and turned to look out the window. Snowflakes fell from the sky, blanketing the parking lot. The flakes were idyllic, and, for a moment, it made me feel like I was staring into a snow globe. I picked up the phone and called my mom. I needed to know what level of support I could count on before I moved. I had no idea if they would come help me or if I would have to hire movers.

"Hello, Amber," she said. She sounded the same every time I called: inconvenienced.

"Hi, Mom."

"So what have you got to say for yourself?" she asked.

"What do you mean?" I hated when she asked me that question. It seemed senseless and stupid, and it was never followed by why she was actually upset. It was my job to know what I did wrong.

"Well. Don't you think Christmas was a bit of a gong show?" she continued.

"I guess," I said.

"You guess? Amber, you could cut the tension with a knife. Why on earth did you bring him home? You guys were rude and disrespectful to Dad and me. And frankly, I feel you ruined Christmas for us all."

I sat in silence while she continued to rant. I supposed she was right. We should not have gone home, but Damian worried about what everyone would think if, once again, we weren't together. I swung my chair back around to look outside but was unable to reach the same serene feeling with Marlene livid in my ear.

The phone fell silent, and I knew it was my turn to speak.

"I'm sorry, Mom. You are right. We shouldn't have come home together."

"Well! I should say so."

"I wanted to ask you something." I interrupted her before she could say anything more.

"What is it?"

"I'm going to move out, and I'm looking for a condo. I wanted to know if you and Dad would bring the truck and help me move?"

She was speechless.

"And when are you thinking of doing this?"

"As soon as possible, but ideally before the end of January. I will be touring a few condos this week and will hopefully get possession of a place right away."

"Have you told Damian this?"

"No, not yet. I wanted to find a place first and have everything lined up before telling him."

"Alright, Amber. We will help you. Just give us enough notice."

"Thanks, Mom."

I hung up the phone, already feeling in debt to my parents for their promised support. Mom had a way of portraying how "put out" she was on the rare occasions I needed her. The furnace kicked on and the humming sound brought back a lull. I scoured the internet for a rental property.

•

I had yet to breach the subject of moving out with Damian. My therapist advised me to get everything set up before mentioning it to him. After a brief search, I found a brand-new two-bedroom condo in southwest Calgary. The area was older, but the condo had been rebuilt after a fire. My landlords were an older couple, and I considered myself the perfect tenant. I signed a one-year contract.

I waited a couple weeks before I told Damian. I approached the subject delicately, telling him that I needed some space and time away to think, that a couple months on my own would be good for us. He agreed and offered to help me look for a place.

"I found one, actually. I get possession of it in a week. I was going to ask my parents to come and help me move a couple of things."

I'd already made the arrangements with my parents. He was shocked. I did all of this without him knowing.

"You can take whatever you want except the dog. She stays with me."

He knew how to cut me the deepest. Sophie was mine. But I agreed to leave her behind. If it meant a safe exit for me, then I needed to succumb to his only request.

"Okay," I said.

•

The next weekend, Mom, Dad, and Chad pulled into the driveway at 9 a.m. with a U-Haul trailer. They'd driven to Calgary the day before and stayed at a hotel nearby. Damian woke up early that morning, took Sophie, and left the house while we packed. We packed up my bed, dresser, and nightstands, the new table and chairs, and the old couches. I took every item of clothing, my toiletries, and a few pieces of decor.

"Aren't you going to take your Barbies?" Mom asked, as she scoured the unfinished basement for items that she had purchased.

"I don't have the space for them. I'll get them later."

Mom had saved all my Barbie dolls and my Barbie dollhouse from when I was a little girl. Numerous boxes filled with clothing and accessories sat there waiting to be played with by my future children.

"Oh no you won't. We're taking them now!"

She instructed Chad to carry the stack of boxes, and we carried the Barbie house out to the truck. They would head back to Saskatoon and wait there for when I had more space.

It took us three hours to get the trailer unpacked and my condo set up. It was small, but it was mine. We ordered pizza and I ate my first meal at my new home.

"So tell me Amber, what was *really* going on with you and Damian?" Mom asked.

Mom had a way of asking questions. She knew she wasn't getting the full truth.

"Meaning what?" I mumbled over a mouthful of ham and pineapple pizza.

"Well, in Maui you said things weren't great. After that, you didn't say much. You told me he was an ass after you fell down the stairs, but what else haven't you told me?"

I looked at her with vulnerability. Mom rarely asked questions from a place of sympathy. Perhaps this time would be different. Maybe she would understand how far I had come and how difficult it was to get here. I opened up and told her about the infidelity accusations, the name calling, the arguments, the blame, the psychological, emotional, and mental abuse, and our recent argument that had landed me on the floor of the closet. She looked at me with a disconcerting expression.

"Well, at least you kept your legs closed!" She laughed and took a bite of her second slice of pizza.

I sat there feeling deflated and lifeless in my own skin, a shell of a human being. I didn't know what to say, so I nodded in agreement. I'd confessed all my struggles and when I wanted her to hold me up, she laughed and took out any stable ground I was standing on. My failures seemed to make her happy.

Emotionally and physically drained, I crawled into bed that night, but I wasn't alone. My mother was sleeping next to me. She had insisted that she and my dad sleep in my bed, while I slept on the inflatable mattress next to Chad on the couch. Thankfully, Dad refused. It was hard enough having Chad in my condo. As I laid there, I thought about what happened with Chad when we were younger. It was a secret that only he and I knew. It popped into my thoughts every time he was around. Unbeknownst to anyone else, these unwanted memories took control of my thoughts, cascading a frigid stiffness of anxiety throughout my limbs and a weight in my chest. Damian had been my escape from both my mom and Chad. And now that I managed to flee my marriage, I found myself caught back in their web.

They left the next day. I found myself alone and safe for the first time in my life. Everything that surrounded me was mine. I cried a lot that first day. I was in awe of what I had just accomplished. I had no intentions of moving back in with Damian, and my next obstacle would be asking him for a divorce.

THERAPY TRAIN WRECK

The reality of being separated or divorced before the age of twenty-seven was starting to set in. I needed to come to terms with my life plan not happening on schedule. I was slowly realizing that everything happens for a reason, and it was up to me to learn the reason and grow from it. Damian and I had been separated and living apart for two months. We had very little communication. Although he tried to reach out, I asked him for space. It was, after all, the reason why I moved out: to have space, gain clarity, and find my strength.

I hadn't seen Sophie or been to the house since I moved. Damian was paying the mortgage and the bills for the house, and I was making the payments on our credit cards and car loans, in addition to my own rent and living expenses.

One Saturday afternoon, I folded laundry in my condo. The patio door was wide open, letting fresh air inside. It was an exceptionally mild winter, a nice change from the frigid temperatures of Saskatchewan. My phone dinged; it was a text message from Damian.

I'm willing to try couples' therapy.

It was a futile attempt to get me to respond or engage. But the more I thought about it, the more I wondered whether a therapist would help him realize we weren't right for each other. I waited a few hours before responding. I didn't want him to think I was readily available to talk.

Okay. I'll book a session and let you know where and when.

I booked a session with a different therapist at the same office I'd been going to since the fall. We arrived separately, and I instructed Damian to sit and wait and that we'd be called in when it was our time.

"How do you know that? Where did you find this place?"

"Because I've been coming here myself for almost six months."

Immediately, I could tell that Damian hated this place. This had to be the reason why I left; my therapist must have told me to get out.

"Damian and Amber?"

A short heavyset woman with shoulder-length hair popped her head out from one of the closed doorways. We both stood up and walked into the room.

"I'm Chantal. Can I get you anything? Water or coffee?"

Chantal gestured for us to sit on the large navy couch or the two armchairs. We politely declined her offer of a drink and sat together on the couch.

"Amber, I want you to tell me why you are here and what you are hoping to get out of our sessions together."

I told her about our challenges with trust and the lack of care I felt after my accident. I let her know about our current living situation and what I needed from Damian in order to move forward.

"Okay, thank you. And Eric, same question to you: What are you hoping to get out of these sessions?"

I turned to look at Damian and could see he was angry. "My name is Damian, not Eric!"

"Oh, I'm sorry. Damian, please, go ahead," she said.

Damian rambled on for ten minutes about my fixation on my career and the lack of care about the promise I made to him to bear children after we were married. He mentioned the anonymous letter that he received and my neediness after I fell down the stairs.

"Thank you, Eric, for sharing that."

I swallowed a large lump in my throat and started laughing inside. She had done it again. She'd called him the wrong name again. I looked over at Damian and he was furious, yet he said nothing. The session ended with the usual love languages homework, but I knew understanding how he received love would not help us at this point. He was pissed and had no intention of returning to therapy.

We managed to go back for two more sessions but by the third session, Chantal looked at me with a look of hopelessness.

"Your husband has no emotional connection to you," she said. "I'm sorry. I think you both would be better off if you divorced."

It was the outcome I was hoping to hear and the reassurance I needed to support my decision to leave. I felt comfort knowing someone else could see what I had been feeling for a very long time.

We left together. As the elevator doors closed, Damian loudly said, "Fucking bitch. She doesn't know what she's talking about. She doesn't even have a degree; did you see that? She's a counsellor. She's not even a psychologist!"

He trailed off as we descended to the main lobby. We said goodbye and went opposite ways.

IF YOU READ THIS...

As our fourth anniversary approached, Damian reached out. We had already been given a professional opinion on the unfavourable outcome of our future, but he wanted to celebrate our anniversary in an attempt to reconcile. I always said a grand apology for how he treated me after my accident was necessary, but it had been almost two years since I'd fallen. By then, I knew that whatever he did or said, it wouldn't change how I felt. Still, I struggled with boundaries and being able to say no, so I accepted his invitation.

Before he came over, I wrote a note: *To whomever reads this, if something happens to me, it was Damian Shrover who did it.* I tucked the note between a stack of sweaters in my dresser drawer.

I loved living in a condo. It had a secure entrance that no one could access. I was on the fourth floor. The elevator worked with a key fob to access each floor, and my parking stall was located right beside the elevator. It was the main reason why I'd chosen this place. I felt safe.

Damian wanted to come over and deliver a few things, pick me up, then take me to dinner. I should have said no but part of me wanted to see what he was capable of and how much effort he thought I was worth.

Hey, I'm here, Damian texted.

Nerves flowed through my body like waves of electricity. I was going to bring him into my safe space. I took the elevator down to the lobby.

"Hey." I greeted him and he immediately hugged me.

We filled the air with idle banter in the elevator. After we arrived on the fourth floor, I unlocked the door to my condo.

"Wow, nice place. It looks a lot fuller than the house now that you took half of everything."

He scoured the place, looking in both rooms and examining the bathrooms and closets. He handed me a bouquet of flowers and two shopping bags. One bag contained a custom cake in the shape of a Jimmy Choo shoe. The other bag held a replica of the skimpy newspaper dress that Sarah Jessica Parker wore in *Sex and the City*, as well as black pearl earrings.

He gave me an envelope with a card and a five-page letter and asked me to read it later, when I was alone. I was already dressed in a conservative outfit, jeans and a nice top, but he insisted that I wear the new dress to dinner.

I went into my room, locked the door, and undressed. I pulled the new dress up over my hips and past my belly button piercing. It reminded me again how I could never say no. The dress was skimpy, at best, and cheap, at worst. It was backless, moderately see-through, and didn't allow for a bra. I compared this dress to the plum dress I'd worn when we first met, and this seemed more deserving of a slut comment. I put the earrings in, grabbed a cardigan, and exited my room to find Damian in the kitchen.

"Ready to go?" I asked.

"Yes."

He ushered me out the door with a hand on the small of my back. When we reached his car, he opened the door for me. We continued with marginal conversation for the entire drive to a restaurant in downtown Calgary. Thankfully, the chefs were cooking right in front of us, and this helped to fill the awkward silence. Multiple times during dinner, Damian referred to the letter he wrote me, as if to say it's all in the letter, rather than sharing his thoughts and feelings in the present moment.

We drove back to my condo in silence. He parked his car and turned off the engine.

"Want to share a piece of cake?" he asked.

"No, I'm actually really full. But thank you. And thank you for tonight. It was nice," I lied.

I knew I couldn't allow him back in my place. Once was enough and I was eager to return to a safe environment. I walked briskly toward the building and got in safely, making sure the doors closed behind me.

I took off the dress and the earrings and curled up in my sweats. I looked over at the letter still sitting on the counter. Spending time with him tonight had been enough. The letter would have to wait until the next day.

The letter was five pages of "I'm sorry," endless promises, and repeated declarations of love. It swirled in confusion and lacked direction. It was like every conversation we had. The letter, more than anything, confirmed that I was done.

YOU'RE NOT INVITED

I avoided Damian like the plague after our anniversary dinner. I let him know that I needed more time, but I thought the absence of **affection and communication would be enough** to let him know that his grand gesture would not win me back. I was up for a big promotion that would require moving to Toronto. It was September, and if I received the promotion, I would move in January. A newly single woman in her twenties, willing to move to climb the corporate ladder, was considered a unicorn in our company. It was the perfect decision and exactly what I needed to present Damian with divorce papers. I was hoping he would be amicable. I thought if I gave him very little resistance on my part that it would be okay. Once again, I wrote a note and left it in my drawer. I texted to let him know I was on my way.

I rang the doorbell even though I still had a key. Damian opened the door and Sophie came running up to me. She squinted her eyes and fluttered her ears. It was how she smiled whenever she saw us. It was the first time I'd been back to the house since moving. It was cold and empty. I fought back the depressing feelings and kept my distance on the other side of the kitchen island.

"So, I'm up for another promotion, but this time it's in Toronto."

"Okay. Well, it worked out the last time; I guess I can talk to my manager and see what's available for me there." I could see the promise in his eyes as he imagined our life together again.

I interrupted him. "I was thinking I'd go alone."

The look on his face said it all. He was angry.

"So what, you want to get a divorce?"

"Yes. I have the papers here. You just need to sign them and then we have to file them at the courthouse."

"Oh. You already have the papers. How thoughtful of you. I'll look at them later."

I could tell the conversation was over. I said goodbye to Sophie and quickly left. We had been separated for a year by this point, so we could file the divorce paperwork immediately.

•

A month later, we met at the Calgary courthouse. I was dressed conservatively in wide-leg suit pants and a blue sweater. I placed my trench coat, purse, shoes, and keys in the plastic bin to be fed through the X-ray scanner and walked through the metal detector.

"You don't have an ass anymore," Damian said as he followed behind me.

"What did you say?" I was entirely caught off guard.

"Your ass. It's gone." Damian repeated himself.

I left it alone, knowing this was one last jab that he had to get in. One more dig to make himself feel better than me. We filed the paperwork and went our separate ways.

I went home and called my parents. We had been speaking almost daily since Damian and I'd separated. We were in a good place for the first time in a very long time. I was telling my mom about the trip to the courthouse when she interrupted me.

"Oh, I didn't tell you what happened on Friday night!"

"No, why, what happened?" I asked.

"Well, your brothers were out drinking at a bar after work on Friday, and Jason let Chad get up and drive home. He got into a car accident on the way home and rear ended a minivan! The cops showed up and by the grace of God he blew less than a point zero eight!"

"What!"

"Yeah, your dad showed up before the cops and told Chad that he better get inhaling as much air as he could because he smelled like booze. And I guess a witness said he didn't even try to stop before he hit them."

"Holy shit."

"Yeah, and I'm beyond pissed at Jason for letting him drive drunk."

"How is it Jason's fault?"

"Well, he's older, and he knows better."

I bit my tongue. Chad was twenty-seven and old enough to know better himself. It turned out that Jason went to the bathroom and Chad left on his own accord and drove home. Mom was relentless with her anger and accusations. She scolded Jason for being in a bar drinking instead of at home with his wife and kids, even though Chad was doing the exact same thing.

This was the first instance where I felt sorry for Jason. He didn't deserve this, and he most certainly was not responsible for Chad's poor decisions. I wished that Chad had blown over the legal limit and had been put in jail and charged. Then he would have finally received a consequence for one of his poor choices. But once again, he walked away unpunished.

THERAPY

I sat back on the couch at my usual Wednesday morning session. I wore joggers and a sweatshirt. I chose comfort today because I knew talking about Damian brought me feelings of angst.

"It feels like your marriage to Damian was a lot to unpack. I commend you for seeking help. Why do you think you ignored all the red flags?" she asked.

"I know now that he was my escape. He was the lesser evil. In the beginning, he didn't have the same hold on me that my mom did, and to me, it seemed more manageable."

"Do you think, subconsciously, you knew that bringing a child into this world with him would be a bad idea?"

"I think it was obvious, and I knew at the time that it wouldn't fix us. I felt like I had these innate maternal instincts that were telling me I wouldn't be able to save my child in that situation."

"That's a very powerful realization. Let's talk about your experiences with Damian on the picnic table, in the bathroom at his parents' house, and after your engagement for a minute. In those moments, were you able to correlate the similarities of what happened between you and Chad at the age of twelve?"

"In those moments? No. I wasn't physically and mentally aware of the correlation between the two, but I felt the same feelings. The physical experience was the same, but after it happened I had the same feelings. I would say when I started to learn about my experiences with Chad is when I understood the likeness of what happened with Damian. I learned about marital rape and consent, two terms that were foreign to me. I never consented to anal sex with Damian."

"Did you ever consider sharing any of this with Damian? Did he have any inclination whatsoever that you had a traumatic sexual past?"

"No. I had no intention of telling anyone. Damian and I didn't have a safe relationship. It was obvious when I fell down the stairs that he wasn't going to be the person I needed. I could only imagine if I ever told him about everything, I would risk being retraumatized by something he could say. Silence and self-preservation were my only choices."

"Okay, I want to revisit this when we start our EMDR sessions. I think it's important."

We ended our session for the day and agreed to meet the next week on the same day at the same time.

NEWFOUND STANDARDS

I've experienced it only twice in my life, the calm feeling that comes over you and guides you to do something you weren't sure of. The first time was when I walked down the aisle to marry Damian. The second was when I introduced myself to Adam.

It was a Friday night, and I was alone in my condo. The room was dimly lit by a lamp, my computer screen, and *How to Lose a Guy in 10 Days* on the TV. Wine in hand, I scrolled through Facebook and saw his profile picture on the side. *People you may know,* I read. I reminded myself of something my dad always told me: "Am, you can get any guy you want."

I didn't truly believe that, but it was enough, in addition to my current buzzed state, to creep on him. I clicked on his profile and was surprised to see he was from Saskatoon and now lived in Calgary. *What are the chances that this guy isn't a total douche bag?* I thought. I quickly studied his photos to see what type of guy he was and whether he was dating anyone. I saw the Star of David illustrated in his coffee, him licking a male mannequin's ear, and him riding a tandem bicycle with another guy. He appeared to be obsessed with golf, and it looked like he loved his mom. Well, worst-case scenario, he would be my Jewish, gay, new best friend. Best case, he's single, respected his mom, and had a wicked sense of humour. Either instance sounded good to me. I clicked on the button to add him as a friend and headed to bed.

Adam accepted my friend request the next day.

Two weeks went by and nothing, no messages. Adam and I were just Facebook friends. Then one day, I was on my way downtown to take a client out for lunch. He'd recently gone on a trip to Africa and wanted to show me pictures of his trip. We met at Joey's and sat at the bar. We perused through the pictures of his safari in between bites of food. Looking up, I glanced across the restaurant, and there he was. The guy I'd added to Facebook. It was Adam. He was tall and slender with dark hair and green eyes. He was dressed in a navy suit with a light blue shirt. No tie. He was out to lunch with a few people all around the same age as himself.

I didn't have the nerve to go and say hello. That would be too awkward. Nothing like showing up at the restaurant and introducing yourself to a guy you've been stalking online, giving off serial killer vibes to him and his colleagues! I went back to work and gathered the girls in my office to tell them about my run-in.

"Pull up his profile again," Rebecca demanded.

She was a feisty and spunky millennial who reported to me. I searched for Adam's profile and saw that it was his birthday.

"You have to send him a message! Just say happy birthday. It's the perfect introduction."

I opened a direct message window to Adam and typed *Hey, Happy Birthday! I think I saw you today.*

He wrote back later that day. *Hey, thanks. Was the scene of the crime Joey's Eau Claire?*

I didn't realize when I typed that message that it left endless possibilities to the receiver so was thankful he had gotten it right. I can just imagine writing back *No, I was driving alongside you and honked but you didn't notice.* Creepy. Dating was new to me. It had been a very long time, and I was nervous. I lacked confidence but had been working with my therapist over the past year to stand in the newfound footing of a single woman living on my own.

Adam and I exchanged a few casual messages and then finally I suggested we meet up for drinks. *Sure, that could work. How does Saturday afternoon or Sunday night work?* It didn't take me more than a second to understand that those time slots were complete bullshit. After all my self-confidence work, I knew I was prime-time material. I deserved to be taken out on a proper date. I thought about what I wanted in a partner and what I wasn't willing to tolerate. This was my first test, so I pushed back. *No, thank you. If you're too busy, then maybe we should find another time or just skip it.*

How does next Friday night work? Dinner and a comedy show?

"Now that's what I'm talking about" is what first came out of my mouth but of course I typed, *Sounds great.*

I wore a white camisole with a black blazer and a long necklace that draped down my front. Dark skinny jeans and heels. Casual sexy was what I was going for. We met at Koi for a beef-and-broccoli dinner prior to heading over to Jack Singer Hall to see Gerry Dee. Stand-up comedy has always been one of my favourite things to watch, even more so than concerts. I had never seen Gerry Dee before, but his show was hilarious. In the moment, I didn't care what Adam thought of me and whether he was laughing, too. Gerry was talking about his wife defecating during childbirth and suddenly everyone else in the room vanished. I started laughing uncontrollably. Tears streamed down my face, and I started sliding out of my chair. This was some funny shit.

I thanked Adam for a wonderful night, and he walked me to my car. Our second date was at a fancier restaurant in Calgary called Alloy.

What are you wearing? I texted.

Mountain Casual.

What the hell is mountain casual? I wondered. I was coming from work and made sure to wear a nice, fitted business dress. It was grey tweed with a small belt that cinched at the waist. Considerably fancier than what I normally wore to work, but I wanted to impress. I walked into the restaurant to find him sitting at a booth.

"Oh, that's what you meant by mountain casual," I said.

He was wearing a hoodie, jeans, and a vest. We sat for over two hours, talking about our views on family, marriage, religion, careers, etc. This seemed too good to be true. We shared the same views on everything. I paid for dinner because he'd paid for the first date and because I wanted him to know that I didn't need a man to pay my way. He gave me a hug and walked me to my car.

CAN HE HAVE HAM?

Adam and I went home for Christmas together in 2011, two months after we started dating. We drove the long, six-hour drive back to Saskatoon from Calgary, exchanging stories about past trips and how we both almost crashed numerous times on the treacherous icy highways. He was staying with his mom, and I was staying with my parents. I had met his mom, Cyd, earlier in December. She seemed warm and intellectual, and made it very clear that she and Adam were close. We planned on staying a week to visit with family and friends. We set aside a day for hometown dates, touring through Saskatoon, and driving past our old schools and homes.

Adam and his mom were coming over for Christmas dinner and would be meeting my family for the first time: Mom, Dad, Jason and Natalie and their two children, and Chad and Libby and their daughter (with another one on the way).

"Amber, I'll need your help in the kitchen tomorrow," Mom said.

What else would I be doing? I thought as my eyes rolled into the back of my head.

"Okay," I said.

I knew it: the two of us would do all the work of preparing Christmas dinner. It was a tradition for us all to come home for

Christmas Day dinner. Jason and Chad would spend Christmas morning at their own homes with their wives and kids, opening gifts and making their own memories. Later in the day they would all come over for dinner and open gifts from my parents.

"I was gonna make a ham, too. Can he have ham?" Mom asked.

"What?"

"Adam! Isn't he Jewish?"

"He's Jewish by descent. Half Jewish!" I said.

"Well, did you know that Jewish people don't eat pork?"

"That's not at all true, Mom. He's an atheist. He'll eat the ham."

"Well, I'm pretty sure it is true."

Her eyebrows were so high they could have touched her hairline. Mom thought she knew everything.

We worked diligently together in the kitchen on Christmas Day. She put the turkey in the oven and a pre-cooked ham on the stove. We made mashed potatoes, stuffing, and her famous orange salad (a combination of cottage cheese, whipped cream, mandarin orange slices, and orange Jell-O powder). I hated cooking. Growing up, I'd never enjoyed food and only ate to stay alive.

Adam and Cyd arrived and immediately offered to help with dinner.

"No, please sit," Mom said.

"I love your snowmen, Marlene," Cyd said.

"The most festive kitchen I've ever seen," Adam chimed in.

Mom was extremely proud of her snowman collection. Every square inch of spare space in the house made the perfect home for another snowman. She had over one thousand snowmen placed throughout the house. They all stared back at you with their rosy, grinning faces.

We all settled in at the table set for twelve. Mom sat at the head of the table, and we said grace. We exchanged niceties and asked various questions of each other, and when the dinner was finished, Adam offered to help clean up.

"Oh, Adam, go sit down. We've got this," Mom said.

"No, it's okay. I'm very capable of doing the dishes," he replied.

Cyd smiled and rubbed his arm with her hand. She'd raised him right. The five women, plus Adam, did all the dishes and packed up the leftovers.

The norm in our house was my dad, Jason, and Chad watching sports on the TV while the women cleaned and the kids ran about playing. It had been this way ever since Natalie and Libby had joined the family. I didn't quite understand my mother's logic. She had different expectations for my dad. He would cook and clean. But the boys were different. It infuriated me to no end. They both sat there laughing and catching up. Chad had an air of arrogance, and Jason joked the kitchen was where women belonged.

*

Before Adam and I headed back to Calgary, we visited with my parents one more time. We sat at the kitchen table, Mom in her usual spot and Dad on the opposite side.

"You okay, Dad?" I asked.

He looked pale. He was exhausted and had a persistent sore throat that had lingered for months without letting up.

"No, my throat is killing me, and I woke up with this."

Dad pulled his sweater to the side to reveal a large lump on the side of his neck. It was massive. My heart fell to my stomach. My dad was only fifty-one.

Dad had a doctor's appointment booked for the following day and assured us there was nothing we could do and we should head back to Calgary. We exchanged hugs and kisses, told them to keep us posted, and got into the car to drive the six hours home.

Two days later, the phone rang. It was Mom and Dad.

I was with Adam at his condo and immediately stood up to find a quiet place to talk. I went down the hall to his bedroom and shut the door. They asked me where I was and whether I was with Adam.

"Yes, I am," I said.

"Okay, good. Am, we've got some bad news," Mom spoke. She and Dad were on speakerphone together.

I started to tremble, and I feared the worst. As my heart sank into my stomach, I almost dropped the phone.

"Dad went to visit his GP yesterday, and they told him to go straight to the hospital. When we got to the hospital Dad was given a scope, a CT scan, and some bloodwork. He has cancer."

I instantly wanted to vomit. My entire world was falling to pieces. I couldn't lose him.

"He needs additional testing and a biopsy, but they believe it's in his tonsils. He's going to be okay, Am."

She tried to console me over my sobs. He was my rock.

"I can't lose you, Dad."

"You won't, Am, I promise," he said.

I let them go and sat alone on Adam's bed, knees to my chest and head buried in my arms. This couldn't be happening. My dad was everything to me. He was the one person who made me feel connected to my family. Adam peeked his head into the bedroom to see if I was okay and hurried over as soon as he saw me. He sat down next to me and wrapped his arms around me. I folded into him and collapsed. He knew how much my dad meant to me, and he knew all too well about loss. Adam had lost his dad to a brain aneurysm when he was seventeen.

A couple days later it was confirmed that Dad had stage four tonsil cancer. He would need to undergo three intensive rounds of chemotherapy and multiple sessions of radiation. He was given a 50 percent chance of survival, and they advised him it was unlikely that he would finish all three rounds of chemo.

Over the next year, Dad endured extensive treatment for his cancer. Mom was always by his side, making sure he took his medications and taking in enough calories. He fought with all he had. He made it through all three rounds of chemotherapy and finished his radiation. He was officially in remission.

A FLOOD OF TEARS

Our love would progress at a rapid pace, but this time it was different. I was on the lookout for every red, crimson, burgundy, or rose-coloured flag. But there weren't any. Adam was kind, he was supportive, he had an air of confidence, and he was very intelligent. He was spontaneous, and he took care of me in ways I never knew I needed. For the many days we laughed together, there were an equal number of nights when I sat on his knee after a good meal and we cried and held onto one another because we were so grateful for this newfound love.

Still, as great as our love was, I found myself struggling with the aftermath of Damian and our divorce. I had issues with trust and would cower on the rare occasion that Adam would raise his voice or get mad. I had a fear of not being loved and chosen. Adam was sensitive to it and reminded me constantly that he was not Damian and shouldn't be punished for someone else's faults.

Our relationship progressed and was built on a foundation of similar core values. We were aligned on all the big things in life, which made life-changing decisions seem like a breeze. We decided to buy a house and move in together after only seven months of dating, and we were engaged fifty-three weeks after our first date. He proposed to me with a ring that he purchased, with his own money, all by himself. There was no need to wait. He was my person, and I was ready to start this new life with him.

Our wedding date was set for June 22, 2013, in Calgary. We booked Rouge as our venue, an old historical house turned into a gourmet, farm-to-table restaurant. They grew herbs and vegetables in the backyard garden. Large trees were dressed with hanging string lights and lanterns. As each guest arrived, they would be given a sparkling Prosecco prior to heading out to the garden. White chairs would form an aisle and we would exchange our own vows under a large birch tree. We planned a happy hour with a signature drink of Saskatoon berry mimosas to pay homage to our roots. There would be sliders, charcuterie, and a risotto station. For dinner, we'd sit amongst the stars under a white tent, tables adorned with white calla lilies and candles. We chose a custom menu with a choice of halibut or rack of lamb, a caprese salad, and a Saskatoon berry goat cheesecake for dessert. And after we danced the night away, a midnight lunch would be served in the form of a gourmet poutine station. It sounded so perfect, and it would be a day to celebrate the two of us.

Mom wasn't privy to our wedding plans. I kept her at arm's length. I couldn't handle her judgment or comments about how excessive it was or how much money it would all cost. I shopped for my dress in Calgary with a couple of friends. Hailey came out for a weekend, and I chose a simple, timeless, ivory lace dress. It had a sweetheart neckline and a trumpet silhouette. It was perfect in its simplicity.

The entire month of June had been rainy, and two days before the wedding, the city began to flood. Panic set in. This wasn't a small flood. This was a once-in-a-hundred-years flood, the biggest since 1897, and twenty-six communities had already been evacuated. We were on high alert to be next. Our venue called and said they were under water. They could not host our wedding. We suddenly had no place to get married or have a reception. We had guests in from out of town and more on the way. We needed to call those who hadn't come in yet and let them know they should stay put because the hotels were full of displaced residents, and many were under water as well. Our photographer was coming in from Saskatoon and bailed at the last minute, in addition to the makeup artist and one bridesmaid. I was speechless.

One of our guests offered up their home in Calgary. They had a large home on Lake Bonavista, far enough away from the flood. My bridesmaids and I brought over our dresses and supplies and got ready in their master suite. It wasn't the dream wedding we'd planned, but if it meant having my dad there, then it was worth it. I made my way down the spiral staircase, careful not to trip. He stood at the bottom of the stairs, looking handsome in his suit. I worried for so long that he wouldn't be there to walk me down the aisle, but he fought tirelessly. I teared up just seeing him. We walked arm in arm for a few steps before meeting Adam under the mantel in the living room where he stood next to our justice of the peace. Adam was in full tears. It wasn't a cute, sweet cry but a full-on ugly cry. Red face and runny nose. I had never seen him like this, and it made my heart melt. We exchanged the vows we wrote for each other. I knew this would be a long-lasting love.

Adam's groomsman brought his DSLR camera and shot some photos out on the dock by the water. We celebrated and ordered pizzas from a food truck, had Spolombos sausages, and Dairy Queen dilly bars for dessert. It was far from perfect. It wasn't even close. It took me a while to overcome the disappointment of the day that we'd dreamt about for a year, but at the end of the day we were married and that was all that mattered.

A FAMILY TRIP

I became pregnant with our first baby just a few months after our wedding. I was ten weeks along when we headed to Maui with my family. Mom and Dad always wanted to take everyone to Maui for a week, so they booked two condos in their usual spot and asked everyone to book their own flight and come down. Jason and his family visited the other islands for a week before coming to Maui. Adam and I came in for one week with everyone, while Chad and his family stayed both weeks. Mom said it was only fair that they host Chad's family for two weeks because they'd hosted me a couple years earlier.

We arrived in Maui late at night and got settled in the condo with Jason, Natalie, and their two kids. Mom, Dad, Chad, Libby, and their two girls were in the condo next door. I was incredibly sensitive to the heat, and sleep was impossible because the condo had no air conditioning.

In the morning, I woke early and watched the sunrise from the lawn chairs by the water. Slowly, everyone trickled out from their rooms.

"Oh, I guess I can see a little belly there," Mom said.

When I told her that I'd been scouring the maternity clearance racks for any shorts left over from the summer season, she'd laughed and said, "I don't think you'll need those just yet." Mom had Jason when she was nineteen, and she was able to hide her pregnancy until she was six months along. She always said that I would likely be the same, and it wasn't until I showed her my swollen belly that she actually believed me and asked if I was sure it was only one baby. I imagined I'd have a cute, tanned belly in a bikini; instead, I was bloated, swollen, and covered in a heat rash.

We visited various parts of the island, following Mom's agenda to a T; it was the same schedule as my previous trip to Maui. The forced regiment of our family was new to Adam. He didn't understand that it wasn't our vacation, it was a *family* vacation. And that meant we would be spending every moment of every day with my family.

The twelve of us piled into two vehicles and took off to tour Lahaina. The air was breezy and much appreciated. We visited the banyan tree, watched the surfers, and saw a manta ray in the glistening water, just off the docks at the harbour. We followed Mom as she led from the forefront like a teacher with a group of students on a field trip. She gathered us together at a desolate green area just off the main strip.

"Okay, let's stop here for some lunch. Who's hungry?" she asked.

We sat down on the grass in the beating hot sun, not a sliver of shade within a mile. Mom dug into her cooler bag and passed out turkey and egg-salad sandwiches. They were on small buns carefully wrapped in Saran Wrap, just like when we were kids.

"You can't eat sandwich meat when you're pregnant!" I said to Adam.

I was shocked that she hadn't asked everyone what they wanted. I should not have been surprised that we were eating sandwiches in a park rather than going out for lunch. It was cheaper that way.

"It's okay, we'll find a spot to get some food," Adam said.

Adam is an exceptionally good cook and showed me what good food tastes like. I knew he wouldn't be satisfied with sweating turkey and mayo sandwiches. He lobbied that we should all get one hour to shop and do our own thing. Mom agreed but it came with a disapproving side-eye and some building resentment. Adam and I hurried to the first pizza shop within sight. I was so thankful that he'd had the courage to speak up. He still, at that point, didn't know what he was really dealing with when it came to my mom.

•

Two days later, Mom offered to take care of all four kids so Chad, Libby, Jason, and Natalie could take the Road to Hana. They asked if Adam and I wanted to join, but I'd been carsick the first time I went with my parents and knew it would be much worse now that I was pregnant. We politely declined and stayed back with my parents and the kids. It was very apparent that Mom had a favourite grandchild. Her favourite was Ella, Chad's youngest daughter. She looked like Chad. She was the youngest, and she was always by my mom's side. I felt bad for the other kids, watching the love from afar. I knew it all too well.

I was able to avoid Chad for most of the trip. Since he and his family were in the other condo, I could mostly steer clear of him. I sat at opposite ends of the table, and every interaction was brief and surface-level.

Mom and I took the kids for shaved ice and to play in the pool. Later in the day, Adam and I popped out for some shopping and a beautiful sunset dinner overlooking the ocean. I didn't see the harm in leaving but it came with raised eyebrows, and I could tell Mom was stirring in her own thoughts. I could read her mind and knew she had a message board running through her head: *She thinks she's better than us* and *Our food isn't good enough for them.* But she said nothing, just continued to let it boil.

•

The week, for the most part, went off without a hitch. We all went to a beautiful spot to take pictures and then had a wonderful dinner at a luau. My belly continued to grow, and I was even asked by complete strangers how many weeks I had left.

On our last day, we went to the pool with my family. We were taking the red-eye back to Calgary. Jason and Natalie were leaving the day after and, of course, Chad and his family were settled in for another week.

I waded slowly into the pool. A small section just off the stairs remained in the shade, and it was the only reprieve I'd felt in days. I stood there silently watching. The kids were all laughing, splashing, and taking turns jumping off the edge into my dad's arms. It was sweet seeing them as grandparents, and it made me think of how they'd be with my own child soon.

"You know, you can't be selfish when that baby comes along," Mom blurted out from the stairs.

She was sitting there sipping on her beer and Clamato juice. I didn't know what to say.

"Why would you say that?" I asked. I was exhausted and didn't have the strength for a fight.

"Well, I'm just letting you know."

"You have no idea what I'm going to be like as a mother," I said.

I stormed out of the pool and into the condo. She didn't know this, but I had already made it my life's goal to be the best mother I could be—and to be nothing like her.

She followed me into the condo and our argument escalated. Yells and screams escaped the open patio door. I sat on the couch with my towel wrapped around me, crying. I pleaded with her once again to go to therapy and work on our relationship. Adam came in, and I immediately felt comforted by his presence.

"Adam, you can leave, this doesn't concern you!" she yelled. Her eyes were black, and her face turned emotionless. She looked unrecognizable.

"It does when you're sitting here yelling at my pregnant wife! She's asking you to go to therapy to work on your relationship. Perhaps you're the one that needs to look in the mirror and figure out who's being selfish," he said.

He was the only one who came to my rescue. Everyone else, including my dad, stayed out by the pool. Adam knew how to ignite her anger and every single time he was able to remain composed. He could return verbal daggers that would make her explode. I admired his composure. I'd tried my entire life to have a sliver of that capability.

By the end of the argument, both of us receded to our own condos. I could tell everyone was mad at me. I had made her mad. It was a common occurrence between us, and every single time it was my fault.

"Fuck, Amber, why did you have to go and do that?" Chad asked.

He was fuming, and Libby wouldn't even speak to me. I wondered why he thought he had the right to confront me. Was it because he was staying with Mom, or because he was her favourite and felt he needed to stand up for her?

"What are you talking about? She's the one who started it in the pool . . ."

"Whatever, there's always an excuse," he said. "You always fucking do this. Why can't you just let shit go!"

I felt defeated. How much could one person just "let go" in a lifetime?

"Oh, yeah, like she ever says shit like that to you," I said.

I started to cry and immediately looked for Adam again. I felt like the black sheep in our family. Every time she was in a mood, they blamed me. This was no different.

•

Adam and I offered to take everyone out to dinner that night to make up for the dramatic afternoon. It was a generous offer that was completely unnecessary. Jason was kind and let me know it would be okay and they'd get over it, but we persisted and took them out for dinner anyway. We had our bags packed and we left shortly after we ate. On our way to the airport, Adam and I vowed that the family we were creating was the only thing that mattered to us, and we would protect it at all costs from Marlene and my family.

A BABY GIRL

I was due on May 23, 2014, with a baby girl. I was elated when I had my sixteen-week ultrasound and heard the news. A girl. It was everything I had ever wanted. A daughter of my own. I had heard recent stories of ultrasound technicians messing up the gender, so I decorated her nursery in teal and kept all the tags on her clothes until I met her in person.

At 6 a.m. on May 24, I awoke with my first contraction. They were manageable and just under ten minutes apart. Adam and I stayed home and continued to binge a TV series while I bounced on a ball. Later that evening, my contractions became more intense; they were now five minutes apart. We drove to the hospital where they confirmed I was only three centimetres dilated, and we were advised to return home to continue labouring.

It was an extremely long night. Our bedroom was lit by the moonlight peeking in through the blinds. It was just enough light to see my husband's face as he snored away in his slumber. I thought about hitting him with a pillow or perhaps smothering him just a little bit until he woke, in hopes he would offer to massage my back or get me some ice water. Anything to get him to utilize the important coaching techniques from our Birth and Babies class. Instead, I went back and forth from the shower to the bed, rocking on my hands and knees, wondering how my grandmother had managed to do this thirteen times.

By early morning, the contractions were becoming unbearable, and we headed back to the hospital. I was still only five centimetres dilated. Feeling extreme fatigue, we went back home to try and get some sleep. As soon as we pulled up to our home, I noticed a small trickle of fluid but thought nothing of it and went back to bed. After a few hours of sleep, we decided to go back to the hospital to check the fluid. My water had torn, and they needed to break the remaining fluid and admit me into the labour and delivery ward. They used what I can only describe as a long coat hanger of an instrument, and a tsunami came flooding out of me. I was relieved to know we were one step closer to seeing our little girl. They admitted me, and I was started on a slow drip of oxytocin and given an epidural.

I didn't understand why an epidural was so sought-after during labour. Mine only froze one side of my body at a time and ended up falling out halfway through my labour. As the hours went on, my contractions became longer, lasting twenty minutes with very little reprieve in between. An outline of my baby was visible in my belly as I experienced each contraction. My blood pressure started to spike at 220/150, and I was still only five centimetres dilated.

The woman in the next room was hysterical. We were fully divided and in two separate rooms, but her moans, groans, and screams were cascading through the halls and into my room.

"Will somebody give that woman a tranquilizer!" I yelled.

I was completely overwhelmed by pain, people, and sounds. She sounded like a farm animal who'd been hit by a semi-truck. At 11 p.m., a new doctor came in and I was delirious. He had asked if I wanted to labour for another hour, with the chance of needing a C-section, or have a C-section then. I couldn't make the decision so I looked to Adam to make it for me, but he wouldn't.

"You can do this, love," he said.

"No, I can't. I can't do it anymore."

The doctor advised that he needed to check me prior to performing a C-section.

"No, you don't need to do that. The nurse over there just checked me. You can go ask her how many centimetres I am," I said. It seemed to me that he was looking for an excuse to feel me up.

"If you want a C-section, I have to make sure you're not past the point," he insisted.

Adam quickly chimed in. "It's okay, honey. He's a doctor."

"I'll give you guys a minute and check back on you shortly," the doctor said, leaving the room.

"What's the matter, hon? Why don't you want him to check you?"

"He doesn't look like a doctor. He's wearing a wife beater and a gold chain with Oakleys on his head. He's just trying to finger me!"

"Hon, I think you're exhausted. We need to let him check you so they can take the baby out safely, okay? The doctor is wearing surgical glasses and scrubs, okay? I'm right here with you."

The doctor came back in, and I reluctantly let him check me to confirm, yet again, that I was only five centimetres dilated. I was prepped and wheeled into the operating room.

They offered to top up my epidural, but seeing as it wasn't working at all, I demanded a spinal. Adam came into the operating room dressed in surgical coveralls. My blood pressure spiked again, and I immediately went into shock. They pulled out a baby girl, blue in colour, and rushed her over to a team of NICU doctors. There were no tears, no sounds. I shook uncontrollably as two doctors pinned me down. One put their knee on my arm and tried to get a blood pressure reading. They wrapped me in a dozen warm blankets and sutured me up before wheeling me over to the post-operative ward.

I had been in labour for forty-two hours. I was depleted of all energy and still shaking. They brought over my baby girl in a small bassinet and told me that once I stopped shaking, I could hold her. "Please, I need to hold her," I pleaded with the nurse. She brought her over and placed her on my chest. The minute we touched, the shaking stopped. Our hearts were reunited. She was eight pounds, four ounces, and her name was Monroe Isla Grray. Because my water tore, our baby was exposed to the Group B strep bacteria. Monroe would spend the next five days in the NICU, being monitored and given antibiotics for a fever that spiked during the C-section. They called her "the big girl."

•

We asked our families to give us a week to ourselves after the baby was born. But with all the commotion and chaos, Mom and Dad decided to drive out to Calgary. They visited me and we took turns seeing Monroe in the NICU. When we finally brought her home, it was time for Dad to head back to work in Saskatoon. Mom stayed an extra week, and while we were in the hospital, she puttered around the house cleaning and washing windows. She cooked meals and was everything I needed her to be during that time. She helped me get dressed, and she put lotion on my legs after I showered. This was the third time in my life that I really needed to be taken care of and she was there.

THE GIFT OF THERAPY

The first year of being a new mom wasn't easy. Monroe was exclusively breastfed and was shy and clingy. She gravitated toward me and rarely let Adam hold her unless she could see me. Yet she was my entire world, and I was determined to be a better mom to her than my mom was to me. Adam and I struggled a lot during that first year. We were completely naive in thinking that a baby wouldn't change our lives.

Adam was taking a brokerage course and was spending hours each night studying. On weekends, he wanted to spend time with his friends, blowing off steam and having a few drinks. I felt so alone. I needed a break. I'd lost my previous identity now that I'd become a mother. I felt like I was drowning in breastmilk stains, dirty diapers, and excess body fat. At the one-year mark, Monroe started daycare, and Adam and I decided to give therapy a chance. I chose a therapist who was highly regarded and specialized in Imago therapy, which incorporates your childhood into your relationship. Imago therapy helps you to understand yourself and your partner better.

We started our first session by expressing our wants and needs, as well as sharing our feelings about the past year. Our sessions gradually started to focus on our childhoods.

"Tell me about your Mom, Amber," our therapist said.

"Well, we haven't always had the best relationship. I feel like she favours my brother Chad. Our arguments are very heated, and she's unpredictable on a good day. She doesn't like it when my dad and I spend time together. She yells and says extremely mean things, but if someone comes over, then she acts like a completely different person."

I looked to Adam to see if that sounded correct and if there was anything he wanted to add.

"Yeah, that sounds right," he said. "The first time she directed it toward me was when we went to Saskatoon when Monroe was six weeks old. I was packing up the car early in the morning while Amber got the baby fed and dressed. Marlene came out of her room and accused me of trying to sneak out without saying goodbye. She was furious with me and, of course, that was never our intent."

"Do you ever feel like you're walking on eggshells around her?"

"Oh, all the time." We both agreed.

"It sounds like what you're describing is borderline personality disorder. And a lot of the time, narcissistic personality disorder will be associated with someone with borderline, especially if you notice them always portraying the victim in any given scenario or argument. Has your mom ever been diagnosed or seen a therapist to confirm that?"

"No, she would never see a therapist. I've asked her to so many times, but she refuses."

"Well, I'd like you to do some reading and learn as much as you can about BPD and NPD to see if it sounds familiar. There are many resources and books that have been written that can help."

This was the first time that I had ever heard of borderline personality disorder or narcissistic personality disorder. For my entire life, I'd thought there must have been some standout moment that flipped the switch in my mom and how she felt about me. It had to be something I did, and for the last twenty-five years, I'd been trying to win her over and make her love me.

•

I did exactly what our therapist suggested. I went straight to Amazon and purchased every book that related to BPD, while keeping an eye out for books that were specific to mothers with BPD. The minor issues in our marriage seemed to be a cake walk in comparison to understanding my mom, and this was such a blessing in disguise.

My mind was completely blown when I started to dive into borderline personality disorder. Monroe napped while I sat on my bed, scattered in books. I was itching to dive fully into each book, like a small child in a candy store, eager to get my hands on every kind of gummy candy. I took one book at a time and read it thoroughly from cover to cover. I highlighted and flagged pages that resonated with me.

I learned that people with BPD have high distress and anger levels and typically have trouble regulating their emotions. They can be unpredictable, causing their loved ones to tiptoe around them, being careful not to upset them. People living with BPD can have an intense fear of instability and abandonment, with an overwhelming sense of emptiness. They tend to be impulsive and act erratically. They try to take control of situations and other people to make their own world seem more predictable and manageable.

This sounded exactly like my mother. As I continued to learn more about BPD, and the correlation of narcissistic personality disorder, I realized that she had these traits, too. People who are diagnosed with NPD lack empathy for other people, are highly insecure with low self-esteem, and can be quite needy. They will typically turn a conversation about someone else around and back toward themselves, creating an opportunity for praise or sympathy. For daughters of NPD mothers who have a good relationship with their fathers, it will create an unsteady relationship with their mothers, fuelled by jealousy and rage. Sons of NPD mothers are typically more liked, until they get married when their new wife may feel the repercussions of jealousy as they compete for her son's attention and influence she has over him.

I sat there with an incredulous expression. This was an earth-shattering revelation to me. It wasn't in my head, and it wasn't something I'd done to make her this way.

"Miiim," a small sweet sound of Monroe calling for me came over the monitor. My baby was awake. I greeted her with my usual good morning song, even though it was the afternoon. She smiled with her few tiny teeth, and I kissed her soft cheek. She was my why, my reason to forge through and heal my inner child so I could be everything she needed me to be.

I began the extremely long process of starting to grieve the mother I wished I had, to understand that she wasn't physically or emotionally capable of being who I needed her to be. She would never be capable of change, and I knew now that it was up to me to change myself. I would learn how to love my inner child the way I deserved to be loved. I would for myself and my daughter.

A NEW HOME

I was eight months pregnant with my second daughter. I was incredibly grateful to find out that she, too, was a girl. I'd developed a fear that if I were to have a son, I wouldn't be able to love him like I could a daughter. I held such resentment for the way my mother loved Chad. She always told me that her mom favoured the boys in her family, and it was obvious that Chad was her chosen one. I worried I would repeat the pattern and end up being just like her. With my second daughter, my most wished upon dream was coming true.

We sold our first home and moved into a townhome rental. Adam had this obscure idea that we could wait out the market while it declined and bottomed out before we'd jump back in and buy our dream house. It seemed elaborate, but I put my full trust in him and went along with his plan. We had been living in the townhome for a few months by the time I became pregnant. This fuelled our desire to find our dream home and we did. It was a newer two-story craftsman home in our desired area, within walking distance from a school.

We took possession in early November and wasted no time getting moved in. Adam was scheduled to be away on a work trip the day after we took possession, so I asked my dad if he would be willing to help me with the move. To my surprise, he said yes. I was waiting for my mom to interject and say he couldn't, but they planned for him to come out for a week, then she would fly out for the weekend and drive home with him. Up until this point, I hadn't spent any consistent amount of time with my dad, just the two of us. When I moved to Calgary, Dad would come out for work on an annual basis. He'd stay in a hotel for three days to meet with head office executives and attend meetings. Mom always told me that he was too busy to see me and not to waste my time trying. But each year, I would text and ask if I could drive him to and from the airport just to have even fifteen minutes with him.

Life is filled with core memories, both good and bad, and this was a great one. Of course, moving comes with its own challenges, especially with a husband that is away, being very pregnant, and having a toddler and a dog to look after. But it was time that I'd never experienced before.

Dad helped me assemble the beds and get the rooms set up. I took three days off work to move. We worked all day and night to unpack the house and still made time to sit in the morning with coffee while we watched the planes fly by.

"This is an exceptional house, Am. Well done."

"Thanks, Dad. I think so, too. It's the house we've always wanted. It seems so surreal. Do you think Mom will like it?"

"What's not to like!"

We sat there brainstorming design ideas and listing our most-liked areas of the house for some time before we agreed we'd better get back to work.

•

We picked Mom up from the airport on Friday. Dad and I both went inside to greet her with a hug. I was beyond tired from our week of work, but there was still so much left to do, and I wanted to get the nursery set up. I needed to start nesting. I could tell something was wrong with Mom when we saw her at the airport. Perhaps she was hoping for Monroe to be there but having her at daycare was my only saving grace to getting anything accomplished that week. We picked her up on our way home and she greeted her grandma with a big hug and a kiss.

We pulled into the garage, unloaded her suitcase, and headed into the house.

"What do you think, Mom?" I asked excitedly.

"Oh, yep, it's a nice house," she said.

She seemed reserved. We ordered pizza and got caught up when it was delivered. But something about her was still off. I went to bed early that night in hopes she would be in a better mood the next day. Sleep wasn't great. I was getting up to pee multiple times each night, and Monroe was fussing at least once because we were in a new space.

Early the next morning, Dad took Monroe to the park. They had legendary park visits, riding each slide multiple times and playing on the swings. She would come back exhausted. I sat down and was eager to finish the kitchen. Numerous casserole dishes and bakeware still needed to be unpacked, so I cozied up to the lazy Susan and started arranging dishes while Mom was getting ready to take a shower.

"Amber! I need a washcloth!"

That sound was all too familiar and sounded exactly as it had when I was a child. It was the way she said it, too. No manners, just the demand that I get it for her.

"They're upstairs in the hall closet," I yelled back.

"Pardon me?"

It was her signature phrase. She was furious about my last comment. I knew that, so I said it again.

"There are a bunch upstairs in the linen closet."

"Well, would you mind getting me one!" she said with irritation.

I huffed a grunt of displeasure. If only I had a working crane in my kitchen to help get my ass up off the floor. I worked my way from my hands and knees to my feet and stomped up the stairs, huffing and puffing. I found a washcloth and threw it downstairs toward her. In retrospect, I should've tossed a dishcloth to her with the hope she wouldn't notice.

"You didn't have to throw it at me!"

"I didn't realize you were standing right there, and you could've gone and gotten it."

Mom had a stare that could kill, and it was all too familiar.

She took a shower and came up to the master bedroom. I was sitting on the floor in the bathroom, unpacking toiletries. She unleashed everything she didn't like about the house: from the amount of cupboard space to the size of the bathroom drawers. She wasn't excited for us. She was angry.

"Why can't you just be happy for us?"

"I never said I wasn't, Amber."

"Yeah, but you don't have anything nice to say about it."

"It's not the house, Amber, it's you! You were pissed that I even came. I could see it in your face at the airport."

Dad was at the park with Monroe, so I knew she would spew hatred with zero hesitation.

"You think you're better than everyone else, don't you? You think you can just sit here and shit on everyone else with your fucking attitude. Well, you can think again. I won't stand for it. I'm not putting up with your shit anymore. You're ungrateful and you don't get to treat me that way."

"What are you talking about? Yeah, I'm tired. I've been moving all week and I'm pregnant. But I wouldn't exactly say giving you an expensive purse yesterday is treating you like shit."

She seemed to forget about the Michael Kors handbag I'd given her the day before after she said she needed a new purse. She stormed down the stairs and headed to the guest room.

"Oh, I know you don't want me here. I bet you and your dad had the best week just talking all kinds of shit about me, didn't you? Well,

I'm done with you, Amber. I'm so fucking tired of you always treating me like shit. We're leaving." She started to frantically pack her bags.

"You go ahead and leave, but Dad can stay."

"Over my dead body!"

Just as our volume started to escalate, my dad walked in the door with Monroe. She was smiling from her fun time with Papa at the park.

"Hi, baby, did you have fun?" I asked as I scooped her up into my arms, tears streaming down my face.

Dad could tell that we were fighting and that tensions were high.

"Ben! Pack your bags, we're leaving!"

She grabbed her suitcase and told him to meet her in the car. She swung the front door open.

"You've gone and done it, Amber. You always treat me like shit. You can be so nice to your dad and everyone else, but when it comes to me, you just shit on me over and over again. But you know what? I'm fucking done with you, you fucking bitch."

Our little dog, Piper, immediately ran out the front door. She tended to bolt and run away. I was holding Monroe through the entire rant and the only thing that I could manage to say was "What is wrong with you?"

I grabbed Piper and put her inside, shutting the door behind me. I could only imagine what a full sprint down the street would do to me at this point. Piper was a runner. I looked at my mom as she marched toward the truck. I took a deep breath and tried to understand what was happening and how exactly this had all escalated. I tried to think of what I learned about BPD, and characteristics started popping into my head. Controlling, insecurities, jealousy, victim mentality, outbursts, boundaries. Yes, boundaries!

"You know, it's one thing to talk to me like that when it's just me, but it's another thing to talk like that in front of my daughter. I'm not going to tolerate it, and I'm done with you, too."

"Good!" she replied as she threw her bags in the backseat of the truck.

She got in and slammed the door. I went back inside, completely frazzled and embarrassed. We were the new people on the block, and I'm sure our neighbours had heard that fight. Dad put on his shoes and held his suitcase. I could tell that he was annoyed and once again I felt like it was because of me.

"You don't have to go, Dad."

"Yes, I do. If I don't, I'll never hear the end of it."

I knew he was right, but I wasn't ready to say goodbye. We both knew that for the next six hours he would listen to her explode about how ungrateful I was. He would be a target, too, for the time we'd just spent together.

"I'm so sorry, Dad."

"I'm sorry, too."

"Thank you for your help this week."

We gave each other a big hug. He told me that he loved me before he walked out the door and headed toward his truck.

I had planned a nice dinner out for the four of us that night, but it was just Monroe and me now. We dressed up and drove to the restaurant.

"Why did Grandma and Papa leave?" Monroe's small voice asked from the backseat.

"I don't know, baby, they just had to go home."

"Cause they had to go see Ella?"

It was clear that even a two-year-old could tell that my mom's most-dearest grandchild was Ella. Every story, or comparison, was always about Ella.

"You know, Monroe, maybe. But I'm happy that it's just you and me, baby girl, because I get you all to myself and I can give you so many hugs and kisses."

She smiled a big smile, with both rows of her tiny teeth showing.

"I love you, Mommy."

"I love you too, baby."

A NEW BOUNDARY

I knew that if I wanted to give my daughters a different life than what I had, I needed to protect them. I wanted to create a shield around them and keep them from my mother, but it wasn't that easy. She was an excellent grandma. She was everything I'd wished for when I was young. When she visited, she sat and played with Monroe and took her to the park. She brought presents every time she and my dad visited. She was physically affectionate, generous with hugs and kisses. *How is she capable of this type of love?* I wondered. It infuriated me. Each moment I saw this version of her poured salt on old wounds. Scars partially healed were cut open once again. I wasn't resentful of my daughter, but I was resentful of my mother. I knew she had love in her to give, she just wasn't willing to give it to me.

•

I pulled into the Toys "R" Us parking lot mid-December of 2016. The heat was on full blast in my car. My belly hung out of my coat, the zipper unable to close. The phone rang and it was her. I'd been ignoring her for the past six weeks, and it had been liberating. Before the fight, we had made plans for my parents to stay with Monroe during my scheduled C-section. I knew that it was the only reason she was calling. I knew she wanted to be here for the birth of my second daughter, and she knew I needed them.

I answered the phone. We both apologized. She apologized for yelling at me in front of Monroe, and I apologized for making her feel unwelcome and for being tired. Saying *I'm sorry* was the easiest way to end arguments with her. I had become an expert at crafting apologies, whatever it took to make the fighting stop and to put her in a better mood. No matter what I did, or how I made her feel, it was always my fault. At the end of the conversation, she asked if we still wanted her and Dad to come out for the birth.

"Sure, that's fine. But I will say this, Mom: if you want a relationship with my children, then you need to have one with me. And if you ever act like that in front of my kids again, you will be out of our lives for good."

"It takes two, Amber."

"I understand that, but I wasn't the one swearing in front of a toddler."

It was the first time I had ever put her back in her place. This boundary was needed for my daughters' sake. We hung up the phone and for the first time in a long time, I felt like I could stand a little taller.

•

A few weeks later, they arrived at my house and settled in to take care of Monroe. I was experiencing a lot of contractions and was slightly worried I would deliver early. Mom was on her best behaviour, and Adam was watching her every move.

Adam and I went to the hospital on January 9 at 6:30 a.m. to get prepped for surgery. By 10:05 a.m., this incredible baby girl was placed beside me. She was beyond perfect. This experience was vastly different from my first delivery. I looked down at her, wrapped in her swaddle, and it was an overwhelming love at first sight. We were both wheeled into our private room, and she nursed for most of the day. Life as I knew it was now complete. I had a beautiful, healthy baby girl named Quinn Presley.

I spent my year of maternity leave in a euphoric bliss. I spoke to my dad on the phone every day. He'd been recently laid off from his job, after returning from his cancer treatment. He was still bringing in a paycheque through severance, and Mom was working. He was free to do what he wanted between the hours of 8 a.m. and 4 p.m. Each of our conversations lasted an hour or more. The sound of our voices on speakerphone soon became Quinn's lullaby as she drifted off to sleep each day.

"Hey, what did you guys get up to last night?" I sat in my rocking chair nursing Quinn before her nap. My phone rested on the edge of her crib, and Dad's voice echoed through her floral nursery.

"Oh, Chad and Libby came over with the kids. Mom asked them to stay for supper."

"Fun," I said in a sarcastic tone. Chad and Libby had been spending a lot of time at my parents' house lately.

"Yeah, they wanted to know if she would babysit this weekend and take the kids for the night. It's the same every time."

I knew exactly what Dad was talking about. Chad was a user.

"Classic Chad. You know I'm never going to be close with Chad ever again," I said.

"Well, you never know."

"No, I do. And I won't."

I didn't have the courage to tell Dad about the abuse in that moment, but by this time, it was festering and simmering inside of me.

"Do you remember when I mentioned we were going to Osoyoos this summer?" I asked.

" Yeah," he said.

"Well, apparently Chad and Libby are going out to British

Columbia around the same time, and they asked if they could stay a night at our house on the way. I said we wouldn't be home, and Mom got mad at me because I wouldn't leave the key so they can stay here while we're gone."

"Seriously?" he said.

I paused for a moment, switching a sleepy Quinn over to my other breast.

"Yeah. She said, 'Well you could do that for him! He's your brother, Amber.' And she got all huffy with me, but I still said no."

"That's bullshit. You don't have to do that. It's your house!" Dad said.

"I know! That's what I said."

"He can pay for his own hotel!"

I placed my perfectly sound-sleeping baby into her crib before turning on her sound machine. I grabbed my phone and closed the door behind me.

"I'm going to let you go now. I have to hop in the shower," I said.

"Okay. Chat tomorrow?"

"You bet!"

"Love you!"

"Love you too, Dad."

I hung up the phone and took a long, much-needed shower. The hot water cascaded down on my shoulders, sore and stiff from being hunched over during feeds. I replayed our conversation in my head. That was the extent of my relationship with Chad and Libby. We exchanged happy birthday text messages twice a year. We saw them once a year if they came out in our direction for summer vacation or to stay one night for a dance showcase. We were a landing pad. They spent most of their spare time shopping at the malls, or occasionally they would rent a hotel for their second night so they could swim, but an invitation to join would never come.

Mom started to get suspicious of my phone calls with Dad. She would look at the phone bills and go over every outgoing call. She would filter through the call log on the phone to see if I was the one to call him. It made her furious to see how much time we spent talking. "What could you possibly talk about for an hour and twenty minutes?" she would ask him.

We started to end every conversation with "We didn't talk today, okay?" Dad would delete my number from the call log, and I would continue with my weekly calls to my parents, pretending we hadn't spoken all week.

It was the beginning of our covert relationship.

MY VERSION OF MOTHERHOOD

Motherhood changes you. It has a way of bringing all your insecurities to the surface. Every decision you make, you question whether you're doing the right thing. Who will have higher therapy bills: them or me? You lose your sense of self in the process and are entirely consumed with this new human being. As I looked in the mirror, I didn't recognize myself: my once perfect breasts were now sagging, and my petite waistline was swollen. But looking down at my baby, I wouldn't change a thing. I am superhuman. I always wanted to be a mother. Having two girls was my dream, and I wanted to do it differently. At first, I thought that if I raised them the opposite of how my mom raised me, they would turn out okay. But I soon realized that wouldn't be enough.

I needed to be cognizant of what really mattered. I wanted to raise strong, independent daughters, daughters who believed in women's rights and equality and not what I was taught, that women should be good wives and housekeepers. My daughters would be raised to speak up when they didn't agree with something or when they felt hurt. They wouldn't have to swallow their feelings and bury them out of fear of affecting someone else. I wanted to raise children who treated everyone with respect no matter the colour of their skin, nationality, gender, religion, or personal beliefs. My mother's opinions about race would not pass on to another generation.

I was never told it was okay to say no. Consent was not something I was taught. I wanted to raise children who were kind and sensitive to the needs of others, but who also had the ability to say no thank you if it didn't suit their own needs. My daughters would learn that there are no gender-specific duties, and they would understand that men can do dishes and cook meals. I wanted my girls to learn the value and privilege of an education and being financially sound on their own two feet. I felt the burden of being the only one in my family who went to university, when it should have been celebrated and supported.

I wanted to provide a safe haven for them. I wanted them to know they can always come to me in person; they do not need to write their concerns in a book. I needed to teach them to value their body and treat it like the temple that it is, not succumb to pressure. And lastly, I wanted them to find someone who truly loves them for all that they are, without reservation; a partner with the strength to stand by them as they grow, stumble, and fall in their life together, just as their dad has done with me. For me, it wasn't enough to just want to do things differently.

One evening, I walked past the bathroom and overheard my mother-in-law bathing my daughter. "Here, take this washcloth and wash your privates, please," she said. It caught me by surprise. Monroe was three. I leaned up against the wall on the other side of the bathroom, still within earshot. I was a thirty-three-year-old mother, and I had never been taught this. My mother-in-law wasn't reaching in with a hand and a bar of soap like my mother had done for so many years. She was teaching Monroe to have autonomy over her own body.

It would take me years to find my way through the fog of young motherhood and realize where these feelings came from. In the moment, they presented themselves as anxiety or shock. But I would eventually make sense of these feelings as my childhood traumas unravelled.

LOSING MYSELF IN THE DARKNESS

I returned to work when my maternity leave ended. I was still working for the same Fortune 500 company. I had turned down the opportunity to transfer to Toronto because my dad was diagnosed with cancer. I needed to be close to him and moving across the country didn't seem like a good idea at the time. I had the same position as an account manager, but unbeknownst to me at the time, I was in a glass box. Over the years I'd applied for multiple positions, even lateral moves. My results were excellent, but I was always passed up.

I struggled to juggle my children, preschool drop-offs and pickups, daycare drop-offs and pickups, a corporate job, laundry, groceries, and doctor appointments. It was all exceedingly too much to handle. I asked my boss if I could work from home two days a week, specifically the days when Monroe needed to be picked up from daycare and taken to junior kindergarten, then picked up three hours later and taken back to daycare. It wasn't an ideal program, but Adam and I were trying to make it work. Unfortunately, my work declined my request and the pressure continued to intensify.

A few months after returning to work, I sat one night with Adam and told him how frustrated and depressed I felt.

"Hon, I've never seen you this upset before. I think you need to consider quitting or finding something else," Adam said.

He was right. I wanted to be home with our children, and I wanted a job that allowed me to give back to others in a positive way. We sat together and Adam did the math of my salary after taxes and the cost of daycare. It made financial sense, but my not having a steady income and purpose weighed on me. I wanted my daughters to see me as an independent woman. I battled with my subconscious and the fear that Adam would own me or that it was his money.

"You need to make this decision, though. I can't make it for you. I can only support you through it," he said.

For most of my life, I'd been told what I could and could not do. This man was pushing and supporting me to be the independent woman I always wanted to be.

As my emotional struggle continued, we noticed that our pup was beginning to act strangely. Initially, we thought she had a UTI when she started to urinate in the house. She was tired and sleeping a lot, but she was four and a half years old, and we were a busy household. We got her medication, and for a few days she seemed to get better, until she plummeted. She started forgetting what she was doing and would stare at the wall until you went over and touched her or called her name. We took her to the vet, and they confirmed she had a neurological deficit and told us to head to the animal hospital right away. After waiting hours, they confirmed she had GME. Granulomatous meningoencephalomyelitis is the medical term for a disease that affects the brain and spinal cord, causing them to swell. Adam and I were devastated.

I resigned from my job to spend time with Piper and to raise our girls. I couldn't handle the additional pressure, the feeling of failing my children, and being constantly surrounded by corporate negativity. A couple of weeks after our dog was diagnosed, she passed away peacefully at home. The girls were surprisingly resilient, but her absence left a large hole of depression in my heart.

THERAPY

"Well, this feels like a nice change to your story!" Dr. M. smiled at me from her usual chair.

It was the first time she had smiled since I'd started seeing her. I smiled back, knowing she was right. My life wasn't all bad.

"How did you feel hearing about borderline and narcissistic personality disorder?" she asked.

"Honestly? Relieved."

"How so?"

"It provided a reason for her behaviour, an external factor. I didn't have to blame her; I could blame the BPD. It wasn't something I did to make her behave and treat me the way she did. If I could look at it that way, then I could find a sense of forgiveness for the relationship that we had."

"That's very big of you to say. Do you feel like you've forgiven her?"

"I'm working on it. I do feel like I have grieved for the mother I wish I had, but I worry that it's hereditary."

"What is?"

"BPD and NPD. I think about it a lot. It's a big fear of mine, actually."

"The fact that you are aware of it, and understand what BPD is, makes me feel comfortable in telling you that you don't have borderline or narcissistic personality disorder."

I felt instant relief. Suddenly I felt like I was on the right track to break the chains of generational trauma. My shoulders relaxed as I sat back on the couch. I looked over to the other chair in the room. It was always empty, and I never chose to sit in it.

"I commend you for your efforts to be a better mother to your children. It's not an easy job, let alone to heal your own trauma and make a conscious effort to give your daughters a different life than the one you had. You should be very proud of yourself."

"Thank you," I said with an authentic smile. It was one of the nicest compliments I had ever received.

"We'll pick this up again next week," she said.

FINDING NEW PURPOSE

As the fog started to lift, I found new purpose and excitement in becoming an entrepreneur. I started my own interior design business, specializing in children's design. Ever since I was young, I'd had a passion for positively affecting the lives of children. I thought being a teacher was the biggest impact I could make, but after growing and becoming a mother, I realized there was another way. When I was a little girl, my safe space was my room. It wasn't my house or my family, it was the four walls that surrounded me when I was alone. My room was my sanctuary. It brought me peace as a child and that peace returned to me as a mother, breastfeeding my babies in their nurseries at night. I knew that I could help provide other children with a safe sanctuary in their lives, even if it was just the four walls that surrounded them.

I set out to build my business slowly, while still taking care of my girls. Room by room, I built up my business and created a vibrant portfolio of beautiful children's spaces, all of which embraced a calm, serene feeling. I still struggled to find time to do it all, to complete an installation or book a consult, with two littles in my full-time care. I tried to give myself forgiveness, to remind myself this was supposed to be a slow build, and to remember that this time with my girls mattered most.

That fall we adopted a Boston terrier, a baby girl we named Lennon. She was feisty and followed me around everywhere. She struggled with training, but we were determined to be consistent. We noticed a couple things that didn't quite make sense: she never came to her name, and she startled when we woke her. I texted Adam at work one day and suggested we get her hearing checked out. We contacted the breeder, and she sent over a team that conducted hearing tests for animals. Lennon was completely deaf, and we were advised to have her re-homed in the hearing-impaired community. I wanted so badly to keep her, but she needed someone who knew sign language in addition to having an older dog that was already trained. We agreed and helped our breeder interview candidates. We found the perfect new home with a family that had recently lost a deaf dog and that had a two-year-old Boston terrier and a ten-year-old daughter. Although it broke my heart to let her go, we knew it was the best decision for her.

UNABLE TO SILENCE

My depression was unpredictable. It was like a bobber on a fishing line; most days it was visible, and on others, it was submerged and out of sight. I tried to distract myself by building a new website for my business, redecorating our house, and organizing every nook and cranny. It was 2020, and we were on lockdown during the pandemic. I found myself surrounded within the walls of our home. My children were taking virtual classes and Adam was down in the basement, trying to keep his company afloat. My health seemed to be declining on top of my depression. I had various symptoms of multiple sclerosis including numbness in all my limbs and vision problems, amongst others. I underwent multiple tests. Every result came back negative, and my doctor more than ever was convinced it was just my depression. What I didn't know at the time was that it was my trauma causing my ailments.

•

I pulled a warm load of clothes from the dryer and felt my body collapse on top of the basket. I began to sob uncontrollably. It finally hit me. I needed help. A few licks on my arm pulled me out of the darkness. It was Kaiser, our Boston terrier, who we'd gotten the summer after Lennon left us. Adam was happy he was a boy, and I was just happy he was mine. I pulled Kaiser into my lap and sat silently, smelling his ears, and kissing his face. The love of a pup has always meant so much to me.

Later that day, I sat with Adam. He was gathering things from the fridge to make dinner.

"I think I'm going to start antidepressants," I said.

"Why, are you depressed?" he asked.

"Yeah, I think so. I have some sad days when I just cry for no reason. Haven't you noticed a change in me?"

"Not really, but if that's what you need, then do it."

That was the extent of our conversation, and my walls instantly became taller and stronger. Our marriage was struggling and had been for a year. Our evenings were spent apart, each one of us drifting to opposite ends of the house for a quiet reprieve at the end of the day. We rarely went out on dates, and when we did, we had surface-level conversations, we fought, or I ended up crying. I didn't realize it at the time, but I knew this was my depression rearing its head and it was my cry for help. I grew inwards and sheltered all my feelings because I didn't feel safe.

Our marriage, from all exterior views, was decent. But what we lacked was the ability to be vulnerable with each other. I don't mean the "I need help, I'm overwhelmed with the kids" type of vulnerability. I mean the real stuff. Deep, emotional vulnerability. We'd previously skidded through aspects of my marriage to Damian, but it was always too much for Adam. He couldn't handle hearing the struggles I'd faced and how much hurt Damian caused, so I concealed everything else.

I booked an appointment with my doctor, and she recommended that I start therapy in addition to Zoloft. My first six sessions with the therapist Alberta Health provided consisted of the typical pandemic-related depression support: suggestions about how to change my lifestyle by working out, eating healthy, getting fresh air, getting enough sleep, and meditating. It all sounded like good ideas, but I knew it wouldn't be enough for me.

I knew it wasn't a lack of sleep, or high stress, or even being in lockdown that was causing my depression. It was the thought that popped into my head like clockwork every morning for the last two years: *my brother had anal sex with me.*

It resurfaced after being buried for the past twenty-five years. Sure, it had reared its head a time or two over the years, but I always managed to snuff it out and bury it even deeper than the time before. I was determined to do the same this time, except now it was an acidic poison burning in my body and permeating through my limbs, causing them to become numb. It was a poison I could no longer ignore.

I was referred to a new therapist who specialized in long-term depression. I felt seen for the first time in a long time. We spent our first two sessions discussing my overall mental health, depression, recent lifestyle changes, and my marriage with Adam. At the end of the second session, she said something that would forever change my life.

"Amber, I want you to take some time over the next week. I'm giving you permission to dig deep into your past. Bring all your emotions and traumas to the surface and sit with them. I'm going to warn you—it's going to get dark—and it is going to be really tough, but I need you to do it."

No one had ever given me permission to do this before. No one ever had the inclination that something was wrong deep inside me. So, I did what she asked. I regurgitated my childhood trauma, and I sat uncomfortably with it for the next five days.

MY TRUTH

Adam's mother, Cyd, came into town during the long weekend in July 2021. She watched the kids while Adam and I went out for a date night. Date nights weren't something we regularly did. We didn't have a roster of babysitters, and my parents hadn't been to visit in over a year because of the pandemic. Mom was worried that Dad would get Covid and become very ill because of his previous cancer. They were skeptical of coming while the kids were in school even though they still managed to visit with Chad and his family.

Three days had passed since I acknowledged my childhood trauma. I was sitting in it. It was like quicksand that kept pulling me down, engulfing my body and snuffing out every breath I tried to take. But I kept treading. I decided to dress for our date in something that would take my mind off everything and make me feel flirty. I settled on a leather pencil skirt with a tight cropped tee and snakeskin heels. The outfit hugged every inch of my curves and oozed sex in its simplicity. I was hoping it would make Adam take a second look.

We headed to a restaurant in the outskirts of Calgary and sat at a table for two in a beautifully designed restaurant. It was quiet, and only a few tables were occupied. Our conversation consisted mostly of discussing Adam's work, as it usually did. My work life always seemed more predictable and insignificant. I juggled a few projects at a time while shuttling the kids to and from school and activities. Every time I began to talk about what was happening in my world, Adam found a way to interrupt me and lead the conversation back to himself.

We nibbled over bites of Brussels sprouts, and my mind started to wander. I began suffocating in the quicksand. In this moment, I felt invisible. As we continued our dinner, tears welled in my eyes. I didn't know how to tell Adam that I was struggling, that I felt weak, that I wanted him to choose me and hold me up from the drowning waters that were pulling me down.

"I just want to feel chosen, that you want to be with me," I said.

We were discussing Adam's next trip. It was in celebration of his fortieth birthday: a weeklong golf trip with his friends.

"You spend all of this time planning trips with your friends, but you can't even book a date night with me, let alone a trip!" I said.

"Why would I want to spend more time with you when all you do is cry in your soup!" he said.

This whole time I thought I was waving a yellow flag, but it turned out to be completely invisible to the male eye.

As we drove home, we threw every dagger possible at each other, each one cutting deeper than the last. There were words that I regret, and words that hurt so deeply they are still burning ash in the lining of my heart. Adam was calling it quits.

"If there is no love there, then what's the point? Why would I stick around?" he asked.

I couldn't fathom what he was saying. He wasn't going to fight for me or our family? He was going to cut and run.

"Aren't we worth fighting for?" I asked.

"Why would I fight for someone who doesn't want me, who isn't attracted to me?"

"That's not what I meant. I'm going through some things right now in therapy. Do you want to know what it is?"

"No. I don't."

It was like a punch in the gut. So cold and harsh.

We went up to our girls' rooms and peeked in while they were sleeping. It broke my heart to think we were about to upend their lives and idea of family as they knew it.

As tears ran down my face, I looked up at Adam and said, "I'm still in this. I don't want to quit. You and our family are worth every ounce of fight I have."

He didn't say anything, but he gave me a hug and I went to bed. I cried most of the night and didn't get more than a few minutes of sleep. Adam spent the rest of the evening talking to his mom before he came to bed. As I laid there, I couldn't help but think of the day Damian had said he'd rather sign a separation agreement than go to therapy together. Here I was in the same situation, wanting my husband to fight for me, but instead, they both chose to walk away. It was me. I was the reason. The commonality between both marriages was me. I was the one person who wasn't worth the fight. I started to spiral in my thoughts and then suddenly stopped myself. *Amber, stop it!* I was working on self-love and positive affirmations through therapy sessions, but sometimes I forgot and regressed to my old ways. *You are gorgeous, and you are incredibly smart. You are the best mother, and your girls adore you. You are a tough-ass bitch, and don't you forget it. You are unforgettable.*

"Unforgettable" was a word a colleague once used to describe me. He preceded it with compliments about being a woman with such beauty and intelligence, and he genuinely tried to assure me that it wasn't meant to sound creepy, but that if he could describe me in one word it would be "unforgettable." It had stuck with me all these years.

The next morning, I awoke with a fresh set of tears rolling down my cheeks, my eyes puffy and red.

"Hey, I think we should go talk outside," Adam said.

He didn't initiate many conversations, but this gave me hope. We sat outside on the front porch, each with a hot cup of coffee.

"I'm so sorry for last night," I said.

"I know, I am, too. But it doesn't change what was said or how I feel. I got to talking with Cyd last night, and she told me I should hear you out about what is going on in therapy. So go ahead. Tell me what's been going on."

I didn't know how to say it. It had haunted me for most of my life, and I hadn't told a single soul. It was my deepest, darkest, most shameful secret. I'd carried it with me all these years. I fumbled as I tried to think of how to say it out loud. I took a deep breath and held it.

"Um, well . . ." I exhaled then continued. "Chad raped me when I was twelve."

As soon as the words left my lips, it felt like poison leaving my body. This feeling of a swarm of thousands of bugs flying out of my mouth. They'd swarmed in me for twenty-five years, and I instantly collapsed.

"No! Jesus, are you fucking serious?" he said.

Adam crouched down with his head between his hands and started to tear up.

"I am so sorry," he said. "I had no idea. I thought it was something to do with your ex when you asked me yesterday if I wanted to know. That's why I said no."

Tears continued to fall down my face.

"I felt so defeated when you said no. It was a lifeline that I was holding out, and I felt like you didn't love me enough to help me or save me," I said.

"I'm so sorry. I had no idea."

"I'm sorry, too."

He wrapped his arms around me, and we stayed on the porch in a long embrace. I cried with every ounce of strength I had, my face nestled into his shoulder, holding on for dear life.

•

Before Cyd left that weekend, I pulled her aside and thanked her. It was because of her that Adam was willing to listen. Had it not been for her, we may have ended up divorced and my secret would still be that: a secret. I shared my trauma with her, and she wrapped me in her arms and gave me one of her legendary hugs. It was no longer my secret to carry alone, and I started to feel a small sense of freedom.

BOMBS AWAY

I had another session with my therapist a few days after I told Adam. I summoned my courage and let her know how far I progressed.

"I have been trying to bury something from my childhood for a long time, and you've given me the courage to say it. My older brother raped me when I was twelve." I blurted it out and it seemed to become easier each time I said it.

"Wow!" she said.

I think she surprised herself with her ability to get through to a patient in such a deep, profound way. I continued to tell her about that moment in detail and how it popped into my mind each morning like clockwork.

"And how did it feel to tell Adam this?"

I rehashed our entire night and the lack of safety I'd felt, the feeling of bugs flying out of my mouth, and how supportive he had been since I'd come forward with my secret.

"I felt such shame and disgust. I felt like no one would love me if they knew. I felt dirty."

"You understand this wasn't your fault, Amber? You didn't choose this for yourself. You did nothing wrong."

Tears overflowed once again. This was the first time I'd ever heard this. I was conditioned to believe that if someone was upset, it must have been something I did or said.

•

Adam and I spent the next week digesting the recent revelations of abuse in my childhood. It was the rape that was on repeat through my mind over the last number of years, but I soon realized that there were other instances that spanned a period of seven years. I blocked every one of them out and buried them as if they were a normal part of childhood. Memories of the flashlight to my genitals and the sleepover where I learned about sex, bathing together in fifth grade, the pornography, and the hand job. It wasn't a normal brother-sister relationship. It wasn't something I wanted.

The next call I needed to make was to my dad. I had no intentions of telling my mom, and I made it clear to Adam that I wasn't a victim, that this secret or story wasn't going to be part of my identity. As much as I accepted or acknowledged that this had happened to me, I wasn't about to let it define me.

I texted my dad an emoji. A single random emoji was our signal to each other that the other one wanted to talk. It was usually a smiley face, nothing too conspicuous. In this way, we prevented my mother from asking questions about why I was contacting my dad instead of her.

The phone rang. It was Dad.

"Hey, whatcha up to?" he asked.

These were the famous words he always said when you answered a call. I made my way up to my bedroom and sat on my bed.

"Dad, do you have a minute to talk?"

"Yeah, sure. Just let me close my door. What's up?"

I could hear a door close from the other side of the phone.

"Do you remember over the last couple of years, every time we'd talk about Chad, I'd say that we would never be close again?"

"Okay, yeah."

"Well, I'm going to tell you something that I've been working through in my therapy, something that happened when I was younger."

Kaiser pushed his way into my room and hopped up onto the bed. He nestled himself in a cinnamon bun position and closed his eyes.

"Am, you're scaring me."

I paused before speaking again, worried that this would forever change us. I had no idea how to soften the words. To make it less of an explosion.

"I know. I'm sorry. I wish I didn't have to be the one to tell you this, but Chad sexually abused me for seven years as a child, and he had anal sex with me when I was twelve."

The phone went silent. I could hear my dad start to cry.

"No," he said, sobbing.

I sat there silently, knowing full well that I'd just broken a piece of my dad's heart. I leaned back toward Kaiser and wrapped my body around his.

"How could he do that to you? I could kill him for touching you. You should have told me. I would have made him stop."

Tears fell from my eyes. I wiped them away and placed my phone back to my ear.

"I know, Dad. I'm sorry."

"You have *nothing* to be sorry about, you understand me? Nothing! I should have protected you and I didn't and for that I am so sorry."

I never expected an apology from my dad. I only blamed Chad and maybe my mom. I felt like she gave Chad access to me as I started going through puberty. She forced us to bathe together and took down any barrier I should have had to my own body.

"I don't have any intention of telling anyone else, okay? Especially Mom. I don't want to cause a huge family uproar or anything. Okay? This doesn't define me. I'm not a survivor or a victim of any kind."

I repeated it out loud, trying to convince my dad and maybe myself. I became adamant that I didn't want to tell a lot of people. I was still dealing with the shame and embarrassment of it. Mom was the type to take advantage of situations or ailments and shine the light on herself, yearning for sympathy in true NPD fashion. I would never be like her. Dad agreed to keep it quiet, and we ended the call with our usual sign off.

"Love you, Am. With all my heart. I hope you know that."

"I love you too, Dad."

"We didn't talk today, okay?" he said.

"Okay, bye," I said.

"Bye."

JUST SAY NO! . . . TO RAPE?

Four days later, I got a text from Dad.
Chat?
Sure.

I ran up to my room and perched on my bed. My bedroom had become my retreat. I'd redesigned it during Covid, and it delivered serenity. The sun cascaded through the sheer blinds, creating a prism of light reflecting on the charcoal walls and up to the vaulted ceiling. I leaned back on the ivory fabric headboard and covered myself with a blanket. This space had served me well, surrounding me with tranquility through this tumultuous time in my life.

The phone rang and immediately I could tell Dad was distraught. The weight of my secret was holding him down and he was struggling to find ways to deal with it.

"How are you doing?" he asked.

"I'm doing okay, actually. I've ordered a ton of books about childhood sexual abuse, and I'm looking forward to seeing Jason, Natalie, and the kids next weekend. How are you?"

The clouds covered the sun, and the room suddenly got a bit darker.

"I'm struggling, Am. I know you said you didn't want to tell

Mom, but I can't keep it from her. I don't know what to do with it. I think about it, and I start crying. It's festering inside me."

The festering feeling was all too familiar to me.

"You can tell her if you want," I said.

I didn't feel like I had a choice in the matter. I could see how throwing this bomb on my father hadn't been entirely fair. I saw the effects it had on Adam, and I couldn't imagine how my dad was managing.

"Okay, I'm going to tell her tonight. We will be alone at the campsite, and we can talk about it together, okay?"

"Sure. Can you send me an emoji or a letter as soon as you do?"

"You bet."

I took a deep breath. "Good luck, Dad."

"Thanks, Am."

"Call you later, okay?"

"Okay."

I hung up the phone and found myself vibrating with nervousness. I never had any intentions of telling her, and this all seemed to be unravelling at lightning-speed pace.

Later that night I received an emoji of a shoe. She knew. I couldn't help but wonder what she'd said. How had she reacted? When was she going to call? I wanted so badly for my dad to steal some time away the next day, but I knew it would be tough. They spent every evening and weekend together. We never spoke outside of work hours, unless it was a FaceTime call and she was on it. Saturday came and went with no call. I thought she probably needed a day to digest it. Take it in. Sunday came and went. No call. Did she not believe me? Or did she not care? I knew she was always Team Chad, but in this instance, I thought she might care enough to call.

•

I dropped my girls off for their first day of Pedalheads bike camp. Four hours of silence and bliss was exactly what I needed. I still hadn't heard from my mom. It had been three days, and my head was spinning. Each time I gave in to thinking about her, I became consumed, spiralling out of control. Suddenly the phone rang. It was her. I wanted to ignore her call, but curiosity got the best of me. My heart pounded as I answered the phone.

"Hello?"

"Hello, Amber." She then paused, and I could tell by her tone that she was angry. "Well, don't you think we should talk about this?"

There were no niceties or formalities. No how's your day going or how have you been. She went straight to the point. I sat at my kitchen island. My body, neck, and throat felt as stiff and hard as the granite countertop. I picked at some of the leftover cereal that had dried on the counter from breakfast.

"Sure, we can talk about it. I was just waiting for you to call."

"Well, you could've called me, you know. Instead of calling your dad and telling him."

Comments like this made me hate her. She was immediately defensive, and I knew this wasn't going to pan out like I'd hoped. She was more upset that I chose to call my dad and confide in him than about what happened to me as a child.

"Start from the beginning," she demanded.

I began with my depression, needing antidepressants, and then going through therapy. I told her how it had haunted me for years and how I tried to keep pushing it down and blocking it out. I explained to her that it wasn't just one time, that it happened numerous times, with multiple sexual coercions, exposure to pornography, and finally rape.

"Well, why didn't you just say *no*!" she said.

Her response knocked the wind out of me. It grabbed me by the throat, and suffocated my air. I held my head up with one hand and turned slightly to see the sun shining through the kitchen window. The birds chirped as they flocked to the feeder under the lilac tree. Happiness was on the other side of the glass. It all seemed to be within reach if I could just finish this call.

"I thought I taught you both to never let anyone touch you?" she continued. "You could've come to me, but instead you went to your dad and he kept it from me for a week."

"Mom, I think you're forgetting the point of this conversation. It's not about me talking to Dad. I did that because he made me feel safe. His first reaction wasn't 'why didn't you say no,' it was 'I'm sorry I didn't protect you'."

"Ha!" she said with a mocking laugh.

"Saying no wasn't something we were taught as kids, Mom."

"Oh, you want to talk about a childhood, well let me tell you something. When I was a little girl, your uncle took me up into his room. It was the one right across from the stairs. He blindfolded me and told me to take off all my clothes and then he rubbed his penis up and down my entire naked body. I went and told my mom, and you know what she said to me? She told me that I was never to mention it or tell anyone again! How do you think that made me feel?"

"Well, I can't imagine," I lied.

This was another instance of Mom making herself out to be the victim. She lacked empathy, and I should have anticipated this.

"I'm sorry that happened to you, Mom. But at the same time, I would've thought since you experienced something similar, perhaps you would have been more sensitive to what was going on in our home. You could have made extra efforts to watch closely, or even just had those conversations about consent and protecting your body."

"Oh, so you think you're a better mother than I am?"

"Yes!" I said, unable to lie. "You should've fucking protected me!"

Emotion overcame me and the words spewed out of my mouth. No filter. Just pure, unbounded candour that I had kept buried along with the abuse.

"You could've told me," I continued. "You could have told me about what happened to you and then maybe it would've provided a safe enough space for me to talk to you. Instead, you just tell me to say no!" My words echoed through the empty house.

Our conversation was spiralling, and our emotions were coming to a boiling point. We always struggled to have heartfelt conversations about anything of significance without overwhelming emotion or anger. She would lash out, and I would become defensive. It was the only way we knew how to communicate.

"Well, I think you need to find purpose in your life," she said. "You've got too much time on your hands, and you need to just get over it and move on."

"I'm not entirely sure what you mean by 'purpose.' I run my own company, and I have two children that I take care of."

"Exactly. You have two beautiful girls that need you and you don't need to be rehashing all of this."

Her words pierced through my scars, reopening them to create a deeper hurt. My face felt hot to the touch. My tears were lava. Two paws reached to the top of the counter stool. It was Kaiser. He had this innate sense to comfort me. I picked him up and sat him next to me on the adjacent stool. Petting him calmed me. If I stopped, he pawed my arm in request for me to continue.

" Okay, Mom. Well, this conversation doesn't seem to be going anywhere. You know everything now."

"That's right, I do. And your dad and I will be calling your brother to deal with this."

"Ah, no you won't!" I blurted out.

"And why not? How do you suppose we deal with this moving forward?"

"Well, it happened to me, so I would like to be a part of that call. Maybe a FaceTime when they're home from their vacation?"

Chad and his family were out in British Columbia for their summer vacation. Every year they'd text the day before heading home and ask to stay with us for a night. Chad was never afraid to ask for something. It was usually accommodations, but occasionally it was a free round of golf, golf merchandise, or balls. Most of the time I obliged, but this time there was no way I could have them in our home, and I was pretty sure Adam would physically hurt Chad if he saw him.

"Let's chat once they get home, but don't say anything to him," I said.

"What? You think I'd say something and wreck their vacation? I don't think so! And just so we are clear, this stays in the family. Do you understand me?" she said.

I replayed the conversation in my head over and over again. She never once told me about her brother, and yet here she was, living life as if it never happened. There were no apologies or condolences, but was I really surprised? For myself and for my girls, I was determined never to be silenced again.

MADNESS

That weekend, Jason, Natalie, and their kids came to visit. They were also on their way out to British Columbia for a family vacation but had no plans to connect with Chad and his family. We went to the zoo, and Adam and Jason got a round of golf in while Natalie and I went shopping with the kids. My relationship with Jason had changed over the last couple years. He and his family visited each year, and we started to get to know each other better, as adults. I valued him as a brother, and I got to know their wonderful children. Adam knew that my number-one goal that weekend was to talk to Jason about everything. He needed to hear it from me, not Mom.

When we got home from a day at the zoo, everyone was exhausted and hungry. Our plates were brimming with food courtesy of Adam and his culinary skills, but my nerves were getting the best of me. Jason and Chad had been close growing up, but ever since Jason was blamed for Chad's drunken indiscretion, they'd drifted apart. Jason was starting to see Chad for who he really was: a user. We finished dinner and Adam offered to do the dishes, motioning for me to take Jason outside. The chill of my wine glass calmed the clamminess in my hands.

"Hey, grab your wine and let's head outside," I said to Jason.

I had already told Natalie that I needed to talk to Jason about something, so she knew to let us have some time alone. We stepped out onto the patio. The shade finally cascaded over the yard, giving us some reprieve from the hot August sun. We sat down next to each other, on separate couches.

"Hey, so there's something that has come up over the last couple of weeks that I need to tell you," I said.

Jason had the same nervous reaction that my dad had, only this time it was in person. I told him everything that had happened with Chad, as well as the struggles that Adam and I had faced and how that led to me confessing it for the first time. I told him how I'd told Dad and how he struggled to keep it a secret before eventually telling Mom.

Jason immediately stood up and walked away. He was enraged. He let out a loud yell, and his hands clenched into fists.

"You're kidding me? What a fucking loser he is. He's fucking dead to me."

He sat down beside me on the patio couch. He scooted closer and wrapped his arms around me. Jason and I were never affectionate or emotional.

"I'm sorry, Amber. That never should have happened."

We sat there embracing, both of us tearing up. He said he felt guilty that he hadn't been there for me during our childhood. He said if he knew what was happening back then, he would have done something about it. I told him about Mom's reaction and what she said during our call, and he immediately vetoed the idea of a FaceTime call.

"No, absolutely not. This is not happening over FaceTime. You'll come to Saskatoon. You'll stay with me, and we will have a meeting as a family in person."

He was eerily calm. The whole idea of an in-person intervention-type meeting seemed daunting, at the very least. The idea that I would confront Chad, let alone in front of my entire family, was overwhelming. I'd thrown this truth grenade out into the open, and now I was not only healing from it on my own but also publicly acknowledging it in front of my family and my abuser. I started regretting my decision to open up about everything, but Jason and Natalie stopped me. They reassured me that this needed to come out, and it needed to be dealt with.

"We've got you, Amber. We won't let him near you. And this is your chance to let him know how it affected you," Natalie said. She was so sweet.

Telling each other how we felt had never been done in my family before. But I trusted Jason, and I was willing to be the trailblazer and keep going.

INTERVENTION

Adam and I arrived with the girls in Saskatoon by 3 p.m. The meeting was set for six o'clock, and we drove straight to Jason's house. We pre-arranged for Cyd to take our two girls and Jason's two kids to her house for supper and to play at Kinsmen Park. I gave my dad specific instructions to be there between five and six. Not at six. I wanted him to be there before Chad and Libby arrived. I needed the additional support.

The doorbell rang at 5:40 p.m. It was Chad. He was by himself. I avoided eye contact with him and headed straight upstairs with Natalie. My limbs were already shaking. Natalie and I sat together on the soft carpeted stairs. My entire body was vibrating. I clasped my hands together to conceal the trembles. Natalie placed her arm around me, and we huddled together, listening to every word being said downstairs.

"Do you know why you're here?" I overheard Jason asking Chad.

"Yeah, it's about some things that happened between Amber and me when we were kids."

"Yeah. Where's Libby?" Jason asked.

"She's not coming."

"No. Call her. She needs to be here for this." Jason was adamant that she needed to hear everything.

"She's at the lake. She said she couldn't be here because of her own mental health. She took the kids with her."

"Pfft. Does she have any idea what's going on here, Chad?" Jason asked.

"Yeah. I told her everything during the weekend."

"Yeah? You told her everything?" Jason said, doubting the words that came out of Chad's mouth. "Well, she will be finding out everything. I can guarantee that."

I heard the doorbell ring again. 6:05 p.m. It had to be my parents. Jason opened the door and greeted them with little emotion. He'd had his own difficulties with my mom recently and this seemed to put him over the edge. Natalie and I came down the stairs and I greeted my dad with a huge hug. It had been over a year since I'd seen him. As soon as he wrapped his arms around me, I burst into tears. I looked over and Mom was watching us, so I let go.

"Hello, Amber," she said.

"Hi, Mom," I said, wiping away my tears.

I could hear her voice inside my head saying "Stop your crying Amber, that's enough. Now wipe your tears off your face." She said this often when I was little. I gave her a quick hug and we walked into the living room where there were seven chairs set in a circle. We had previously agreed where each person would sit. I sat in the middle, with Adam and Jason on either side of me. Their chairs were close to mine, propping me up on both sides. Mom and Dad sat on the loveseat together, with Natalie's chair opposite them. Chad was facing me. The plan was that we would all take turns telling Chad how we felt about his actions. I went first, followed by Adam, Jason, and then my parents.

I've never felt more scared. My body was no longer my own in that moment. I felt physically debilitated. My entire body shook uncontrollably, and I could barely get through the words I'd prepared. Before this moment, there was so much I'd wanted to say to him. I wanted to tell him how what he did broke me, how it shaped me, and how it haunted me for most of my life. But as I sat there, Adam's hand on my knee, I wished that my speech was condensed to just a few lines of spite.

I had no idea what to expect from this, and I was no longer in control of the situation. I relinquished control the moment Jason suggested we have this family meeting. Every book I read about sexual abuse recommended that you not confront your abuser. Most abusers deny what happened, minimize it, or cause additional trauma to those abused.

And so, I began to speak in front of my family. I read all five pages of my letter, stopping briefly to wipe away tears and to see if Chad showed any emotion. I spoke about every single detail of the abuse and what I remembered of it. I told him how it had led me down a path of destruction and promiscuity at a young age. How it took me down a spiral of depression and created a lack of self-worth. I spoke of wanting to commit suicide in university. I spoke of wondering if I'd been protected by my family, perhaps I would not have married an abusive husband. I indirectly chastised my mom for creating an environment where Chad was "untouchable" and the "favourite." He was someone so incapable and incompetent that I had to do his homework, clean up after him, and make his bed for him. As I finished this elaborate declaration of pain, I looked up at him. The look on his face is burned in my memory forever. He sat with one leg slightly up on the chair, his arms crossed over his chest, and his head tilted downward. His eyes frowned and his lips pouted. He was crumbling, but in a childlike way.

Jason acted as the moderator and instructed each person to proceed with what they had to say. Adam articulated how this impacted him and our family. He said that it almost broke us and that if anyone should have to bear the weight and shame, it should be Chad.

Jason went next and his response was much the same as when I first told him. His fists were clenched, and he let out a yell. I became sad while listening to what my parents had to say. Dad spoke softly;

he was unsure about what to say because the idea of it all made him sick and disappointed. Mom had a script written out. She held several pages of paper covered in scribbles. This was her opportunity, in front of everyone, to say the right thing. She started slowly and began to draw similarities between Chad and the devil, but she then took a sharp turn and steered her speech to how she never had any favourites and how she was proud of all her children. She emphasized that she still wanted to be a part of her grandchildren's lives and how she loved them all equally. As she spoke, it became apparent that she wasn't mad about the situation. She was upset because she knew it would disrupt our seemingly perfect family to outsiders. Each sentence she spoke left me dumbfounded and in shock.

Lastly, Jason turned it over to Chad. This was the moment we'd all been waiting for. Would he deny it? Would he try to save face and minimize it? He sat up but never made eye contact. He stared at the floor, arms still crossed, pout still on his face.

"I'm sorry, Amber. What I did was wrong."

He admitted everything.

He said that he'd wanted to address what happened between us for the last few years but could never find the right time.

"I've been dealing with depression, too. I'm on a prescription that I take every now and then when I have bad days."

Our mom got up and walked out the front door. She'd had enough. No goodbye, no apology, nothing. Dad sat still.

"Chad, you can leave, too," Jason stated.

Chad stood up and sulked toward the door.

"Sorry, Amber," he said, and then he was gone.

We had a moment with Dad before he left.

"Her walking out like that, that's fucking bullshit, Dad." Jason was upset. "She can't even give Amber a hug?"

"Yeah, I know." Dad came over and gave me a hug. "I'm proud of you, Am."

I held him tight. "Thanks, Dad, I'm proud of me, too."

After everyone was gone, I took out my phone and emailed Libby. *I wish that you came tonight. I felt compelled to speak up and agree to this meeting because of you and your girls.* Her oldest daughter was twelve at the time and one of my main reasons for coming forward. I could never live with myself if Chad touched her and I hadn't warned them. I signed off my email with *You have every right to know this and use it to make your own decisions for you and your family.* I let her know that I was available to talk any time. I attached my entire speech and clicked send.

She responded later with a text message. *Chad told me everything. It was a long time ago and it was before my time. It has nothing to do with me.* Whether she read the email in its entirety, I'll never know. But she was dismissive in her response, and it was obvious that she didn't care.

I took a sip of wine and fell into Adam's arms. He physically held me up as I balanced on what felt like baby deer legs.

"I've got you," he whispered.

I squeezed him tighter.

He looked down at me. "Hey," he said.

I looked up, and his green eyes met mine.

"You are safe." He leaned in and kissed my forehead.

HEALING SEPARATION

The next day, my mother texted to ask if we'd stop by with the girls to see her and Dad before we drove home. We'd already left. We'd left first thing in the morning. I had no intention of visiting and making a trip out of it. It was surreal that she was ignoring everything that had just happened. I replied: *No, I'm exhausted and that was a lot to process. We left this morning at eight.*

As we drove home, I sat there depleted of all energy and strength. I watched the farmers' fields for miles, stretches of nothing but beige wheat with the odd grouping of steers. It left me mesmerized. I took out my phone and texted my Aunt Beth. *What's your email address?*

She texted back. I was determined that no one would ever silence me again. Not him, not my mom. I sent my speech to her and within minutes she called.

"Oh my god. Amber, I'm so sorry that this happened. I had no idea," she said. She went on to talk, saying everything that a mother should say in this situation. She didn't wait three days. She waited three minutes, the time it took her to read the email. This was love. It was her love and support that showed me what a mother's love and support could look like. Our conversation was brief. The girls were in the backseat, and I didn't want to talk about the last twenty-four hours in front of them.

"Okay, I'll let you go. I'll call you later."

"Okay."

"Hey, I love you."

"I love you too, Auntie Beth."

After having a hot bath and a good sleep, I awoke to an early morning call from my dad. He was already at work. I sat on the couch, coffee cup in hand, Kaiser curled up between my legs. We skipped the niceties and jumped right to digesting the intervention, along with Mom's reaction.

"Why did she get up and walk out?" I asked.

"I don't know, Am. She said she had to puke and that she was done talking."

"Puke?"

"Yeah, she said she puked in the bushes, but I don't know."

"That seems a little far-fetched, don't you think?"

"Yeah, it does."

"What did she say when you got in the car?"

"She asked me if I knew Chad was on antidepressants."

I was stunned.

"You mean to tell me that after everything I told her about my sexual abuse, promiscuity, depression, wanting to commit suicide, and being raped that the first thought she had was about Chad taking periodic antidepressants? That's not even how they work! You have to take them every day for fuck's sake! He's probably taking benzos and is too stupid to know the difference."

"I know, Am. I don't get any of it."

His agreement helped back me off the ledge. I looked out on our patio and saw a bird wading in a pool of water that sat stagnant on one of the chair covers. I took a deep breath and let Dad get back to work. He had started working for a competitor to ride out the years until his retirement.

Two weeks after the intervention, Dad called to tell me that Chad had sent him and Mom an email with an apology. Dad read the email to me over the phone. Chad minimized everything. He said each time he tried to write the email, he cried. He said there was not a day in his life that he disrespected his family. He said he'd spent his whole life not worrying about himself, just trying to make everyone happy. He said that while what happened when we were children lingered in his mind, he'd dealt with it. He hoped the meeting was what I'd needed to heal. He thanked my parents for their love and support and made it clear that he had other ideas about what happened back then but would keep those to himself.

His email made my blood boil. He was trying to minimize what he had done and reclaim his place as the perfect son. I was curious what he meant by saying he had other ideas about what happened, but not curious enough to dig into it. He no longer occupied a place in my life and reaching out to ask would open a door that was now permanently closed and locked.

I found out that Mom visited him shortly after he sent the email. She dropped off his kids at his work and went inside for a quick visit. I assumed that she had words of forgiveness and support for him, followed by a hug goodbye. She still hadn't reached out to me since the intervention. It was clear that she was taking a firm stance on Team Chad.

A few days later the phone rang, and it was Marlene on FaceTime. I couldn't help but feel betrayed at this point. The feelings I had were compounding daily, and my anger festered.

"Hello?" I said.

"Hello, Amber."

Mom always said *Hello, Amber* in a specific tone. Every single call and voicemail started that way, like I had done something wrong or was a small child who had been caught stealing candy.

"What have you been up to?" she asked.

I mentioned the usual, being busy with the kids and their activities, then tiptoed into the healing conversation I'd been reading about in books on childhood sexual abuse.

"Oh yeah, and has it been hot there?" she asked.

I stopped in my tracks and the stuffed animal fell from my hands. I was down in our playroom tidying it up. The conversation and topic of sexual abuse just floated on past her without a pause.

As the conversation came near the end, I asked her, "Aren't you going to acknowledge any part of what happened?"

"No, I'm done talking about it. I won't be talking about it with anyone anymore. We all just need to move on," she said. Her tone was rigid and callous.

My body was steaming. How could she possibly feel entitled to make that decision for me? I was a thirty-seven-year-old woman who was being silenced again.

"Oh, well, I didn't realize that it was your call to make," I said.

"I think it's best that we leave it at that," she said.

She was smoke-bombing the entire conversation. She'd dropped her bomb, and she was out. I ended our call. Fuelled by rage, I power cleaned the entire basement. After holding this secret for twenty-five years, it wasn't that I needed to shout it from the rooftops, but I was determined not to be silenced about it ever again. It was my story. Telling it to others was not about gaining sympathy; in fact, that part made me feel anxious and uncomfortable. I hated telling people because they always said they were sorry. I didn't need their apologies. I needed them to understand me. I wanted them to understand who I was and why I made some of the choices I had growing up. I wanted to inspire others to speak up and feel a sense of freedom by releasing their burden.

I thought long and hard about my mom's reaction, her words, and her behaviour over the past two months. For me to be able to properly heal and move forward from this, I needed a "healing separation." It was a term I'd learned from the books I was reading. A healing separation was separating from those who caused pain during the process of opening up.

I told my dad that I was going to ask Mom for this, and he was supportive of the idea. I knew that I was done with her until she changed her ways. This was *the* hill I was willing to die on. If I didn't do it for myself, then who would? And if I didn't stand up for myself, then what kind of role model was I being for my girls? I always preached a strong female lead. If I didn't fight this fight, I'd be a doormat who allowed someone who hurt me to be in my kids' lives. I wasn't sure how long it was going to be, but I thought we could all use some time away from each other. We needed time to really understand everything that just had happened in our family. I had high hopes that my mother would somehow come to terms with her actions.

I texted Mom and told her I wanted to have a conversation. We arranged for a Tuesday night at 8 p.m. after the kids went to bed. There was no way Adam was going to miss being on the call. He was my strength during the entire ordeal. Each day he would physically hold me up with a hug and let me know that I was loved and that I was safe.

We sat up at the counter together, side by side. I put the phone on speaker. Adam kept his hand on my lap, just as he had during the intervention. It gave me the physical sensation that he was there for me.

"Hi, Mom."

"Amber."

"I wanted to speak tonight to ask a few questions that I have in hopes that they will help in my healing journey."

"Okay. Go ahead," she said. I could tell by her voice that she seemed inconvenienced.

I had written down all my questions in advance. I didn't want to forget anything.

"The first question I'd like to know is why did it take you three days to call me after you found out everything?"

She stumbled with her words. "Three days, so what! I reached out when I did; why does it matter how long it took me to reach out? I'm not sure why that matters."

Understanding that I wasn't going to get the answer I hoped for, I moved on to the next question.

"Okay, why did you say in your speech that you had no favourites and that you were proud of all your children?"

"Why is that always an issue with you? It's the truth. I don't have any favourites, I never have."

It became clear that I wasn't going to get what I needed from her. She had no intention of being sympathetic, or accountable for her actions or words, so I continued to stoke the fire by asking the rest of my questions.

"Why did you feel like it was okay to walk out of Jason's house without saying goodbye or giving me a hug?"

"The conversation was over. I was sick to my stomach with everything that just happened."

She started to get short and heated, and the conversation began escalating to a full-blown fight. She was belittling every emotion I had.

"You just need to forget all of this and get over it, Amber. I went through exactly what you did, and I was able to get over it and move on."

Adam suddenly stood fully erect, like he'd been hit with a bolt of lightning. He had been on edge, waiting for the right time to step in.

"Oh, I'm sorry Marlene, I didn't realize you were raped," he said. He was calm but sarcastic.

"Who was raped?" she asked.

"Your daughter was Marlene, when your son Chad put his penis wrapped in Saran Wrap inside her anus when she was twelve!"

"Oh, that's enough! It wasn't rape, it was just kid stuff."

She continued to gaslight me, and as she did, Adam made it clear that she was a narcissist and a poor excuse for a mother. She battled back, calling him an alcoholic and a gambling addict. He just laughed. He handled her insults with nonchalance and grace. Her words didn't hurt him, they motivated him as he orchestrated every rebuttal.

I looked over to the stairs, fearful that the girls would be standing there listening, awoken by our yelling, but there was no one there.

"What would you have me do Amber, huh? Do you think I knew what was going on? It was twenty-five years ago!" she said.

I was suddenly overcome with unbridled rage. After twenty-five years, it was bubbling in my throat like acid.

"You are a lousy fucking mother! You should have protected me!" I wept in my chair, Adam's arm around me. I was completely broken.

"Ben! Aren't you going to say something or are you just going to sit there?"

"Yeah, no." Dad was speechless.

We'd never had such an emotional, heated conversation before, and for the first time in my life, I'd brought ammunition. Adam was my strength and could talk circles around her. He held me up and helped fight my battle. This was the love I'd been waiting a lifetime for.

As the emotions died down, we all took a deep breath.

"I didn't expect you to suddenly love me more than Chad after finding this all out. What I was hoping for is that you'd support me through this, be by my side, and check in with me like a mother should. Especially now, knowing that you experienced similar trauma. It took every single ounce of strength I had to come forward with this truth, and this is the mountain I'm willing to die on. I need to start creating boundaries that allow me to heal in a safe environment, and unfortunately, Mom, that does not include you right now. I am asking you for space and a healing separation for a while."

"Okay, so what—you don't want me in your life anymore?"

"Not right now, no."

"Okay, Amber. I'll be sure not to call or message you. Best of luck in your healing journey," she said, then hung up the phone.

Adam picked me up from my chair and held me.

"I'm proud of you," he said.

I took the last sip of my peppermint tea, then Adam led me upstairs and tucked me into bed. He pulled the covers up and wiped a tear away from my face.

"Thank you. Thank you for loving me and for helping me through that conversation."

"You never need to thank me for that. It's part of the contract." He smiled and kissed my forehead. "I love you, Amber Nicole."

He turned out the lights and left the room. Every last tear fell from my eyes and onto my pillow. I laid there in silence, proud of the strength it took to stand up to my mother. I was no longer the obedient daughter she expected me to be. It was the last step that I needed before really being able to start my healing process.

CONSENT

We sat waiting together in the doctor's office. Monroe was four and Quinn was two. The sterile smell filled the air and the paper crinkled as they fidgeted on the table. They were both stripped down to their underwear and playing with stickers I'd brought to keep them busy.

There was a knock at the door.

"Hi, girls!" Our female GP entered the room for the annual checkups.

She listened to their lungs and looked inside their ears and throats. She felt their tonsils and then asked Monroe to lie down so she could feel her stomach.

"Can I take a look inside your panties?" the doctor asked.

Monroe froze and looked at me. She shook her head no. My mind flashed back to a core memory from my childhood, the grey-haired doctor who lifted my panties and placed his hand inside.

"No, thank you," I said to Monroe's doctor. This was the start of our conversations around consent and boundaries and having the autonomy to say no.

"Okay, that's fine. Do you have any concerns?" she asked.

"No concerns," I said.

As I started to wrestle with my childhood trauma, it became clear that I wasn't hiding it as well as I hoped. There were days with lots of tears and endless hugs from Adam. There were days with phone calls behind closed doors. I knew I had to address this with my girls, but I needed to be in a stronger mental state before I did.

The morning after my healing separation call with my mom, I was still struggling with what was said and how heated it got.

"Mommy, how come you're so sad?" Monroe asked as she wrapped her arms around me and gave me a big hug. "Are you sad with us? Did we do something wrong?"

"No, baby, not at all."

Her question and hug broke me. Monroe was eight years old and reminded me of myself: introverted and shy. She liked to sit back and watch people, trying to get a read on the room or situation. She knew something was wrong, and I needed to use this as a teaching moment.

"Okay, Mo, come with me," I said.

We went upstairs to her room. We sat on her bed, cross-legged, her hands in mine like schoolgirls playing Miss Mary Mack.

"First, I want you to know that Mommy's sadness was never about you, Quinnie, or Daddy, okay?"

"Okay," she nodded.

"I've been working with a therapist on some feelings that I've been having. Do you remember when we went to Saskatoon a few weeks back?"

"When we only spent one night? It was too short."

"I know, baby. But there was a reason for that trip. Mommy's family was having a meeting that night when you and Quinnie and your cousins went for supper with Grandma Cyd."

"What was the meeting about?"

"Well, when Mommy was a little girl, Uncle Chad touched me

in an inappropriate way and it made me very sad. The meeting was to talk about it."

"Did he touch your privates?"

"Yes, he did."

"Oh." She stared down at her bed with a troubled look.

"I'm sorry he did that to you, Mommy."

"Honey, I don't want you to say sorry for him, okay? What I need you to know is that you can say no to anyone at any time, okay? It is your body, so you and only you make the rules. No one is allowed to touch your body."

"I know, Mommy," she said. We had been discussing this for years now.

"And when you're older and you find a partner that you love and want to be with, then you may change your mind and want to explore a bit more. But even at that point, Mo, you are still in charge and can say 'No,' or 'I'm not comfortable,' or' I'm not ready yet,' okay?"

"Okay, Mommy. I'm not sure that I even want a husband. I think I'm just going to adopt a baby like Bella and have four dogs."

I laughed and said okay. Bella was her favourite baby doll that I'd given her after George Floyd's death. She had a dark skin tone and was part of our conversations around anti-racism. Bella was everything to Monroe.

"Who should we trust to talk to about our bodies, or something that makes us feel uncomfortable?"

"You or Daddy. Or a teacher, a grandparent, or someone I trust like a therapist or doctor."

"That's right, baby." I gave her a hug and promised her that I was going to be just fine.

"Are we ever going to see Uncle Chad and our cousins again?"

"Uncle Chad won't be in our lives, but if your cousins want to be when they get older, then they're more than welcome."

"I don't want to see him ever again, Mommy."

"Then you don't have to. You know why?"

"Why?"

"Because it's your body, your rules!"

She smiled and leaned back, resting her head on my chest, her arms wrapped tightly around my waist. She took a deep breath and let out a loud exhale.

"Ah, I love the way you smell," she said.

I squeezed her back and ran my fingers through her curly hair.

•

Monroe and I decided that Quinn was a bit too young to learn all the details about our meeting in Saskatoon. Instead, we reviewed consent and boundaries with children's books. She was quick to pick up the "my body, my rules" phrase, especially when she didn't want to eat her vegetables.

Creating self-autonomy has always been a priority for me. My girls have always known that they can choose who gives them a bath and when they are ready to move on to showers by themselves. They have never been forced to do something they are uncomfortable with and are never judged when they come to me with concerns. These are the things they've been taught since they were little. It is the opposite of what I had growing up. My girls deserve to feel safe.

THERAPY

"Okay. I think we need to talk about the intervention. Undoubtedly, I feel like that was a bad idea and probably risked causing more trauma. Whose idea was it to have this meeting?"

I knew Dr. M. was right.

"It was my brother Jason's idea."

"I see. Knowing you and everything you've been through, I could imagine you didn't feel like you could have said no to that. Am I right?"

Finally. It felt like someone understood me. She didn't say "Why didn't you just say no?" like Marlene had.

"Yes, you're right."

"Was there anyone in your life at the time who tried to convince you otherwise? A therapist perhaps? Or even Adam?"

"No. I had just finished up my allotted sessions through Alberta Health with my previous therapist, and since my needs had changed from depression to sexual abuse, I was no longer a fit for their expertise. Therapists were in such high demand because of Covid, which is why I went through Alberta Health. I had reached out to CCASA, and their waitlist for support was a year. I found you, but by the time we had our first session, a month had passed since the intervention."

"I see. I'm sorry that you were put in that position."

"I'm not entirely sure what the alternative would've been, though."

Exhaustion had taken over and I contemplated lying down on the couch. It seemed too cliché, though, so I leaned back, crossed my legs, and folded my arms across my chest.

"What do you mean?" she asked.

"Well, if we didn't have the intervention, what would have happened? A FaceTime call with my parents and Chad in the room? Who knows what he would've said to convince them otherwise. The trauma of the meeting was worth the apology and the admittance in front of everyone."

"That's an interesting way of looking at it. Did you ever have any doubts that your family wouldn't believe you?"

"Of course I did. Doesn't everyone who's been through sexual abuse?"

"I suppose so."

She looked down at her notebook and started to lift her pen to write something but stopped before she could. I sat there silently staring at her, awaiting her next question.

"Next session, I'd like to start with EMDR, if that's okay with you. Unless there's anything else you'd like to talk about?"

"Nope, I think I've covered most of it."

"Okay, well that's all the time we have for today. Our next session we'll begin with EMDR. I will explain everything in full detail before we start. I think you will benefit greatly from it."

I left her office feeling slightly skeptical but also hopeful that EMDR could really help me erase my emotions.

EMDR

The next week, Dr M. greeted me in the waiting room with a smile and a sense of urgency. She was running two minutes behind, but I wasn't bothered by it. I was a little nervous, not for the session, but that EMDR would be a futile attempt to erase my trauma.

As I entered her office, I saw she had an odd contraption set up. It was a metre-long light bar sitting atop a tripod. It faced the couch at eye level.

"Okay, you can have a seat," she said.

She ushered me around the wires, and I took my usual place on the couch. She adjusted the tripod slightly lower to my eye level. Then she handed me two small, black handheld devices that were connected by wires. She sat down in her usual chair and explained what would happen.

"Okay, I know this looks intense, but trust me it's all part of the process. The process of EMDR is just that: eye movement desensitization and reprocessing. This bar will have a red light that travels back and forth. Left to right and in a constant motion. The paddles you are holding will vibrate in accordance with the light. I will be the only one speaking unless I ask you a question. During this entire time, I want you to follow the light with your eyes. Does that make sense?"

I nodded my head in agreement.

"The process mimics what happens to your brain during your REM sleep phase. It mimics the dream state. But as you recall your memories of trauma, EMDR allows your brain to process these traumatic memories and shift from the front part of your brain in your amygdala where they have been stuck. It allows them to be processed by the brain like any other non-traumatic memory."

"Okay," I said, still feeling nervous.

"Do I have your consent to this EMDR session today? And if yes, would you mind signing your name here?"

She handed me a consent form and I signed my name. I sat back and tried to get as comfortable as possible. I crossed my legs and kept my hands on my knees, holding the small devices.

"We will do a series of short light sessions during the time we have today. We will do as many as we can in our ninety minutes together. Each one will take approximately ten to fifteen minutes, and we will go through each traumatic memory starting with the memory at the age of twelve. I will check in with you after each light session, and we can repeat the session until there is no physical feeling associated with it."

She started up the light bar, and without delay, the paddles started vibrating back and forth in my hands.

"Now, keep your eyes following the light. Allow yourself to go back to when you were twelve years old. I want you to relive that memory. Feel present in the moment."

I concentrated on the light and brought the pastel armchair to my mind. I felt a weight in my chest, and it became harder to breathe. A lump swelled in my throat and tears ran down my face. I let them run long, dripping onto my shirt. I replayed the memory over and over again until the light stopped, and I could force a blink and wipe away my tears.

"Tell me how you feel right now. Where do you feel it in your body?"

"My chest mostly. And my throat. It's hard to breathe right now."

We took a couple minutes for me to compose myself and find some sense of safety before beginning another round. Dr. M. asked me to go back to the same memory over and over again, adding in different outcomes until the physical feelings became bearable. After the end of that session, I was completely exhausted. It felt like I had been through a physical fight.

"The exhaustion is normal. You can expect to feel this way for the rest of today and possibly tomorrow as well." She assured me that I would feel better in time.

•

We continued with three more sessions of EMDR therapy. Each time, I dove back into my deepest traumas, including memories of Damian. At the end of my fourth EMDR session, she looked at me with a small smile of admiration.

"You know, it's okay to take a break from therapy," she said.

I could tell she knew how long I had been fighting, how impatient I was to rid myself of this toxicity.

"It's normal in therapy to go for a few months and then take some time off just to live and use what you have learned; to find and live in a state of calm for a while," she continued.

Her words were so reassuring. I feared that if I stopped, I'd never find freedom from my trauma. But I could tell already that I felt a sense of healing. My emotions surrounding my trauma had started to dwindle, so I decided to trust her.

I agreed to give myself a break from therapy. She was right. She was, after all, the third therapist I'd seen this year, and I had come a very long way since the beginning.

THE WORK

I swung as hard as I could, punching the centre of the punching bag. Once with my right fist, then my left, and back to my right, repeatedly, as hard as I could. I pictured his face each time I punched. The expression, that pout on his face during the family intervention. The childhood that he took from me. My grunts turned to sobs, and I fell to the ground, tears fleeing my eyes. I'd never cried this much before in my life and was shocked to find I still had an available supply of tears inside of me. I grieved for my inner child. I was fighting for her. Wiping my tears and sweat away, I picked myself up and did it all over again.

Even though I had recently finished my EMDR therapy, I was determined to sit in my trauma for as long as it took to heal. I kept a picture of myself as a child on my bedroom nightstand. My five-year-old self. She was my motivation, my constant reminder to keep going and fight for her.

I felt considerably better since my EMDR sessions, but I wanted to try something else as well. I was curious if hypnotherapy might also help to erase my trauma. Many practitioners were only seeing clients online because of the pandemic, and this was the case for my hypnotherapist. I felt most comfortable in my own home anyway, and considering he was male, this made me feel the safest. My hypnotherapist gave me a recording of a meditation journey. For thirty days, each night before I fell asleep, I closed my eyes and listened. His voice was now familiar. I listened with intent to every word he said. His words created a veil of tranquility over me, and within a few minutes, I was in a peaceful trance.

After thirty days, we met virtually for a one-on-one session. His words took me back to the summer I was twelve. To that exact day on the armchair. I could see both myself and Chad. Next, the hypnotherapist instructed me to barge through the front door. It was me as an adult. I needed to get twelve-year-old me out unscathed. I broke the front door down by kicking it in and immediately saw myself on the pastel armchair. I could see that everything was the same as it had been in that moment. The decor, the smells. It brought back every memory of that day. I grabbed fourteen-year-old Chad and started wailing on him, beating him to the ground. My younger self, fearful, was curled up in the fetal position on the chair. As Chad laid there lifeless, I picked up my younger self and held her tight. We clung to each other fiercely. "I've got you. You're safe," I whispered to her. We ran through this scene multiple times. Each time was different—I'd beat Chad up or I'd burn the house down—but every single time, I rescued my child-self and prevented it all from happening. It was extremely powerful.

We continued the rest of the session, repeating multiple scenes from my childhood. Each time, I allowed myself to say whatever I wanted to say, to either Chad or to my mother. My hypnotherapist instructed me to bag up every single harmful emotion. I bagged up every ounce of pain and tossed them away like trash. I bagged up my mother's anger and her destructive words and threw them away. When the session ended, I had a new sense of power.

•

I took Dr. M.'s advice and tried to find happiness. I tried to live in the moment with my girls and Adam, and to live without the burden of my secret, the trauma, or Marlene. It took me three months to feel like I was no longer being controlled by her. Every Sunday, I felt pressure to call her. The guilt was heavy and tangible. It flowed through every cell of my body. I'd never established personal boundaries before then. I was just learning what boundaries were. Throughout this journey of healing, I learned that it was imperative to create a barrier of protection around myself. Those who judged, minimized, or disregarded my truth were discarded. My supporters were brought even closer.

Dad and I continued to chat weekly. After the separation, Mom was known as M, not for Mom but for Marlene. He knew that her words, actions, and position on Team Chad made her my birth mother. She would never be my mom again. Our family was now divided in two: Team Chad and Team Amber.

My dad was in the toughest position. He was living with her. They fought constantly, and it was a fight I wasn't sure he could win. She relentlessly tried to push Chad and his family onto my dad. She wanted things to go back to the way they were. She tried calling me, but I ignored every call. I ignored her on her birthday and at Christmas. She called and left happy birthday voicemails for my girls, but I never returned her calls or said thank you.

In the spring of 2022, I felt a strong urge to buy a dress for her funeral. It was an overwhelming feeling. Perhaps it was a tangible sign that she was dead to me. I picked out a beautiful pink and green floral chiffon tea-length dress. It had long translucent sleeves, a sweetheart neckline, and a ruched bodice. It was stunning and likely more appropriate for a wedding, but I knew Marlene was always one to overdress for an occasion. As I stood in my closet with the dress on, swaying back and forth, I recalled Jason and Natalie's wedding and the dress that M made me wear. This felt perfect for the occasion.

•

As the months went by, I continued to ask my dad to come to Calgary for a visit. Each time I hoped he would't have the heart to say no. I texted him to extend an invitation for Father's Day weekend.

Let me think about it, he texted back.

Three days later he texted again. *I won't be coming for the weekend. The girls should be spending this time with their own dad. Not with me.*

I knew she wrote it. It had her tone.

I called him the next day.

"Why won't you come visit?"

"I can't, Am. I'm sorry. I really want to, though."

"Why not, Dad? I miss you. This is bullshit."

Dad explained that they were at odds and had been fighting a lot. She hated that he was on my team and was hurt that he hadn't stuck up for her during our last conversation.

"She tore a strip off me. Said I didn't support her when you called her 'the worst fucking mother in the world,' and I should be standing by her instead of wanting to come see you."

"I didn't say she was the worst! I said she was lousy! Big difference. And what about my kids? Just because she can't see them, now you can't? She's going to hold you hostage?"

I was raging once again. She'd dismissed everything that had happened with Chad and now she was the victim because of one comment, a comment that was sparked by the hurt and anger she'd caused. I was disappointed with my dad. I knew he was in a tough position, but wasn't I worth fighting for? Given his cancer treatments, shouldn't he know that life is too short? I left it alone for the moment and reached out to Jason for help to get Dad to visit.

CANCER

Twelve months and eight days passed since I'd last spoken to her. Though she tried. Multiple text messages and phone calls all came and went unanswered. I was no longer hers to control. I would never forgive her for her stance on Team Chad. I knew that a couple of months without speaking would not be enough to undo all the hurt she'd caused. I thought maybe, at some point, she could be in my life at arm's length. But not yet. I told Dad that if she wanted to say anything to me, she should write me a letter, but a letter never came.

•

In early September 2022, my girls were back at school and I was enjoying a beautiful sunny day, sourcing items for a client project. My feet were perched on the patio couch and Kaiser lay beside me in the shade. My phone rang and I glanced to see who it was. It was Dad. Every time I saw his name pop up on my phone, it brought an instant smile to my face.

"Hey, how are you?" he asked.

"Good! You?"

"Not bad. So, there is something I need to tell you," he said.

I could tell something was wrong. He seemed nervous.

"Your mom went to see her GP, and he admitted her to the hospital for some tests. She's got a lump in her stomach, and her bloodwork doesn't look great."

"Okay, so what does that mean exactly? Are we thinking it's something like a hernia or more serious?"

"Well, we don't know for sure what's going on, but I don't think it's good."

"So, what? Cancer?"

"I don't know, Am."

"Okay, well keep me posted please, okay? How are you doing with all of it?"

"I'm okay for now. Trying not to stress about it before we know for sure."

I left our call feeling confused and suspicious. Was she making this up? Was it just a ploy to get us all together again? It seemed like something she would do. I wasn't convinced it would develop into something serious.

•

A week later, Dad called again. It was a Thursday afternoon, and I had just picked up Monroe from school. I gave her and Quinn a snack before they settled in for their quiet time. I answered the call and went upstairs. I closed the door to my bedroom behind me. M had undergone tests over the past week, and I was sure he was calling with her results.

"Hello, Amber."

I was on speakerphone. It was a voice I recognized but hadn't heard in over a year. She was her same hardened self, although she sounded a bit smaller and frailer. I felt slightly betrayed in that moment, but Dad knew I wouldn't answer if she called me.

"Hi, Mom. How have you been?"

"I have liver cancer and, well, you know, it's fatal," she said.

I didn't know what to say. There was no tiptoeing into the subject, no niceties.

"I'm sorry to hear that, Mom."

It was the only appropriate thing to say, but as I said it, I felt like this might have been a gift from God. I took a deep breath and let out a long exhale.

"Yeah, well, I just thought you should hear it from me."

"You know, Mom, we've been through this before. We can do it again, right?"

"That's right," Dad said, chiming in.

"Yep, I know," she said.

"Don't lose faith, Mom. Keep me posted on what your treatment plan is and what the doctors say, okay?"

"Okay."

"I love you, Mom."

"I love you, too."

"Bye."

I told her I loved her because I knew she expected to hear it. It was another one of her unwritten rules. Growing up, each night before bed, we'd tell her we loved her and give her a kiss. It was something we had been doing ever since I can remember, and even when she visited me as an adult, she still had the same expectation.

•

Over the next few weeks, she underwent additional tests and a liver biopsy that confirmed it was a rare, atypical lung carcinoid that had metastasized to her liver and bones. She had multiple tumours on her liver, all of which were inoperable. They wouldn't give her a prognosis, or a survival rate, and their sense of urgency seemed nonexistent. Conversations around chemotherapy and a liver transplant started to surface, but they were always initiated by my parents. She was a ticking time bomb that no one could snuff out.

Dad and I talked daily, and he always kept me updated on her appointments and tests. He sent Jason and me photos of her to show us how quickly her health was declining. She was frail. Her skin had turned yellow and draped her body in excess. She'd lost thirty pounds. The reality of her cancer was starting to set in. Still, I was in disbelief. And being so far away allowed me to disassociate and put it in the back of my mind, except for when I spoke to Dad.

"Hey, how is she doing?" I asked.

Dad and I usually spoke when Mom wasn't around and my girls were at school.

"Not great. We've been talking a lot about travelling," he said. "She wants to go out east and see the Maritimes. I even said we should get on a plane now and head to Maui for a couple of weeks. Her first chemo appointment is just after Thanksgiving and then she'll have two weeks ideally between rounds and bloodwork, if all goes well. She wants to see how she feels after her first round and then we'll plan a trip somewhere."

He shared his mild frustrations about her unwillingness to pack up and leave immediately and for the lack of clarity around her treatment plan.

"She reached out to her siblings to ask if they would test to see if they are a positive match for a donor transfer."

"Is that even an option at this point?" I asked.

She hadn't asked any of us kids, but if she did, my answer would be no.

I ended the conversation by asking him one question that had been on my mind since her diagnosis.

"Dad? Can I ask you something?"

"Yeah, sure. What's on your mind?"

"Has she, or anyone else, blamed me for this?"

"Why would you ever think such a stupid thing like that?" he said.

"Because it has always been that way, and I just thought—"

He interrupted me with a resounding no that calmed my heart and put my soul at ease.

I found myself feeling depressed after our call. I sat on my bed, stirring in my own thoughts, only to be interrupted by Kaiser's loud snores. I wasn't entirely sure what was bothering me. Maybe it was that she wanted one of her siblings to be a donor. I couldn't imagine anyone offering to give her half of their liver. Maybe it bothered me that she wanted to spend her remaining time travelling instead of repairing our family. Or maybe it was because her timeline was still undetermined and there was no end in sight.

Adam arrived home from work and greeted me with a smile. I reached to him and nestled into his chest for a long hug. I took a deep breath and lingered on the sweet smell of his musk. With his arms wrapped around me, I felt safe. He was exceptional throughout all of this, patient and always willing to listen. He was everything I needed him to be.

"Group hug!" Monroe said with excitement.

Both girls came running from around the corner. We wrapped our arms around them and shared one of our remarkable family hugs. This was all that mattered.

CHEMO

It had been a couple of weeks with mixed emotions. She had stage four lung cancer. It was aggressive and spreading rapidly. Her oncologist would not provide her with a timeline. And typical of our family, we were not discussing the inevitable outcome of her death.

I succumbed to the expectation and pressure of being there for her during this time. It was not in my nature to lack empathy, and I did not want to have regrets. She started her first chemo treatment, and my girls and I put together a chemo care package for her. I explained to them what cancer was and what chemotherapy entailed. I told them about my dad's experience with cancer so as not to scare them. We shopped for items that could provide her comfort during her treatment: a blanket, sweater, lounge pants, socks, items to help with nausea, head scarves, creams, reading materials, and two cards, amongst other things.

M and I spoke several times that week. We didn't speak of the past, and we didn't acknowledge the past year. For the first time in my life, she spoke about me as a child.

"I remember one time when you were about four. You sat outside, under the big weeping birch tree in our front yard. You made a hammock for your baby out of a blanket tied to the branches. Your hair was blonde and curly, and the wind was blowing. You were so independent. So happy just being by yourself with your babies."

I remember that exact moment and day. She had seen me for who I was, and who I should have remained. A young child with innocence. Untouched and unscathed. It was heart wrenching to hear her mention it to me. Her heart seemed to be working overtime now that her liver was failing. In this small moment, I saw her as a mother.

She completed one round of chemotherapy at 30 percent strength. Her bloodwork was retested, and the treatment was working against her. Her oncologist advised that she would not be able to handle another round. It would be too much and would kill her. The only other option was immunotherapy.

GRANDCHILDREN'S GOODBYE

In November, we headed to Saskatoon for our first visit with my parents in over a year. I was nervous to see my mother. Our conversations had been brief, and they usually revolved around her treatment or diagnosis. I had no idea if she would bring up that conversation from a year ago or if she would simply ignore everything like she had always done.

Although no one was actually saying it, I knew this would be the last time my kids would see her. This visit would be their final goodbye. I'd spent the better part of the last year opening up to my children about what had happened to me when I was young, and we were able to grieve the relationship we'd had with her and the place she held in our family. Her life expectancy had been narrowed down to eight weeks; if she was lucky, she might make it past Christmas. Her first immunotherapy treatment would be an injection that she would receive once a month starting the week after.

We loaded up the car with small Christmas gifts from the kids. Inside the car, the smells of pine needles from a small plant and mandarin oranges surrounded us while Christmas songs played through the speakers. Outside, the frosted flatlands of Saskatchewan's oblivion enveloped our car. So desolate and cold. We tried to bring a sense of normalcy and joy to the trip for the sake of the girls. I only hoped they wouldn't bring up all the truths we'd discussed with them.

I caught my reflection in the rearview mirror. *Do I look okay?* I wondered. I zipped up my sweater, covering a small coffee stain that had dripped from my cup. I hadn't seen them for so long, and I had this obsessive feeling that I needed to look perfect. I didn't want M to think I missed her or that I'd needed her over the last year. I worked tirelessly to heal from everything that happened. I thought my shield of perfection would protect me from feeling weak or hurt. I had freshly washed and curled hair. My nails were done with a French manicure. My brows were waxed, and my skin looked dewy. *Am I skinny enough, though?* Dad told me she'd lost a lot of weight. *What if she thinks I'm fat in comparison? Maybe I should have worked out more leading up to this visit.* I never seemed to obtain her approval, and no matter how hard I tried, she always criticized. I was reminded of the time I called to tell her I received a raise at my job. I was twenty-six and bursting with excitement and pride.

"Hey, Mom! Guess what? I got a raise today!" I told her.

"Oh."

It was her classic minimal response with the least amount of engagement or excitement she could put forth in a conversation.

"Yeah! I got a twelve percent raise!"

"Good for you. How much money do you make now?"

"Just over $87,000!"

"What do you need all of that money for anyways? You should give some to me."

It wasn't what I thought she would say, and she wasn't joking either. She was never happy and had no intention of celebrating my life wins.

As Adam pulled up to the lake house, we got out of the car and walked up the steps to the front door. Before we could knock, the door swung open to a smiling Dad with wide-open arms.

"Hi, Dad!"

"Hi, Am."

He wrapped his arms around me and squeezed tight. Dad's hugs were one of my favourite things. His shoulders, neck, and arms were always so rigid. They reminded me of his handshake. "You have to have a firm grip and shake like you mean it" he would tell me. Dad always hugged like he meant it.

She stood just past the door in the hallway: a small, feeble woman. Her sagging skin was a honey-wheat colour. Her glasses were propped up on her nose and overwhelmed her face. Her hair was now just mere whisps over her scalp.

"Hi, Am," she said as she shuffled toward me with her arms open.

I wrapped her in my arms and embraced her in what would be the longest hug I'd ever have from her. It felt different than any other hug we shared. It came from love.

"Thank you," she said.

One of her last wishes was to see her grandchildren again, and I felt her gratitude for making her wish come true.

The kids decorated the Christmas tree, and we exchanged some small gifts that the girls had picked out. It was an early Christmas celebration. It was one thing Mom and I had in common: Christmas was our favourite time of the year.

"Would you girls like to come out next summer and Papa and Grandma will take you for a boat ride?"

Cheers rang loudly from both of my girls. Next summer? Why would she ask them that? We didn't talk about her dying. We didn't talk about her funeral wishes, or about what would happen after she died. It was a delicate matter that we could not acknowledge.

•

We spent the rest of the weekend at Jason's house. Mom and Dad came over for dinner on Saturday night but needed to leave early because Mom was tired and not feeling well.

"Will you stop by on your way home tomorrow?" Dad asked.

"You bet," I said.

Before we called it a night and went to bed, Jason told us how much she'd declined since they last saw her on Halloween, just two weeks earlier.

"It's happening fast. I don't know if she's going to make it until Christmas, to be honest."

"You'll call me, though, when the time comes?" I asked.

"Yeah, of course. Do you think you'll come?"

"Maybe. I'm not sure yet. I'm nervous about seeing Chad."

"You should come," he insisted.

We left it at that.

•

In the morning, we headed back to the lake for a final visit. I asked Adam if he would be willing to take my dad and the girls out for a walk so Mom and I could talk.

"Take as much time as you need," he said.

His support was incomparable. A week prior to this visit, he had sat down with me and asked me to start thinking about what I needed to hear from her to find closure and be at peace with her passing. "Have no regrets, Amber," he said. Adam was exceedingly mature around the subject of death. He'd lost his dad, and it wasn't until now that I understood his pain and loss in such a profound way.

When we arrived, Mom was still sleeping. Dad had just woken and put on a fresh pot of coffee. When she woke up, we ate breakfast together. And then the kids dressed up in their winter suits to head out for a hike in the hoar-frosted trees to look for wildlife.

"Come, Mom, grab your tea. Come sit," I said. I knew if I didn't initiate a conversation with her, it would never happen.

We tiptoed into it with questions about my work and the girls at school. I started to cry, and as tears fluttered down my face, I looked up and said, "Mom, I'm really sorry that this happened to you, and I also want to tell you how sorry I am for what I said during that conversation in August."

"Well, it certainly isn't ideal," she said. An uncomfortable silence encapsulated the small loveseat that we were sitting on together. "I'm sorry that your brother did that to you. If I knew it was going on, I would have stopped it. Oh, and I'm not a narcissist!"

This wasn't the time for an argument, so I just replied, "Okay."

"And I don't favour your brother," she continued.

"Okay."

"And I don't think I was the worst effing mother in the world."

"I know," I said.

I always imagined this type of conversation would be filled with life lessons or advice that your elder wanted to pass on. How to live your life to the fullest and to forge forward after they have passed. Perhaps even shared regrets for not being exactly who I needed them to be. But it wasn't that. I didn't realize it at the time, but that would be our last real conversation before she passed. It wasn't long after that that she stopped answering her text messages and slept most of the day.

"WILL" YOU HELP

To say we were unfamiliar with dying would be an understatement. As each member of my family floated in their own bubble of denial, it was apparent that she was dying. Still, we didn't talk about it, and she refused to sit down and make a will.

Please, just tell me what to write. I wouldn't ask unless I really needed your help.

I received this text message from my dad and three images of a lasting will and testament that looked like a template found on google. I had never seen my dad this broken before, not even during his own cancer journey.

Okay, let me work on it and I'll email it over, I replied.

The quickest, most efficient way was to modify my own will and send it over. I opened and then copied the file, filled in her name, and deleted everything that pertained to me and my family. I placed Dad as her sole beneficiary and executor and listed Jason as a second executor and trustee should anything happen to my dad within thirty days of her passing. I listed myself as third executor and trustee in the improbable chance that anything happened to both my dad and Jason within thirty days of her passing. I saved it as a pdf and sent it off to my dad.

The phone rang. It was my dad.

"Hey, what's up? Was there a typo?"

I was still at my desk, now working on a nursery project for a client.

"No." He paused, and by the sound of his voice I knew he was trying to find the right words. "I showed it to Mom. She read it over, and she would like your name to be removed as executor and trustee and have Chad's added."

I was speechless and felt like I'd just been slapped.

"What! Are you fucking kidding me? Doesn't she know the likelihood of needing a third executor is never going to happen?"

"I know, Am. I'm so sorry. I didn't want to have to call you and ask that. I tried explaining it to her, but she was adamant. She said that's the birth order."

"Well, fuck. I guess I'm smart enough to write a will, just not smart enough to execute it after she dies."

I hung up the phone engulfed in fury. She was sleeping twenty-two hours a day and yet she still had enough brain capacity to keep throwing daggers. I edited her will and sent it over. It would be over a week until she finally signed it, and she would never provide a thank you to me for preparing it.

BYE FELICIA

At the beginning of December, she was still at home. My dad and her sisters were providing around-the-clock care. Jason stayed a number of nights to help in the middle of the night, and he showed up every day to make sure Dad got a break. Mom was flooded with visitors during the last few weeks: family members, old friends, coworkers, and neighbours.

Hey, you should come. Dad could use the help, Jason texted.

Jason and I had become closer since our family divide. We'd been in similar positions during the past year. We'd both gone into self-preservation mode and had distanced ourselves from Mom.

Okay, sure. I'll look into flights. I might stay with Cyd, though, just to give them some space. What do you think?

No, you need to stay with Dad. He needs the help. It's too much for him to do by himself.

The benefit of living in another city is not having to see firsthand how dire the situation was.

•

As my flight landed, I gathered my things and headed to the car rental counter.

"Hello, Mrs. Hayes. What brings you to Saskatoon today?" the rental agent asked.

Not thinking, I blurted out, "Um, my mother is dying."

The look of horror on her face told me I should have filtered my response. Perhaps "visiting family" or "I'm actually from here" would have been better, but in that moment, she got my most unrefined honesty.

"Oh, I'm so sorry. Here are your keys. Please let us know if there is anything we can do for you, okay? Best of luck!" she said.

I grabbed my luggage and made my way to the parking lot. Calgary was cold, but Saskatoon was frigid. If hell froze over, it would be as cold as it was that day in Saskatoon. Negative thirty-eight degrees Celsius. I sat in the car shivering while I waited for it to warm up. My teeth chattered, and I felt my face start to burn as it thawed slightly from the windchill.

I drove slowly along the icy roads. The snow blanketed the highways and the fields leading up the winding road to their lake house. A few unknown vehicles scattered their driveway. I didn't know what to expect when I walked into their house. The house was completely quiet with an eerie silence. I stepped into the living room where Mom slept on the couch. Surrounding her were numerous chairs filled with close relatives: aunts and cousins. Jason was there, and so was Dad. I scanned the room. There was no sign of Chad, and I exhaled in relief.

"Amber's here," my dad whispered into her ear.

She groaned, and without saying a word, she opened her eyes. She was barely recognizable. She'd lost even more weight and bore only a skeletal resemblance to her old self. Her face was hollowed, and her eyes bulged. They were the same shade of pale yellow that matched the housecoat she was wearing. Her skin had darkened, and her teeth sparkled the whitest I'd ever seen them. Dad sat beside her, his hand running through her fine feathered hair, leaning in each time she tried to speak.

I sat there watching while she slept, not looking at her but watching my dad. The way he looked at her and cared for her. The way he discreetly wiped away a tear running down his face and turned away so no one could see his sadness.

"Hon, how about we get up and get something to eat?"

Dad refused to let her wither away.

"No, just some chocolates," she replied.

Since her diagnosis, she had been on a steady diet of Kraft macaroni and cheese, chocolate, cakes, cinnamon buns, candy, and anything that resembled dessert. He placed a box of Toffifee on the coffee table and offered up a piece to everyone. Some declined, but Dad assured everyone that he had three more boxes in the pantry so there was more than enough.

I spent the afternoon and early evening watching Jason and Dad lift her from the couch to the wheelchair, to the toilet, to the bed, back to the wheelchair, then back to the couch. She became restless. I learned the routine of medications, what she liked to drink, and how to get her tucked into bed with the bed rail so she wouldn't fall out.

We said goodbye to each visitor and then Dad and I fed her Rice Krispies for dinner, gave her some Dilaudid, and tucked her into bed. Dad closed the bedroom door, grabbed his cup of tea, then sat down on the couch. He looked at me. His face was exhausted. His eyes were strained and puffy, his shoulders hunched as he placed his hand on my knee.

"Thank you for coming," he said.

I could tell he was barely holding it together. I put my arm out and he folded in and started to sob. We sat together in silence until I mustered some words of comfort.

"I'm sorry, Dad. I know this is tough."

We were both very much in disbelief at the severity of her cancer. It seemed so surreal. It was still the beginning of December, and we were told she would have until Christmas.

"Has anyone called the palliative care nurses yet for an assessment?"

"No, not yet."

"Okay, I'm going to ask Jason to do that. They will come to the house and let us know what to do. She should probably be in hospice, Dad."

"I know. But then it's really final, you know? I'd be fine if she wanted to stay at home until the end."

"I know, Dad. But this is a lot of work for you, and that's not what she wanted."

"Okay, let me ask her again tomorrow if that's what she really wants still, and if it is, we will call the nurses, okay?"

I agreed, but in my heart, I knew that there was a purpose to my visit. I needed to get her into hospice or palliative care. This was not sustainable for him, and it would only become more difficult. Eventually, she wouldn't be able to consume her medications and her pain levels would become unbearable. He could not be the one to make the call to have her assessed and moved.

The next day was spent visiting again with anyone who wanted to stop by and see her. She drifted in and out while we sat around her in the living room and caught up with those who came to visit. That night after she had her dinner, Dad asked her if she still wanted to go to palliative care, and she assured him that she did. We gave her some Dilaudid, and she perked up and demanded we plan a trip to Waterton for a family vacation right away. She was heavily delirious, but it was the most lively she'd been since I'd arrived. The morning after, Dad and I lifted her to go to the bathroom. I could tell by the look on his face when he stood her up that it wasn't good. The toilet was full of blood.

"Maybe she just has a UTI, Dad, and that's why she's so delirious."

I had no idea if that would actually be the case, but I knew she was prone to them over the years.

"Let's call the nurses and see what they say."

I made the call, and they advised us to call an ambulance and have her admitted into the hospital. It took forty-five minutes for the ambulance to arrive, and in that time, Dad laid next to Mom and explained that she must have a UTI and that we needed to get her checked out.

"How do you know I have a UTI?" she asked.

"Amber said so," he said.

"Oh," she replied.

The paramedics were nothing short of exceptional. They gave her additional pain medication and wrapped her up into a small cocoon to transport her onto the hydraulic stretcher that was at the bottom of the porch stairs outside.

As they transported her onto the stretcher and into the ambulance, I could tell that she didn't want to go. As Jason and I stood there, she stared deeply into my eyes and gave me a look of detest, as if I were trying to get rid of her.

Jason and I packed up some things to take to the hospital: a few toiletries for Mom and a phone charger for Dad, Mom's medications, plus her living will, slippers, glasses, and housecoat. We arrived at St. Paul's and grabbed a tea for Dad because we knew it would be some time before she was admitted. At this point, only one person could be with her in the hallway. Jason and I waited together in the emergency waiting room. This hospital was in the heart of Saskatoon's most impoverished area and was heavily populated with drug users. We watched while people slept on the floor of the emergency room, soiling themselves in their drug-induced high. Security and the custodian team would never get a rest.

Not long after, they moved Mom into a generously sized closet within the emergency department. It was a small room that they used to house additional equipment and could fit one bed and one chair. Dad invited Jason and me to come in and say hi to Mom while he stepped out to make some calls and take a few minutes for himself. There was a knock at the door and a younger female doctor came in.

She explained that she was the leading physician in the emergency room, that she'd reviewed Mom's file, and that she had three days left to live.

"Three days!" I said to Jason, completely shocked.

He looked back at me. "What do you mean three days?"

Jason's hearing had started to take a turn for the worse over the last couple years.

"The doctor said Mom has three days left to live!"

I was in shock. This was the first time during her diagnosis that a doctor had been completely raw and honest with us. I texted Dad to come back as soon as the doctor entered the room, but she was long gone by the time he returned.

"Dad, I have to tell you something."

I gathered every ounce of courage I had to tell him about the doctor's prognosis.

"What! That doesn't seem right, does it? Didn't she seem good to you yesterday?"

Denial and fatigue were the only common factors that we all shared at this point. I agreed with Dad, and we sat silently watching Mom sleep, just the four of us in this tiny room. It was dark, the blinds were drawn, and there was constant commotion in the emergency room. An older gentleman named Steven was fighting with the paramedics, yelling at the top of his lungs, demanding that he needed to poop. Oddly enough, it kept the mood light, all things considered. I kept waiting for Chad to show up, but he never did.

Jason and I went home around 10 p.m., and at that point, we were still waiting for Mom to be admitted into palliative care. It wasn't until 2:30 a.m. that she was moved to a private room on the fifth floor in the palliative care ward.

I arrived the next morning with a tea for Dad and saw Chad out of the corner of my eye. The doctor was in the middle of explaining that no treatment would be provided for her UTI, and going forward, only pain medication would be given. It was what Mom requested in her living will. The doctor wrapped up her visit with us and proceeded to finish her rounds.

I said hello to Mom. Chad approached and wrapped his arms around me, hugging me tightly. I froze. My heart pounded in my chest, and I couldn't breathe. What was he doing? Why was he hugging me? It seemed like his life hadn't changed much in the last year, that he'd simply forgotten about the intervention meeting.

"Hi, Am, thanks for coming," Chad said.

"Thanks for coming?" I repeated to myself.

He said it as though I had just gotten off a plane and driven straight to the hospital. Did he not realize I'd been there for days helping Dad? Did he not know that I was the one making the arrangements with the crematorium? That it was me who wrote her obituary, not to mention her will? Where the hell was *he* during all of this?

I broke free from his hug and sat in a chair across the room. As I sat there in silence watching Chad hold her hand, my mind turned to the night before when I was alone at their lake house. I was searching for her birth certificate, marriage licence, SIN, and health card—everything that was needed for her file at the crematorium. I came across several sticky notes in her wallet. Written on them were arguments that both Jason and I'd had with her, and some of the harsh things that we'd said over the last couple years. It made me sad. There were no mentions of all the good we ever said or did. It was just the bad that she carried with her every day as a reminder to herself. Alongside the notes were six pictures of Chad's two children and two pictures of Jason's kids. None of mine.

We took turns sitting with Mom, holding her hand, making coffee runs to Tim Hortons to grab food for everyone, and visiting with the family members that stopped by to say their last goodbyes. For these three days, we acted as if nothing ever happened between Chad and me. I buried every emotion inside me because I knew Dad needed me to be there for him.

Hey, I'm really proud of you and how you're dealing with everything, Jason texted.

It was the reassurance I needed. I knew he still supported me and hadn't forgotten about everything that happened.

As each day went on, Mom became more restless. Visitors came and went, including one of her brothers who looked at me, said nothing, and then gave Chad a hug. Nothing ever stayed quiet in her family. Her sisters were there on rotation to help take care of her. They'd taken shifts ever since she'd been diagnosed and were a godsend to our family. The whole week was a depressing vortex-type of waiting game that never seemed to end.

Now she wanted to get up every twenty minutes. I asked the nurses to give her a sedative and a catheter to calm her and make it easier for Dad to be able to step out for a shower or to eat some food. The doctors came in and checked her knees and feet daily. I researched signs of imminent death to prepare myself, so I knew they were checking to see if her extremities were becoming mottled.

It was now Tuesday night, the end of the second day, and she was still hanging on. I had just returned to the lake house when my phone rang. It was my girls on FaceTime.

"Mommy!" they both squealed.

The sound of their voices instantly revived my exhausted body.

"When are you coming home? We miss you!" Monroe said.

Adam and his mom were with the girls and had been all week. He assured me that the girls were fine, even though each time we spoke they cried.

"How do you know I'm fine! I'm not fine! I cry in my bed every night. Mommy, I miss you, please come home," Quinn said.

I couldn't help but chuckle at her electrifying declaration of emotion. Quinn has always been my feisty, precocious child.

I missed them so much. Their Christmas concert was scheduled for that Thursday, and they were adamant that I not miss it. I needed to come home to do their hair, they said. I told them I loved them, sang both of their bedtime songs, and said good night.

I sat alone on my parents' couch and thought about what I should do. If I left, I wouldn't be there by her side when she passed. I wouldn't be able to hug my dad and help him cope. I would never see her again. If I went home, I could see Quinn's first Christmas concert. I could see Monroe play the xylophone. I pictured Quinn taking centre stage and adding impromptu spins like she did at her first ballet recital, and Monroe's shy face and finger point that she used to do when she was in junior kindergarten.

They were my entire world. But most importantly, they would feel loved and chosen if I was there. I'd spent the last thirty-eight years wishing my mom would have chosen me just once. My deliberating was short-lived. I chose my girls. They deserved a mother who would always put them first, no matter what. I booked a flight for Thursday at noon.

•

The next day was much of the same. More family and friends came to say their goodbyes, as did Natalie and Libby and the kids. I left the hospital that night and headed back to my parents' house. Completely exhausted, both emotionally and physically, I started to clean. I cleaned every inch of their home: bathrooms, kitchen, the floors, their bedroom. I imagined what it would be like for my dad to come home alone and what I could do to make it easier for him. I got rid of everything that would make him sad. The medications and hospital records. The oxygen tanks, the walker, and the wheelchair. The exercise bike that she thought she'd be able to ride to keep up her strength, and all the medical supplies.

As I was cleaning, the phone rang. It was Natalie.

"Hey, you doing okay?" she asked.

"Yeah, I'm okay. I'm just cleaning up the house. I don't want Dad to come home to all the medical supplies, so I thought I should clear it all out."

"That's a good idea."

"How are the kids doing?" I asked.

"Not great. They're taking tomorrow off from school, too. I thought I'd take them for ice cream or to a movie to distract them."

"I'm sure a distraction would be welcomed right now," I said.

At the hospital that day, her kids had been visibly upset. They were much closer to my mom than my kids were. They'd had more years with her and had seen her more often. I'd wrapped my arms around them, trying to console them.

Natalie and I continued to talk while I cleaned the rest of the house. She agreed to come by and return all the oxygen tanks to the supplier before my dad came home. After three hours, I collapsed into bed. I woke the next morning still exhausted but relieved that I was going home to see Adam and my girls. I packed my suitcase and loaded it into the car. I knew this morning would be tough, but I was ready for it.

When I got to the hospital, my dad and Chad were there.

"Can I have a minute alone with Mom, please?" I asked.

They closed the door on their way out.

I thought a lot about what I wanted to say to her before she passed. I wondered if she even knew that she was dying, or if she would understand what I was saying. I had so much pent-up anger and hatred inside me, but I sat down on the chair next to her. Her eyes were closed. I grabbed her hand and sat silently for a minute. I'd spent the last five days watching her sleep. I tried to capture a mental picture of her hands and her face. Her body was disintegrating. She startled awake and looked over at me.

"Mom, I'm going home to be with my girls. Their Christmas concert is tonight."

"Oh. Okay."

"I wanted to say thank you, Mom, for making me who I am today. You have made me stronger than I ever thought possible. It's because of you that I have become the mother I am."

I gave her a kiss and told her I loved her.

"Don't cry, Am. I love you, too," she responded.

•

I left the hospital feeling an overwhelming heaviness. I'd had heart palpitations and a weight in my chest all week, but this was much more. I drove straight to the airport, took a sigh of relief, and boarded my plane. I felt guilty for leaving my dad, but I knew this was the right choice.

I arrived home and met Adam's mom at the house. I fell into her arms, and she gave me a much-needed motherly hug. I picked up the girls after school. As soon as I saw them, I bent down, arms wide open, and we shared a long embrace. The smell of their tousled, unbrushed hair gave me a shot of pure euphoria. We walked home, and that night, before the concert, I helped them get ready.

I brushed and pulled their hair back from their faces, adding soft curls in the back and a small bow. I sat in the front row gleaming, Adam and Cyd next to me. The girls performed multiple songs and played instruments that they'd studied throughout the year. Their innocence and purity shone as they danced and sang. Quinn's look of brazen confidence and Monroe's infamous shy smile; they were mine and they would always be worth it.

•

The next day I received a text from Jason at 6:20 p.m.

Mom passed away just now.

Disbelief came over me. Was she really gone? Was it really over? For most of my life, I wondered if I would cry when she died. I did. I cried for my dad and his pain, and I cried for the young child inside me that still longed to have a mother who loved me. As much as I had grieved over the last decade, hope never left me that she would someday be someone who was capable of more.

FINALLY FREE

The real healing started for me after she died. It was Christmas time, and Dad had come to stay with us. He hadn't been to our house in years, and I was overjoyed with excitement. For the first time in my life, we didn't need to hide our relationship. There would be no deleting of text messages, or skirting the truth about why I called, or reminding each other at the end of our conversation that "we didn't talk today okay?"

We didn't have to hide any of it out of fear that she would find out and be upset. This was the first time in my life I could spend time with my dad and be unapologetically happy. We stayed up late every night during the holidays, sharing stories and memories of Mom. I couldn't help but think about how hard we both fought to survive for years, and here we were, on the other side. Finally free. But Dad was at an all-time low of sadness and disbelief. He missed her.

We sat together with cups of peppermint tea in hand, curled up on the couch. The room was dimly lit by the Christmas tree, and the fireplace was humming away.

"I have something I need to tell you, but I don't want it to wreck your Christmas," he said.

"Trust me, Dad. You won't ruin my Christmas. Having you here and being able to spend time with you is all I've ever wanted."

"Okay, well, do you remember me telling you that Mom put aside some envelopes after she got the terminal diagnosis? We weren't sure if she was going to write letters to everyone, but instead, she wrote each grandchild's name along with a piece of jewellery on the envelope. She wanted her wedding rings to go to Chad's children, Amber. Her newest set to his oldest and her original set to his youngest daughter."

"Why would she do that?" I asked. I was in shock. "Was there an envelope with my name on it?"

"No, I'm sorry, there wasn't. Just the grandchildren."

"What did she leave for my kids?"

"She had a necklace written down for Monroe, but she hadn't gotten to writing down something for Quinn, but don't worry, I will find her something."

I'd always thought her wedding rings would be handed down to me, and so did my dad. She'd asked me five or so years prior if I wanted anything when she died, and I just said some of her jewellery. But in true Marlene fashion, she managed to keep hurting people even after she was gone. I didn't know why it bothered me. I wanted nothing from her.

•

The next four months were rough and full of ups and downs for Dad. Jason and I tried our best to keep him busy with trips to Florida and Palm Springs. On Sundays he went to Jason's house for supper, and we talked every other day. I travelled back to Saskatoon in early April for Mom's celebration of life service and to scatter some of her ashes. Dad wanted to wait until the snow melted so we could spread her cremains around the lake, like she wanted. He bought all the grandchildren necklaces to hold a portion of her cremains. I accepted the necklaces for my girls, but I wouldn't allow her to stay in our home forever.

I took Dad out the night before the service and picked him out a new sports coat, shirt, and dress pants. I wore the dress I'd bought the last year for her funeral. Some eyebrows were raised, but I joked to Adam that it was better than wearing a "Mom's favourite" sweatshirt as an alternative. It was a beautiful tea celebration hosted and put together by my aunts. Two sections of tables lined in rows, the family divide clearly apparent. Jason, Natalie, and their kids sat at the front with Dad, me, Adam, and our kids. Chad, Libby, and their two daughters sat on the other side, halfway back with Libby's parents. I always wondered if they knew what caused the divide.

We scattered her ashes separately. Each one of us had a small urn and a portion of her cremains. I sat there alone at the lakeside campsite where they loved to go camping. It was a site that we'd occupied when we were young kids. The ground was still slightly frozen and covered with leaves, branches, and odd pieces of trash. I scattered her ashes around the campsite, and the only polite thoughts that came to my mind were these: *Thank you. Thank you for making me the mother I am today. Thank you for forcing me to develop myself into a strong and independent woman. Because of you, I will be the mother I always wanted and the mother every child deserves. Because of me, this generational abuse will stop here. I have made it my life's goal to be nothing like you. Upon your passing, I hope you are able to understand the impact in every way that your life and your behaviour had. I'm sorry you had to endure such a painful, abusive life, and I'm sorry that you weren't strong enough to break the chain. I hope that the young girl inside of you will finally be able to heal and be at peace. Rest in peace, Mom.*

I sat down on the top of the picnic table and took a moment of silence to acknowledge her passing. I let out a sigh of disbelief and exhaustion. I could let go now. She couldn't hurt me anymore. I wouldn't let her. I stood up from the picnic table and walked over to the park where my girls were playing. Quinn came running up to me, her long hair blowing in the wind. I scooped her up, spun her around, and reached out to hug Monroe. We walked hand in hand back to the park to meet Adam.

My girls were my reason. The reason I had to keep fighting. To heal, to break the cycle of generational abuse, and to be everything they needed me to be.

Adam wrapped his arm around me and whispered, "We love you."

I was officially free.

EPILOGUE

I believe in the power of manifestation. Do I think I manifested my mother's death? No, but wouldn't that be one hell of a superpower? I feel like we all have a divine purpose in life. Mine was to break the generational cycle of abuse and to speak up for victims of abuse. The impact that we all have on each other is profound, and most of us don't even know it. Whether you are a therapist, a teacher, an aunt, a parent, a partner, or a friend, your effort, love, and kindness can save someone's life. You can contribute to a ripple effect that will change the lives of others. For those individuals mentioned in this book, I give you my endless gratitude.

To those who have been through something similar, I encourage you to find your voice and speak your truth. The act of speaking up and releasing the toxicity circulating in your body will help start your healing. In the beginning, I was determined that sexual abuse would not define me, and I didn't want anyone to know about it. Yet here I am. I've tried many avenues of healing—hypnosis, traditional therapy, EMDR, reading books, psychic mediums—but for me, the biggest release came from using my voice and speaking my truth.

Abuse is something that stays with you forever. I do not consider myself "fixed" or "cured," but as I stand here today, my eyes have been opened and I am consciously aware of what I've been through. I speak my story from a place of truth and honesty. I'm not sharing my story out of malice or with any intent to harm those who have caused me harm. This is my story. These are my memories. For those that have yet to find their voice, I stand with you. My words can be your words, and this book is for you.

ACKNOWLEDGEMENTS

To my husband, Adam: I thank you endlessly for accepting me with all my traumas and for loving me just the way I am. You were the first person to stand up for me. You caught me as I stumbled throughout this journey. I will forever be grateful to you and the safe haven you've provided for us. I couldn't think of a better father and role model for our girls. Thank you for choosing me in this life. I love you.

To my daughters, Monroe and Quinn: You have always been the light in my life that I run toward. You gave me a reason to heal, and a reason to be a better mother. You are my motivation in living a life full of happiness and laughter. Because of you, I can stand proudly and confidently, knowing that I will not pass along the traumas that happened before you. You are my entire world, and I love you more than life itself.

To my dad: Thank you for fighting as hard as you did throughout your life. I know it wasn't easy for you, either. You stood beside me and showed me what love looked like from the day I was born. You allowed me to open up and be myself. No one knows me better than you. You are my best friend, and I love you.

To Jason and Natalie: Thank you for your unwavering support over the last number of years. You never doubted me and always had my back. You made me feel safe and for that, I'm forever grateful.

To Auntie Beth: Thank you for being the mother I always wished I had. You never forgot about me. I love you.

To my mother-in-law, Cyd: Thank you for raising a strong, feminist son. It is because of you that he came to me with a listening ear and never gave up on our family. Your relationship with Adam has shown me what a mother-son relationship should look like. You can laugh and joke together, and more importantly, you respect and love each other. Thank you for accepting me into your family.

To Alex March: I booked a reading with you as an avenue of healing. I had no idea that by the time I spoke with you, my mother would pass away from cancer. You validated my childhood, the relationship that I had with my mother, and the abuse that occurred in our home. You changed my life and passed on words from my mom that I longed to hear as a child. You are an alchemist and the cherry on top of my healing.

To Shasta Grant, my editor: Thank you for continually pushing me to dig deeper than I ever thought I was capable of doing. You helped me tell my story in its most authentic form. You never once tried to steer me away from my truth or silence me. You held my voice and story safely in your trusting arms. I will never forget the support and love you've shown throughout the writing of this book.

RESOURCES

BORDERLINE PERSONALITY DISORDER

Barlow, Don. 2021. *Gaslighting & Narcissistic Abuse Recovery.*

Forward, Susan. 2014. *Mothers Who Can't Love: A Healing Guide for Daughters.* New York: Harper.

Kreger, Randy. 2008. *The Essential Family Guide to Borderline Personality Disorder: New Tools and Techniques to Stop Walking on Eggshells.* Center City, MN: Hazelden.

McBride, Karyl. 2009. *Will I Ever Be Good Enough? Healing the Daughters of Narcissistic Mothers.* New York: Atria.

Roth, Kimberlee and Freda B. Friedman. 2004. *Surviving a Borderline Parent: How to Heal Your Childhood Wounds & Build Trust, Boundaries and Self-Esteem.* Oakland, CA: New Harbinger,

Streep, Peg. 2017. *Daughter Detox: Recovering from an Unloving Mother and Reclaiming Your Life.* Ile D'Espoir Press.

SEXUAL ABUSE

Bass, Ellen and Laura Davis. 2008. *The Courage to Heal: A Guide for Women Survivors of Child Sexual Abuse.* William Morrow: New York.

Duncan, Karen A. 2004. *Healing from the Trauma of Childhood Sexual Abuse: The Journey for Women.* Praeger: Westport, CT.

Feuereisen, Patti. 2018. *Invisible Girls: Speaking the Truth about Sexual Abuse.* Seal Press: New York.

ADDITIONAL RESOURCES

Gibson, Lindsay C. 2015. *Adult Children of Emotionally Immature Parents: How to Heal from Distant, Rejecting, or Self-Involved Parents.* Oakland, CA: New Harbinger.

———. 2019. *Recovering from Emotionally Immature Parents: Practical Tools to Establish Boundaries & Reclaim Your Emotional Autonomy.* Oakland, CA: New Harbinger.

———. 2021. *Self-Care for Adult Children of Emotionally Immature Parents: Honor Your Emotions, Nurture Your Self & Live with Confidence.* Oakland, CA: New Harbinger.

March, Alex. www.alexmarchenergy.com

AMBER NICOLE HAYES has always been a masterful keeper of secrets. For twenty-five long years, silence was her dogged companion. But if Amber could carry such a heavy burden and appear to rest of the world as a contented mother, wife, and business owner, how many others were doing the same?

Amber's memoir, The Obedient Daughter, leaves no stone unturned as she explores the sibling sexual assault she experienced throughout childhood, under the shadow of a mother with undiagnosed borderline personality disorder. Compelled to break the chain of inter-generational trauma, Amber speaks to the unspeakable, proving that no secret is too heavy to share.

Now the owner of a successful interior design studio, Amber specializes in creating safe and inspiring spaces for children and volunteering her time for causes she believes in. Amber lives in Alberta, Canada with two great kids, a saintly husband, and a Boston Terrier who is the perfect writing companion.